AMERICAN BIG GAME FISHING

From a painting by Lynn Bogue Hunt   *Courtesy of the Artist*

SAILFISH

Tapping the bait off Miami Beach.

American Big Game Fishing

Edited by Eugene V. Connett III

THE DERRYDALE PRESS

LANHAM AND NEW YORK

T H E   D E R R Y D A L E   P R E S S

Published in the United States of America
by The Derrydale Press
4720 Boston Way, Lanham, Maryland 20706

Distributed by NATIONAL BOOK NETWORK, INC.

Original Derrydale printing 1993
First paperback printing with french folds 1999

EDITOR'S PREFACE

The sport of big game fishing is a comparatively new development in angling. In recent years a group of amateur sportsmen and professional boat captains have studied this thrilling sport with unremitting enthusiasm, and their efforts have now reached a point where the best methods, tackle, baits, etc., are sufficiently understood to make a volume of this sort invaluable.

In treating a sport which is of comparatively recent origin (in contrast, for instance, to trout fishing or wing shooting), one naturally finds a fairly wide divergence of opinion among the men who are most experienced in it. Such differences will be found in this volume. In editing it I have made no attempt to bring the authors to any common body of opinion, as I feel that readers will gain more from having the individual results of each author's experience.

It is quite natural that the men who have pioneered in taking these monster fighters of the sea should jealously guard their hard-won knowledge of the best methods and localities for taking the various species. It is high proof of their sportsmanship that they should divulge these secrets in the greatest detail in this volume.

I am sure that all those who read it will join me in thanking the authors for their efforts to advance the sport of big game fishing by so generously contributing their knowledge.

In particular I wish to express my gratitude to Lynn Bogue Hunt who has made all the decorations, paintings, drawings and maps which add so greatly to the beauty, interest and value of this book. Thanks are also due Ray Schrenkeisen for his assistance in reading proofs.

EUGENE V. CONNETT.

New York, May 1, 1935.

TABLE OF CONTENTS

LIST OF ILLUSTRATIONS

LIST OF ILLUSTRATIONS

LIST OF ILLUSTRATIONS

LIST OF ILLUSTRATIONS

LIST OF ILLUSTRATIONS

LIST OF ILLUSTRATIONS

By Lynn Bogue Hunt

WHITE MARLIN

INTRODUCTION

BY

MRS. OLIVER C. GRINNELL

IG game fishing has at last come into its own. While a few scattered sportsmen have angled for a quarter of a century for big game fish there have been less than a hundred who have fished seriously as a major sport until the last five years.

Big game fishing is destined, and rightly so, to become one of the greatest, if not the greatest sport of all nations. Originating mainly on the Pacific Coast for tuna and swordfish and on the Florida coast for tarpon, today sportsmen are following the game fish wherever they migrate and records are being made at points heretofore unknown as sources for sport fishing.

It is not merely *fishing* that attracts our men and women to this grand sport — environment plays a mighty part. No other sport offers such panorama of beauty, never twice alike. Each day out there on the ocean is different from its predecessor. Some days are so calm that seaweed floats in masses and the submerged reefs are visible. On such days it seems as though the wheeling of the gulls and the flight of the man-of-war birds is lazy and slow, fitting in with the glassy sea. On other days, the waves are choppy-bright and white with foam. Your boat dances up and down and sidewise all at once. Then there are times when sudden squalls darken the skies, sunshine and shadows intermingle to produce kaleidoscopic effects of seascape that are surpassingly gorgeous. Often from these blue waters one may be fortunate in seeing a school of flying fish rise, bits of shining silver gliding through the air a hundred feet, their brilliant bodies glistening in the sun. No money could buy a framed painting half as beautiful.

INTRODUCTION

Then there is always the fresh, stinging, tangy, salty air; the vastness and beauty of ever-changing blue waters, the indescribable sunrises and sunsets, the meeting of the sky and the water on the horizon, the intangible something that levels the problems of life, that makes real men and real women, that puts deep sea anglers in a class by themselves; and I predict that the devotees will in time be as vast as the sea itself.

There is nothing in history to tell us just when and how a rod, a line and a hook were used for the first time to catch either fresh or salt water fish.

Whoever first opened up the sport of deep sea fishing should have a great and lasting monument dedicated to him, for he gave to thousands recreation and pleasure that grows and will continue to grow as the years go by.

He of faint heart should not take up the sport of big game fishing, for the taking of large and stubborn sea monsters presents thrills and problems that call for good generalship and a hefty brand of stick-to-it-iveness on the part of the enthusiast who is handling the rod. It takes patience, for days upon days are sometimes passed without even sighting one of these prized fish. Generally speaking, big game angling should never be taken up where backbone and grit are lacking.

By big game fishing is specifically meant the pursuit of broadbill swordfish, marlin, tarpon, sailfish, tuna, wahoo, bonefish and striped bass, each having their devotees and each meriting all their devotees say of them.

Authentic angling records of the first catches of all these species are confused and incomplete, as no official records have ever been kept or published, and unfortunately there has always been the serious handicap of no national standardization of tackle. Obviously a sailfish caught on a 12 thread line could not be recognized as a record by a Club specifying 9 thread as light tackle, or a 12 ounce tip as against a 6 ounce tip.

The ethics of angling are even more important than the tackle used. The hooking of a fish on tackle light enough to give the quarry a fighting chance, enhances the thrill of the strike, the ensuing battle and playing the fish to boat, whether the game is large or small; and it would be a pity to allow this sport to degenerate to a point of losing a single thrill to the angler, and it is so obviously unfair to compete for records, except on standardized tackle and standardized methods or ethics.

As long ago as October 27th, 1930, Erl Roman, Fishing Editor of the

INTRODUCTION

Miami *Herald*, pleaded through his column for anglers to affiliate and to agree upon and adopt some set rules and specifications and ethics so that an angler from any part of the world might establish a record that would be recognized and go down in history *as* a record. His plea was not then carried out but it bore fruit, for in 1934 there was so much pressure brought to bear on the Salt Water Anglers of America, a national body dedicated to research, conservation, restoration, to combat polluted water and to promote sportsmanlike methods of angling, — that they finally agreed to sponsor this standardization. They therefore created a committee drawn from the most experienced anglers from all parts of the country who have laid down a set of rules and specifications and ethics, which were culled from the best of those obtaining at old established existing Clubs. Records are to stand until beaten by new records made under the new national rules, and all records will be filed with the American Museum of Natural History.

Every true sportsman should lend his support to these rulings, not only as to the tackle used for competitive angling, but to the ethics and the sportsmanship pertaining to the boating of a fish. Otherwise competitive records will remain a joke. No other major sport is conducted in the hit-and-miss manner that angling is today and every Club should lay aside local club rules in order that their members may be recognized in national competitive angling.

Angling for tarpon (*Tarpon atlanticus*) was unquestionably the beginning of big game angling in this country. The first tarpon of which there is any record was caught on rod and reel as far back as the late 80's in Indian River Inlet by Wm. S. Jones of Philadelphia. This fish weighed 130 pounds. This tarpon was a topic for conversation for all fishermen wherever they congregated, and the sport immediately became popular at the Inlet and has extended since to both the East and the West Coasts of Florida. Grover Cleveland, Joseph Jefferson and A. W. and Julian Dimock followed this sport feverishly for years and helped to make it popular.

The tarpon is a magnificent game fish and has been taken weighing up to 350 pounds, but not on rod and reel. No other large game fish has the brilliant burnished silver color of the tarpon which earned for him the name of Silver King, by which name he is known the world over.

Although the tarpon has long been a favorite with big game anglers, practically nothing of a definite nature has been verified regarding its habits. The question of its origin and its breeding grounds is a matter of dispute and although small specimens have been found, these have been found alike in ocean, bay and river. In one instance at least, an angler found tiny tarpon in the stomach of dolphin, a fish which is known to inhabit only the blue waters of both the Atlantic and Pacific oceans. These specimens measured only 1 ½" to 2" in length.

Cuvier and Valenciennes state "Tarpon have been found from Long Island to Brazil, abundant off the coast of Florida, the species being known since 1846."

Next in line came the tuna (*Tunnus thynnus*), the first on record having been landed on rod and reel in 1898 by Charles F. Holder. This specimen, weighing 183 pounds, was taken from the waters near Avalon, California. It was this catch that resulted in the forming of the Tuna Club of Catalina, of which club Mr. Holder became first President. This club is still in existence and holds a prominent place in the angling world.

Many tuna have been taken on the Pacific Coast since that time but they do not run so large as in other localities, specifically on the North Atlantic Coast up as far as Nova Scotia where specimens have been taken commercially weighing up to 2000 pounds.

The tuna is a powerful swimmer. To encounter him with rod and reel calls for endurance and brute strength on the part of the angler rather than great skill. This fish is also a deep swimmer, and the playing of this fish does not possess the fascination that does playing surface fighting fish like the swordfish, marlin and sailfish.

Broadbill swordfish (*Xiphias gladius*) evidently was so named because of the peculiar sword-like projection protruding from the upper jaw, which is roughly a third of the length of the entire fish, and is the weapon with which he kills his prey. The fact that this giant invariably travels alone, never schooling together as do even whales, has given him the name of "Lone Wolf of the Sea."

In a recent report of the Fish and Game Group of the Food Survey conducted by the S.W.S. workers in co-operation with the New York City Department of Public Works, is an interesting paragraph: "Secluded among the hills of Tuscany in Central Italy lies the ancient city of Siena. It should have a peculiar interest for Americans. Christopher Columbus received his education here and in the height of his triumphs as a discoverer he chose to deposit a memento of his first voyage across the seas. His votive offering hangs over the portal of the old collegiate church, closed for many years and rarely visited save by enterprising American tourists. It consists of the helmet and armor the discoverer wore when he first planted his feet on the earth of the New World, his weapons, and the weapon of a 'warrior' killed by his party when approaching the American Coast — the sword of a swordfish.

"It is natural to assume that Columbus, or some of his crew, seafaring men of the Mediterranean, had seen the swordfish before. Still, its sword was treasured by them and for the past five centuries has formed a striking feature in one of the best preserved monuments to the discoverer of America."

Much has been said regarding the pugnacity and the ferocity of these fish, and weird tales have been told of their attacks on vessels. It has never been proved that a swordfish attacked a boat except in instances when they are harpooned and are crazed with pain, or because of their habit of breaching, they come zooming up from the bottom of the sea — and happen to come up under a vessel. The tales of deliberate attacks are fantastic and can only be classed with the legend of the Banshee.

There is much mystery regarding the habits and breeding places of this fish; no fish of this species ever having been caught in our waters bearing spawn, notwithstanding the thousands that are dressed for market each year, and no really small fish are found in our waters. The smallest we have on this coast average 50 or 60 pounds. There are one or two exceptions to this statement. A young fish weighing only 7⅜ pounds was taken by a commercial fisherman presumably by harpoon on Georges Bank by the schooner "Anna" on August 9, 1922. Last year 9 tiny but perfect specimens of swordfish were taken from the stomach of a dolphin which was hooked off Miami. The smallest of these was 5 inches in length, the largest 21 inches. This might indicate that swordfish spawn in the deep sea areas near Miami, — or the small swordfish may have floated in seaweed from some Southern point, possibly the Isle of Pines, to a point opposite Miami, where they were devoured by dolphin. It is generally believed that swordfish spawn in the Mediterranean Sea off the coast of Sicily.

Swordfish were first taken commercially as far back as 1845, the first one recorded at Barnstable, Mass. It was then shipped in small quantities to foreign countries, mostly salted, but later it found a market in this country without the curing process, as the flesh of even these giant fish was found to be delicate and of great food value. Today there is a large commercial industry, the swordfish fleet following the swordfish the entire length of the North Atlantic Coast and as far as Prince Edward's Island. It is a curious fact, however, that swordfish was not served in our leading hotels in New York until about 1930 when Oscar of the Waldorf finally placed it on his menu.

Notwithstanding swordfish have been known commercially since 1845, it was not until 1913 that one of these weird fish was taken by an angler on rod and reel. W. C. Boschen took at Catalina this first fish, which weighed 355 pounds. Since that time these fish have constantly been sought on the Pacific Coast, but in 22 years there have been less than 150 fish taken. Anglers from Eastern States travelled 3000 miles to try their luck on these grand battling game fish, but it remained for Oliver Cromwell Grinnell to pioneer the sport on the North Atlantic Coast. On the Pacific Coast, swordfish fed mostly on flying fish which are most plentiful there, but on the Atlantic Coast there are comparatively few flying fish, and a new bait had to be devised.

To begin with, the small sport fishing boats on the Atlantic Coast were not designed to go to sea in quest of these mighty fish; so, in 1924, Mr. Grinnell designed a specially sturdy, sea-going Lawley built boat, the "Oligrin," and for three years he experimented first with one bait and then another. Success crowned his efforts, when, in September, 1927, he landed the first broadbill swordfish to be taken on the Atlantic Coast on rod and reel. This fish weighed 193 pounds and he caught four more fish weighing up to 369 pounds before his death in 1930. Captain Billy Hatch and Captain Wally Baker were his crew, his companions and his colleagues during the period of experiments and later in the landing of the five fish. To these men Mr. Grinnell gave unstinting praise for their part in the development of the sport which has in the past five years grown to such tremendous importance.

The mackerel bait which these three men developed, which takes an experienced guide an hour to prepare, is so lifelike in its appearance in the water that Sir Broadbill does not hesitate to attack. It is this mackerel bait (and as second choice the squid or ink fish) that all anglers for swordfish are using today.

Mr. Grinnell was one of the first men to use the now famous white feathered bait on the Atlantic Coast. During the early spring of 1926, his friend, John Philip Sousa, son of the famous band master, sent him a small box from Japan.

Mrs. Oliver C. Grinnell with the first broadbill to be landed by a woman on the North Atlantic Coast. It was taken off Montauk, August 2, 1931, in one hour and a quarter and weighed 245½ lbs.

Oliver Cromwell Grinnell with the first broadbill swordfish taken on the North Atlantic Coast, September 1, 1927. At the left, Capt. Wally Baker; at the right, Capt. Bill Hatch.

INTRODUCTION

This little box contained four curious feathered baits or lures, the heads being crude handmade lead with a painted eye. Mr. Sousa wrote that these baits were being used by the Japanese in tuna fishing with splendid results. These baits were so crude that it was almost unbelievable that a tuna would strike them, so they were relegated to the tackle box and forgotten for the nonce. Midsummer, the waters teemed with tuna weighing up to 60 pounds but they could not be induced to take a hook. In desperation, but with no confidence, the little feathered hooks were taken from the tackle box and affixed to our lines. No sooner did the line pay out than we were each hooked to tuna. This was repeated until we were tired and ashamed to take more from the water.

Certain it is that the landing of the first broadbill swordfish on the Atlantic Coast gave great impetus to all big game fishing. Immediately anglers swarmed the seas, and this type of angling has developed more during the past five years than ever before.

Big game fishing has not been confined to man alone. Mrs. Keith Spalding of Catalina landed in 1921 the first and only broadbill swordfish taken by a woman on the Pacific Coast, while the writer was fortunate in being the first woman to land one of these game fish on the Atlantic Coast. This fish was taken on August 2, 1931. There have been but five swordfish taken by women, of which two were caught by myself.

Today marlin have become an important factor in the angling world. They appear to be more plentiful than swordfish and while the majority weigh in the neighborhood of a hundred pounds, large specimens are encountered on occasion.

At Bimini, a British Island, 45 miles east of Miami, during certain seasons of the year, marlin of prodigious size — some of them estimated at 1000 to 1200 pounds, have been sighted. Large specimens are found off New Zealand, various points in the South Seas, and Tahiti Island, where "Carrie Fin" (Mrs. Eastham Guild) landed a monster specimen weighing 856 pounds. Because of the close proximity of Bimini Island to Miami it is to be expected that some worth while records will be made there.

The first marlin to be taken on rod and reel of which we have record was one taken in 1903 by Edward Llewellyn of Los Angeles; while the first one to be taken in the North Atlantic was taken by Julian Crandall off Block Island.

There has been much discussion as to how many varieties of marlin are known. The marlin has erroneously been referred to as a swordfish. The marlin does not belong to the swordfish family but to the spearfish family and it is generally conceded there are at least four varieties; the black marlin, the blue marlin, the striped marlin and the common or white marlin.

The differences in opinion on every variety of salt water fish force upon us the realization of the crying necessity for more research and study — their habits, their feeding and breeding places and where they migrate, as all our pelagic fishes are known to do. Again, we have no authentic record and no real knowledge is available of the origin or habits of this grand game fish.

Marlin are surface feeding fish and are perhaps the most spectacular of all our game fishes. When hooked, their leaps, their tail-walking on the surface of the water, their runs at prodigious speed, give the angler who is fortunate enough to hook one of these beauties, a thrill that will forever linger in his angling memories.

Sailfish and marlin belong to the same spearfish family and there is no fish that swims that is as popular with the angler as the sailfish, and none more beautiful. It is impossible properly to describe this loveliest of all game fish, — its great sail which it sometimes uses in flight, the heavenly blue and silver of its vivid coloring, and the slight and graceful form. To hook one of these fish on really light tackle and watch his repeated great flying leaps in the air is a thrill that must be experienced first hand to appreciate.

The first sailfish was seen in Brazil as early as 1648. The first specimen in the U. S. National Museum was taken off Newport in August, 1872. No others were observed until March, 1878, when two were taken on hand lines by a vessel between Savannah and Indian River, Florida. Commercial fishermen took several on hand lines while fishing for kingfish off the coast of Florida, but the real start of the sport of sailfishing on rod and reel was inaugurated by Captain Bill Hatch in the Gulf Stream off Miami late in November, 1916.

Captain Hatch is notoriously bashful. He knew that commercial kingfishermen had caught sailfish on hand lines, but it was he who figured out the "cut bait," fashioned the first one (as it is used for trolling) and also figured out the proper method of enticing the sailfish to this bait, the "drop-back" and the hooking. Captain Hatch was catching sailfish on rod and reel regularly many years before it became a recognized sport among other guides.

Sailfish are to be found on the East Coast of Florida and in the tropical waters throughout the world. Off the coast of Florida the average weight is 40 to 60 pounds, although in some cases larger fish have been caught, — notably one of 119½ pounds caught from the cruiser "Pilar" owned by Ernest Hemingway. Further south, however, in the Perlas Islands off Panama, one sailfish was landed that weighed 187 pounds.

Striped bass is decidedly a game fish but it is not necessary to go to sea to catch this species. They are fairly plentiful on both the Atlantic and the Pacific coasts and are mostly caught by casting from the shore. They put up a fight that makes them very popular from the angler's point of view, and they have the advantage of being edible.

Striped bass are not natives of the Pacific Coast. They were transplanted by the government to the Pacific waters and now they are possibly more numerous there than in their original home, the Atlantic Ocean.

The mako shark is not at this time regarded as a game fish for we all have our pet aversion to classing sharks among our game fish, but this particular variety differs so greatly from the other members of the shark family that I predict the mako will be classed as one of our game fishes in the near future. The mako is a surface-feeding, surface-fighting fish, giving the angler plenty of spectacular play, and he has only one characteristic of the shark — the gills. Off New Zealand the mako is highly prized as a game fish and he is not to be despised by the angler looking for action.

Last, but not least, we mention bonefishing. He who has not angled for these game little fish has certainly missed something from life. The largest on record weighed 13 pounds 12 ounces, while the average size is nearer 6 pounds. The fascinating thing about bonefish is the manner of fishing. It is of little wonder that seasoned anglers are flocking to this particular angling, for the game is comparatively new. My first experience of angling for these fish will forever remain a high spot in my memory. We rowed a small skiff out on the flats just before dead low water. We anchored, our hooks were baited with live shrimp, we cast out according to our guide's instruction. Long we waited, when our guide said "Look." What I saw were tiny bits of old silver lace protruding from the water. As I watched, they disappeared, to appear in another spot. Our guide whispered "They're coming in." They came, nearer and nearer, until angling instinct told me to strike. That was all I was expected to do, — the bonefish, for these lovely bits of old silver lace were the tails of feeding fish, did all the rest. I do not believe there is a fish in existence that will put up the fight for his size or will show the speed of these little gems.

But these details are only part of the story that will unfold itself within your actual experience when you cruise the deep sea for game fish. For there are more than 600 varieties of fighting fish (all worthy of your time), outside of those listed as game fishes; and who can describe by mere words the smashing speedy grace of this great variety of fishes. No one can guess what the next strike will be, — perhaps the bulldog rush of the fighting amberjack, the lightning leaps of the matchless and brilliantly colored dolphin, the wicked barracuda or the stubborn, streamlined wahoo with brilliant stripings encircling his torpedo-like body, or the snapping bluefish.

But, again, all is not in the number of fish to your credit at the end of the day, when, replete with angling thrills, your craft anchors in some quiet spot and you watch the sun dying in the West, — you will know that in all the world of sports, there are none others that compare. And when you finally crawl into your bunk to be lulled to sleep by the gentle lapping of waves against the sides of your vessel, you pass into a dreamless rest undisturbed by worrisome thoughts that are accustomed to accumulate in the work-a-day world.

Truly it is a great sport!

AMERICAN BIG GAME FISHING

Ernest Hemingway with the largest sailfish ever caught in the Atlantic. The fish was hooked by Thomas J. S. McGrath and landed by Mr. Hemingway. It weighed 119½ pounds and was caught about eight miles from Key West on what is called the Ten Fathom Bar, just off the Western Dry Rocks.

CHAPTER I.

SAILFISH

BY

LYNN BOGUE HUNT

THERE is a report from some source that the first sailfish to come under the eye of a white man was caught from a Spanish or Portuguese adventure ship off the east coast of South America in 1648. No one knows the truth of this tale, but the ships were certainly in those waters then, and so were the sailfish; also, sailors in lazy weather have for all time tried their luck for fish as a change of fare by trolling from their ships. The first scientific record is from the Indian Ocean, and the date is 1786. In the Pacific and Indian Oceans, especially in the regions of Malaya and the South Seas, sailfish must have been known to the venturesome, fish-loving races of men a long time back, but it is within a few years only that the world-wide distribution of sails has been understood, classification by scientists has been undertaken, and sailfish have won a high place among anglers as big-game fish.

By studying the map of world distribution of sailfish, the reader will see that the Atlantic sails are completely cut off from all the other seas where sailfish are found, and by a glance at the drawings of the Atlantic fish, he will see that this fish shows consistent differences in outline and dimensions from sailfish shown from the rest of the world. After spending a lot of time pursuing every source of information I could come at, I conclude that if the sailfish of the world can be divided into species, I would admit only two: the Atlantic as one, and the sailfish of the rest of the world as the other. The science of ichthyology, however, creates several species from both regions, and I am giving them here because of my personal interest in this grand fish, and because the species of sailfish has ever been a living question among the anglers and guides whom I know, and I feel sure the readers of this book will have the same curiosity.

Sailfish of the Pacific and Indian Oceans and all their tributary seas, as the reader will note from the drawings of them, are long slim chaps with slender bills and huge sailfins. The color runs, in general, to steel blue in the dorsal and body, as compared with the purple dorsal and gulf blue body of the Atlantic, and these Pacific fish show consistently the same variations as to spots, stripes, shape of dorsal, length of pectorals, and what not, among themselves, as do the Atlantic sailfish among themselves. These exotic sails average much larger in size than the Atlantic. In weight they seem to run about twice the poundage of the Atlantic fish, with proportionately greater length. In the Atlantic, sailfish average around 45 to 55 pounds, while the sails of other waters run from 125 pounds to nearly 200 pounds, as the records stand today. Authentic records at the moment show heaviest Atlantic fish 119½ pounds, an extraordinary weight, as against 187 pounds from the Pacific. It is a question whether a bigger sailfish will ever be taken from the Atlantic, but tales are rife of sailfish in the Indian Ocean reaching a length of 20 feet; weight, anybody's guess. Here is a field for the well-to-do sportsman to investigate, and his reward may be such a sailfish as will give him world renown.

In the science of zoölogy, the first-named creature is given the type scientific name, so this honor goes to the sailfish from the Indian Ocean, examined, described and named *Istiophorus gladius*, in 1786, by Broussonnet in his work *La Mer des Indies*, and pictured in colors by Cuvier and Valenciennes, from which plate the drawing was made of the typical sailfish for this book. All other sailfish are here recognized as sub-species only and bear trinomials as is the custom of science. This I do at the suggestion of John T. Nichols, Curator of Ichthyology of the American Museum of Natural History in New York, as against the usage of other scientists whose observations have been of the greatest help to me, and who have given all their sailfish the rank of full species.

So, under this arrangement, the typical Atlantic sail becomes *Istiophorus americanus*, and is the usual sailfish of our Gulf Coast, the east coast of Florida and the West Indies, as the world map shows. It is also the sailfish of the east coast of Central and South America, where it is found to the mouth of the River Plata, the southern boundary of Uruguay. This sailfish probably occurs off all the Atlantic islands within the areas indicated on the map, and is recorded on the west coast of Africa and north to the Bay of Biscay on the coast of France. Strangely enough, it does not appear to enter the Mediterranean, though conditions here would seem to be congenial for sailfish.

The sailfish runs pretty well north on our own eastern seaboard. From "The Marine Fishes of New York and Southern New England," by J. T. Nichols and C. M. Breder, Jr., the following quotation about sailfish in the region of New York State:

"Casual, Summer and early Fall, six or seven records. *Woods Hole, Massachusetts*, casual, a half dozen records in early Fall during twenty-five years. *New York* one record, August."

This little book, by the way, is most complete. Each species is illustrated with line drawings of great accuracy and is of the greatest value to the sportsman in identifying the fish he may take anywhere on our eastern coast from Maine to the Dry Tortugas, since it figures many of the tropical game fish which stray into the region of New York in summer and early Fall. It should be aboard every fishing cruiser of either the sportsman or the fishing guide. Copies may be had from the New York Aquarium, Battery Park, New York City, and the cost is one dollar and forty cents.

None of the sailfish noted above as being recorded near New York, were taken by sportsmen, I believe, and so far as I can find none have been so taken north of Florida. During the very hot Summer of 1930, when dolphin, little tunny and flying fish were abundant offshore from Barnegat Ridge off New Jersey to Martha's Vineyard, this writer fully expected to learn of the taking of a sailfish within these waters by rod and reel. The nearest this expectation came to fulfilment was the single reported instance of a sailfish being hooked and played for a half hour from the charter boat of the late Captain Brooks Van Orden on Barnegat Ridge. The fish was on long enough and leaped near enough to the boat to make it seem impossible for it to be mistaken for a marlin, and a sailfish it was declared to be. I have no doubt any sportsman ambitious enough to cruise the Gulf Stream in the latitude of Cape Cod would find sailfish there and possibly as far north as Georges Banks, where commercial fishermen, sailing from Gloucester and Portland to Georges Banks for broadbill swordfish, report flying fish and dolphin on the Banks, and these fish are a fair indication that conditions are right for sails at least in the Stream, which crosses the Banks. It will interest the big game angler to know that these same commercial chaps report big tuna and marlin on Georges Banks in abundance.

In the Gulf of Mexico the Atlantic sailfish is reported from southern Texas to Louisiana, but it is probably well offshore in the Gulf Stream as a usual thing, though it might well approach the coast in summer.

The Atlantic sailfish is more robustly built than species from other parts of the world. The depth and diameter is greater in proportion to the length, and the bill and pectorals are shorter and less slender. In color, the Atlantic sail is much richer than the Pacific, Indian and Oriental sails, though like all fishes of high color, the variation is great with the season and the waters in which it is taken. A prime Atlantic sail from the blue water will usually show a dorsal running from a pinkish purple or lilac shade, on the front of the fin, into a deeper true purple backward and toward the outer edges, becoming darker as it approaches the tips of the rays. The entire dorsal, with the exception of the first few rays, will show a greater or less profusion of roundish, half-inch spots of a very deep blackish purple, usually following with some regularity the webbed spaces between the rays, but in many instances appearing over the rays also.

The sword is a deep, blackish purple, until it reaches the enlargement which carries it into the head, where it merges into the Gulf Stream blue of the back. The entire back, to the base of the tail and about one-third of the way down the side, is a gorgeous deep blue. Between this and the silver of the sides, the fish has a band of grass green, merging imperceptibly into the blue above, but ending on the lower edge in an irregular and fairly well-defined line. The silver of the sides of a prime Atlantic sailfish is as bright as a newly-coined dime, and runs the entire length of the fish into the tail, where it spreads a little upward and quite likely more than half way downward on the tail fin itself. Forward, the silver of the side overcomes the green band just at the gill covers and continues, including the eye, to the sword, on which it appears to about the tip of the lower jaw. The line between the dark upper color and the silver from the gill covers forward is very sharply defined. The eye is silvery, with purple shades, and the triangular pupil of the eye is more or less opalescent. The silver of the sides includes the sides of the lower jaw, which darken at the tip to the

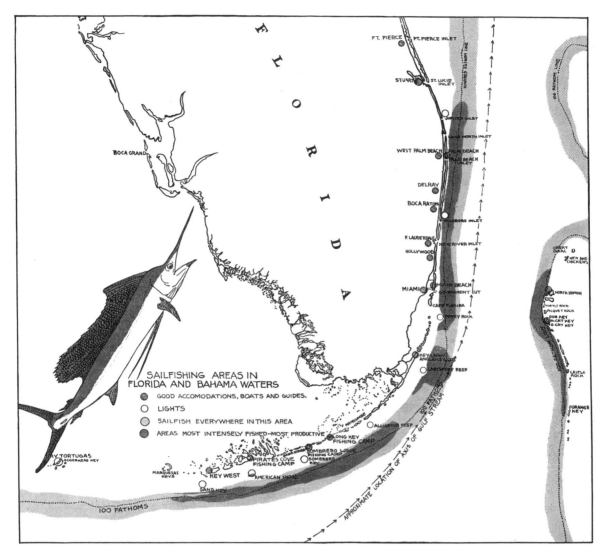

SAILFISHING AREAS IN
FLORIDA AND BAHAMA WATERS

● GOOD ACCOMODATIONS, BOATS AND GUIDES.
○ LIGHTS
● SAILFISH EVERYWHERE IN THIS AREA
● AREAS MOST INTENSELY FISHED—MOST PRODUCTIVE

Drawn by Lynn Bogue Hunt.

color of the sword. The belly is white. The pectoral fins are varying shades of blue above and silvery bluish-white below. The breast or ventral fins are extremely long, flexible affairs of a deep purple color and appear as slender, almost, as wires, until one takes the trouble to unroll them, when they become thin, membranous paddles, nearly two inches wide at the extreme ends. The anal fin is silvery white, with front rays and tips showing blackish purple. The larger part of the upper half of the tail fin is deep, purplish black, as is the tip of the lower half. Down the whole length of the fish, from the gill covers to the base of the tail, appear vertical stripes about three to four inches apart, of a dazzling turquoise blue arranged in a series of dots and dashes having the appearance, at a short distance, of continuous lines. Altogether, one of the most beautiful fishes in the world, colored and patterned in the same exquisite taste as is the wood duck, which I consider the most truly beautiful of all birds.

Aside from this fine color in the prime Atlantic sailfish, the genus is possessed throughout the world of the very finest speed lines imaginable. Long and lean, driven by a powerful tail, long sword in front broadening back to the eyes, at which point the sail has its greatest diameter and from there tapers back to knife-thin after edges of the tail fin. His great sail reefed down in the dorsal slot, long ventrals neatly stowed below, pectorals folded back snug in their depressions, the sailfish becomes an animated torpedo and like a torpedo, rips through the sea at express speed. Jordan and Evermann in "A Review of the Giant Mackerel-like Fishes, Tunnies, Spearfishes and Swordfishes," quote Mr. Hamilton M. Wright on the sailfish: "These fishes have been known to attain a speed of 60 miles an hour and to leap across 40 feet of water on a loose line." From a bulletin of the Long Key Fishing Camp, Long Key, Florida, dated February 17, 1934: "The speed of a sailfish has been estimated variously by experts, as between 40 and 60 miles an hour, and men who have timed the rushes of a sailfish on a loose line with a stop watch, say that it would take out 100 yards of line in three seconds. This would be at the rate of over 60 miles an hour." At any rate, in my experience, the sail is a fast fish in his earliest runs — even faster than any marlin I have had on, though my experience with marlin is limited to a few that were not large, and I have never fought a marlin with a drag so light as merely to prevent backlash, as I like to do with sails until the early rushes are over.

Beside *americanus*, the type sailfish of the Atlantic, three other species have recently been given a place in our own waters by Jordan and Evermann. Wright's sailfish, *Istiophorus americanus wrighti*; Voladora, *Istiophorus americanus volador*, both of Florida, and Maguire's sailfish *Istiophorus americanus maguiri* from the West Indies. The drawings of Atlantic sailfish here shown portray the differences found by these scientists and are made from specimens taken in Florida waters by the writer of this chapter. With all respect for these great scientists, it is my lay opinion that the four sailfish here figured are one species.

All sailfish anglers and guides have noticed the great variations in color, markings, length of sword, shape of dorsal and general form of sailfish taken off the Florida Coast, and I have personally observed as great differences among the sailfish caught in one day from the same waters as one would see in the figures and faces of as many white men. Yet science makes all colors and breeds of men, one species, *Homo sapiens*, divided into races which cross freely, the offspring of such crosses remaining fertile, a circumstance which, in my understanding, is quite final in determining true species.

Anyway, since I have landed from the same spot off Florida and on the same day, sailfish that could be classed as species *volador*, *wrighti* and *americanus* and at one time took from a school of four sails one of twenty-six pounds which answered perfectly to the description by Jordan and Evermann of the species *maguiri*, although another hooked at the same time from the same school was the usual type and weighed 55 pounds; I can but feel that if these scientific differences really exist, the sailfish are not aware if it, especially in the instance of the *volador*, *wrighti* and *americanus* above, which were haunting the same waters during what is supposed to be the breeding season off Florida, at which time many females are caught containing ripe roe. It is difficult for me to believe that a male *americanus*, coming upon a female *volador* in the act of discharging her eggs, would hesitate for an instant in getting busy with his fertilizing milt, or that the young of such a mésalliance would not take on the characters of either or both parents as they grew to maturity, and go merrily and ignorantly on their way, increasing and multiplying and filling the warm waters of the Atlantic Ocean and all the seas and gulfs and bays adjacent thereto.

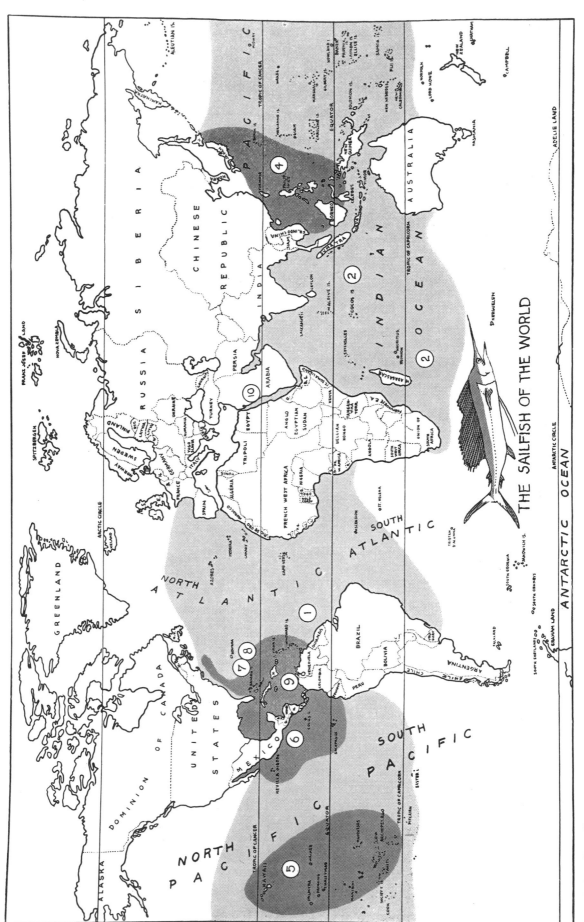

THE SAILFISH OF THE WORLD

Drawn by Lynn Bogue Hunt.

SAILFISH

In the following series of drawings showing the essential likeness existing among sailfish from widely separated points in the Pacific and Indian Oceans and all their tributary seas, the four named species from the Atlantic are also shown. The first drawing among the series is of the Atlantic sailfish, *Istiophorus gladius americanus,* and is placed in this position to give the reader at a glance the main differences between all the Atlantic species and those from the Pacific, Indian and Oriental seas. The three remaining species of sailfish from the Atlantic close the series and will be found as consistently alike among themselves as are the exotic sails among themselves. By comparing lengths and weights as given in the records at the end of this chapter the reader will be impressed by the extreme length as compared with weight of the exotic sails in contrast to the shorter heavy build of the Atlantic sail. For example, a sailfish caught at Cocos Island, Pacific Ocean, weighed only 65 pounds but was 9'6" long whereas the Hemingway-McGrath Key West sailfish weighed 119½ pounds and was but 9'¾" long, a difference of 56 pounds in weight and only 5¼" in length with the balance in favor of the lighter fish.

It will be noted that the specific names of the sailfish that appear in the following drawings are all the trinomials of subspecies with the exception of the Indian sail which is the type sailfish of the world and bears the *full species* name, *Istiophorus gladius,* and the Atlantic sailfish, *Istiophorus americanus,* the true species of our waters. The scientists whose names accompany the captions of the drawings gave each sailfish pictured the rank of *full* species and used binomials only; thus, *Istiophorus orientalis, Istiophorus greyi,* and so on right through their classifications. The names of these men are given as the namers of the species throughout the series of the pictures but they are not responsible for the introduction of the name *gladius* or *americanus* as interposed by the author in making all but the Indian sailfish and Atlantic, subspecies. This arrangement lies at the door of the author only, justified by the advice of Mr. John T. Nichols, Curator of Ichthyology, American Museum of Natural History, New York City.

The reader will see that the numbers accompanying the drawings are not in sequence. This is because they are numbered according to their placement in the world map of the distribution of the sailfish. This map was prepared with the advice and help of Mr. Nichols and of Mr. Henry W. Fowler of the Philadelphia Academy of Sciences and I wish to give both these men my thanks for their co-operation on the sailfish world map and on several others which appear in this book.

The artist makes no pretense to *scientific* accuracy in these drawings. He has neither counted rays in the fins nor measured by other means than the eye, the various relative lengths, depths and diameters used by ichthyologists in the study of fishes. The whole idea has been to give the reader at a glance the general characteristics of the sailfishes of the world as at present designated by the scientists. He has leaned heavily upon Jordan and Evermann and John T. Nichols in his search for knowledge of the sailfish in other parts of the world than Southern Florida, where his own knowledge and experience cover a period of years and even here his interest has been that of angler and artist with no real scientific qualifications. However, the drawings will show to the sportsman's eye accurately enough, the great similarity existing among sailfish from the two great, and so far as the sailfish is found, definitely separated salt water areas of the world.

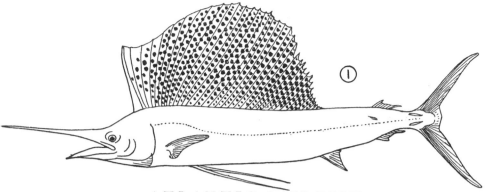

1. ATLANTIC SAILFISH

Istiophorus americanus   (Cuvier and Valenciennes)
Angler: Lynn Bogue Hunt. *Location:* off Miami, Florida. *Weight:* 68½ lb.
Length: 7′ 1″. June, 1932.

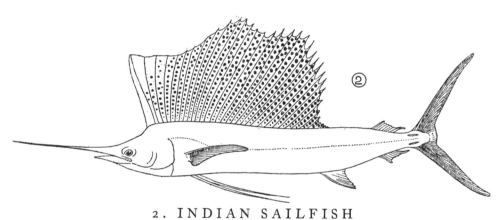

2. INDIAN SAILFISH

Istiophorus gladius   (Brousonnet)
The type species of all sailfish. Named from the Indian Ocean by Brousonnet in 1876
in his work *La Mer des Indies*

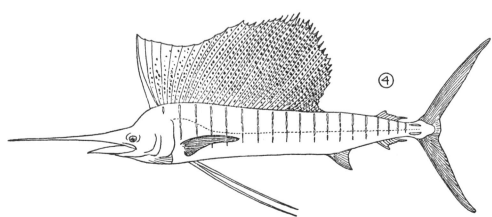

4. PHILIPPINE SAILFISH

Istiophorus gladius orientalis   (Temminck and Schlegel)
Taken by a commercial fisherman. *Location:* Manila, Philippine Islands.
Weight, length and date unknown.

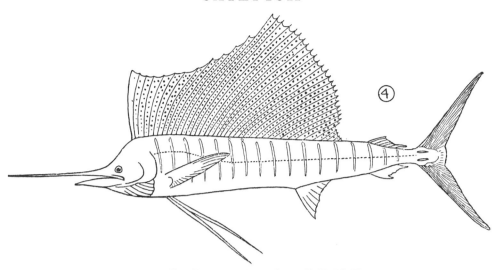

4. JAPANESE SAILFISH

Istiophorus gladius orientalis   Picture basing species (Temminck and Schlegel)
Locality: Japanese waters. No photographs accessible. This drawing from a color plate
by Temminck and Schlegel.

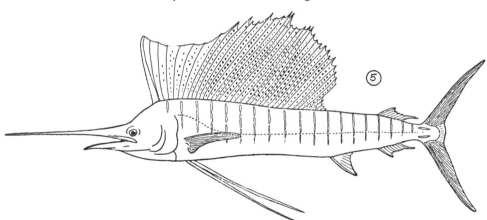

5. TAHITIAN SAILFISH

Istiophorus gladius greyi   (Jordan and Evermann)
Angler: Eastham Guild.
Location: Papeete, Tahiti. *Weight:* 160 lb. *Length:* 10′ 2″. September, 1928.

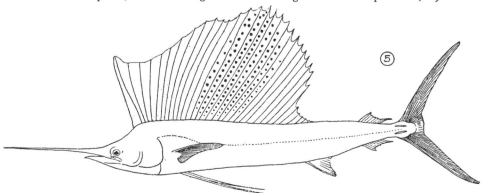

5. HAWAIIAN SAILFISH

Istiophorus gladius eriquius   (Jordan and Ball)
From a photograph. Weight, length, date, location and angler unknown.

SAILFISH

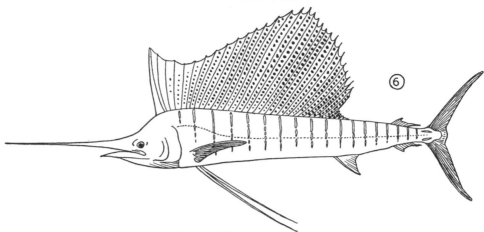

6. GREY'S SAILFISH

Istiophorus gladius greyi   (Jordan and Evermann)
Angler: Zane Grey. *Location:* off Cape San Lucas, Lower California.
Weight: 138 lb. *Length:* 10′1″. September, 1925.

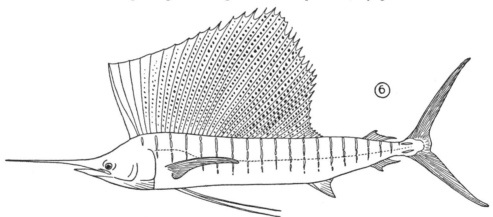

6. PANAMA SAILFISH

Istiophorus gladius greyi   (Jordan and Evermann)
From photograph furnished by Edmund S. Whitman of the United Fruit Co.
Angler: unknown. *Location:* Pacific Sailfish Club, Bay of Panama.
Weight, length and date unknown.

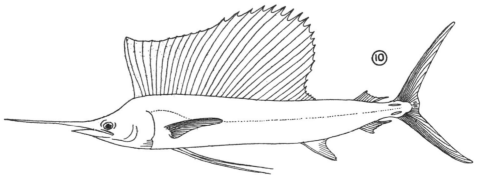

10. RED SEA SAILFISH

Istiophorus gladius immaculatus   (Ruppell)
Described from the Red Sea. Considered identical with the Indian Sailfish. Color
described as gray and silver with no spots on the dorsal fin. Probably
from a fish sometime dead.

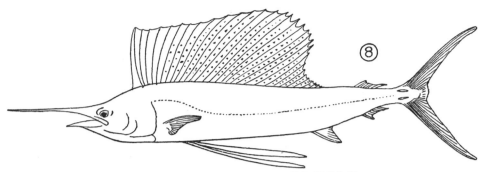

8. WRIGHT'S SAILFISH

Istiophorus americanus wrighti (Jordan and Evermann)
Angler: Lynn Bogue Hunt. *Location:* Key Largo Anglers Club, Key Largo, Florida.
Weight: 26 lb. *Length:* 5'10". December, 1932.

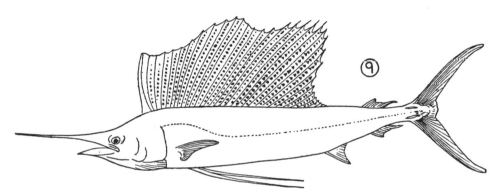

9. MAGUIRE'S SAILFISH

Istiophorus americanus maguiri (Jordan and Evermann)
Angler: Lynn Bogue Hunt. *Location:* off Miami, Florida. *Weight:* 32 lb.
Length: 6'. April, 1929.

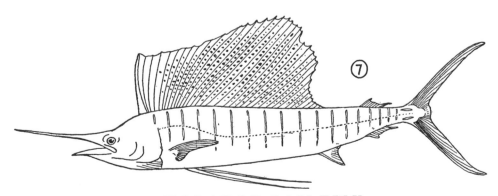

7. VOLADOR SAILFISH

Istiophorus americanus volador (Jordan and Evermann)
Angler: Lynn Bogue Hunt. *Location:* off Miami, Florida. *Weight:* 42½ lb.
Length: 6'8½". April, 1929.

BIG GAME FISHING

Three very interesting, apparently intermediate forms, showing characteristics of both the sailfish and the marlin. Drawn from photographs and descriptions by Jordan and Evermann of specimens found in the markets of Honolulu in 1925.

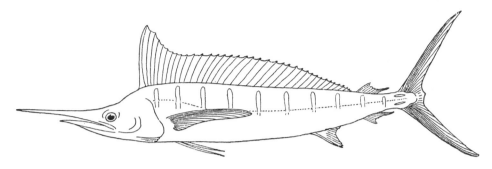

MAKAIRA GRAMMATICA

Note the height of the after part of the dorsal fin as compared with the dorsals of the black, blue, striped and white marlins; also the big marlin tail and pectoral.

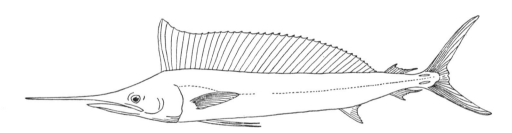

TETRAPTURUS ILLINGWORTHI

Note the sailfish-like slender body, the sailfish tail, the intermediate character of the dorsal fin, the short pectoral fin, and the marlin-like ventrals.

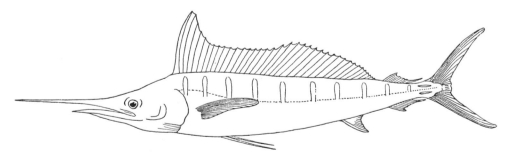

TETRAPTURUS ECTENES

Note the marlin-like body, short ventrals, long pectoral, sailfish-like tail and the dorsal showing a tendency to become sail-like aft; also the sailfish-like head.

SAILFISH

It is to be hoped that more sportsmen in the future will invite scientists to accompany them on their sailfishing expeditions, thus giving these men the opportunity to study these fish as specimens fresh from the water, instead of being obliged to confine their researches to skins, mounted specimens, photographs, and too often, mere parts of the fish of which they are seeking knowledge. Ernest Hemingway did this during the summer of 1934, when he invited C. M. B. Cadwalader and Henry W. Fowler, of the Philadelphia Academy of Sciences, to study the marlin of the coast of Cuba aboard his cruiser "Pilar." Some quotations from the book, "A Review of the Giant Mackerel-like Fishes, Tunnies, Spearfishes and Swordfishes," by Jordan and Evermann, and published by the California Academy of Sciences, will give the reader an idea of the chaotic nature of scientific knowledge of sailfish. In the second paragraph of their introduction to the chapter on sailfish, they say: "Lütken recognizes as valid species of *Istiophorus*, only *gladius* and one other, apparently *orientalis*, the last not stated clearly." In the third paragraph of this introduction they say: "No one knows what changes sailfishes undergo in the process of development and it is quite possible that some characters used by us in the following key are matters of age instead of differing with species." And later, in the same paragraph: "The color may also change with age instead of differing with species." It appears in some places in this book that species have been named from photographs and descriptions sent in by sportsmen and from other rather meager sources, which seems hardly fair to the fish if better opportunities can be afforded scientific men, interested in the study of sailfish.

Very few anglers have had the curiosity or patience or whatever it requires to dissect their sailfish with an eye to determining by infallible means the sex of the fish they have taken, and so learn to distinguish the male from the female by their outward appearance. The taxidermists, however, are in a different category, and I have found them men who are much interested students of fish from the natural history point of view, aside from the commercial angle, and have explored the sailfish from end to end, finding out what they could of the outward differences between the sexes, having determined by dissection which is male and which is female. Another important item they investigate is the kinds of fish the sail has been killing for food, and in addition to this, the parasites he carries about with him in his gills and in his digestive tract.

These taxidermists and such anglers as have looked for themselves are agreed that the heaviest but not the longest of the sails brought in are females; the long slender sails under sixty-five pounds being males. To quote a letter from Mr. Henry U. Birdseye of Miami Beach, an ardent sailfish angler of long and studious experience: "According to my experience all the real heavy (not long) sailfish are females, and sixty-five pounds seems to be the limit of weight of males in this vicinity. The females run here up to eighty-nine pounds which is the largest taken in these waters. The Miami Beach Rod and Reel Club's record is seventy-six pounds caught on a fly rod by yours truly." And again, from the same letter: "The female fish are very broad and heavy set. The seventy-six pound female was seven feet eight inches long, while I have seen a fifty-four pound male fish which was eight feet four and a half inches long."

Mr. Albert Pflueger, noted naturalist and taxidermist of Miami, tells me that female sailfish average much heavier than the males, as he has determined from the study of hundreds of specimens which have been sent to the Pflueger Museum Company for mounting. He also adds that he has never observed any difference in color between the sexes.

Mr. Fred C. N. Parke, who halves the honors as naturalist and taxidermist, with Mr. Pflueger, writes me from his Parke Marine Museum at Palm Beach: "I have never detected any difference in the colors of the male and female sailfish. I have found through close observation that the female fish is usually larger and appears to possess more muscular appearance. They usually run larger in size and it is quite easy to determine the difference between the male and female without dissecting them."

It is generally accepted by the guides that the heavy-bodied (short for weight) sails are females, and that the longer, slender fish are males, and it is a common thing to hear them pronounce the fish a male or a female in no uncertain terms as it comes aboard. Color has never seemed to be a determining sex character in the opinion of these men.

It is certain that sailfish breed in the waters off Florida, and it seems likely that the breeding takes place wherever the sails may be at the right season throughout the world. How they go about it I have never been able to learn. It is certain of course that the sexes do not get together in the same sense that they do among mammals, birds, reptiles and insects, but there is reason to believe that they run in pairs or with two or three males following one female which is carrying ripe roe. Perhaps, being allied fish, sailfish do as Ernest Hemingway

Sailfish doing a "tail walk."

The tired sailfish.

This sailfish came clear out and is going in head first.

Baby sailfish taken from the stomach of a dolphin.

states about marlin. In this case, the male and female lie head to tail, discharging the roe and the milt at the same time. If this is true, the eggs must be pelagic, but I have not been able to make sure about this. It may be that the eggs are deposited on sandy bottom, on the coral rock, or attached to gulf weed, or merely cast free anywhere, to drift and take their chances in a ravenous world. All the sailfish anglers of experience, and all the guides and taxidermists I know are agreed that the breeding season off Florida is during late June, July and August, when females are taken filled with roe so ripe that it frequently pours forth from the body as the fish are being hauled aboard. At this season also, it has been noted that a female may be closely followed by one or more other sailfish, presumably male, while she is being played by the angler, these fish sometimes hanging about close alongside while she is being landed. This might indicate that fertilization may take place in the stream but the fish may go into shoal water to spawn, as indicated by observations by John Mahony of Miami, a keen angler, who writes as follows: "Chub Wafford and I, together and separately, have repeatedly seen sails milling about in the summer months, four to six in a bunch, in clear white sandy patches in the green water, 'way inside the reef, in holes forty to sixty feet in diameter, ten to twenty feet deep. They act very much like black bass when the latter are nesting, though they seemed neither boat shy, nor pugnacious. To me, they look to be doing what bass do when they 'fan' the spawn."

The presence of numbers of tiny sails in the waters off Florida is only secondary evidence of local breeding, since the very young of many ocean fishes appear at enormous distances from the places where it is known the eggs are deposited. I have never had the good fortune to take any tiny sails from the stomachs of other fish or to see schools of them in the water, so I have gone to the best possible sources of which I know, for what information is to be had on baby sailfish. Little sails of a few inches in length have been taken from the stomachs of dolphin and bonito off Miami. Taxidermist Al Pflueger, of that city, has some of these little ones preserved in alcohol. He writes me of one such specimen taken from a dolphin by Captain Hutter, and five taken from the stomach of an eight-pound bonito, which were from nine and a half to eleven inches overall. Captain Herman Gray, who fishes from Palm Beach, and is one of the best-known charter boatmen of North America, writes me: "I know of one sailfish seven inches long that was caught in a net here about three years ago.

Another instance where a school of fifty or sixty, none over a foot long, were around a boat for twenty minutes or more after baits, but they failed to hook one as the baits were too large." Which must have been a sight to remember! John Mahony writes from Miami: "Many instances are known of sailfish measuring six to ten inches having been taken by the guides from the bellies of other fish. They have been found in dolphin, tuna, bonito and possibly others, but these I know about. In these little specimens, the colors are bright and the body quite fresh, indicating that they must have been killed in the immediate vicinity, for otherwise they would be partially decomposed, as food disintegrates very rapidly in a fish's stomach. Except that the eyes and sail are disproportionately large, the rest of the proportions seem perfect, though the coloring is rather more vivid than in the adults."

From taxidermist Fred C. N. Parke of Palm Beach, I have a letter which says in part: "I have known of three small sailfish being taken from the stomach of the dolphin. This occurred near Long Key during the month of February, 1931, if I am correct in the year. One of these little specimens was in almost a perfect state of preservation, the other two more or less digested but with sufficient undigested portions to establish beyond a doubt that they were sailfish. These three were taken from one fish, which seems definitely to establish the fact that they travel in schools when small in size."

Here are some little sailfish which probably were eggs the previous summer. Apparently no one knows the interval between the laying of the eggs and the hatching of the larval sailfish, nor the length of the larval stage. Once the larva has changed to the final stage, the little sail, like all fishes where food is abundant, probably grows very rapidly to a size where he is able to take a regular sail bait, though it may be some years before he is big enough to excite pride of achievement in the angler who gets him.

Sailfish were known off Florida, among commercial fishermen, a long time ago, and probably one was occasionally snagged by them because he fouled himself in striking the bait which was being trolled for other fish, or was fairly hooked by taking it directly in his mouth without the preliminary tap, as sails sometimes do. It began to be noticed that sailfish always returned to pick up the bait when it had been knocked free by the strike, and when one wanted to hook a sail it became the practice, about 1904 or 1905, to carry a loose coil of the line on the stern while holding the hand line with the fingers and letting the coil run out after the strike. Who actually started this coiled line business is the subject of much discussion, but the honor seems to belong to Captain Charlie Thompson, a great fisherman and a man of enormous reputation in the history of offshore fishing when the sailfish was a curiosity, had no significance among sportsmen and was only a nuisance to the commercial men.

As to who started sport fishing for sails as practiced today, all the old-time anglers and guides are agreed. Somewhere in the middle teens of 1900, a man began to be talked of everywhere among offshore anglers as the keenest, most observing, hardest-working and most successful of all the angling guides of America: Captain W. D. ("Bill") Hatch. The history of sailfishing with rod and reel began in 1915, when Captain Hatch became peeved because sailfish were continually mangling his kingfish baits. Now kingfish were the prime off-shore game fish of these ancient days, and anything that ruined the kingfish bait was public enemy number one. Bill Hatch was not the man to let this sort of thing go on without trying to turn the tables on an occasional sail. So, having observed that the sail almost invariably struck the bait with his sword as he rushed it, and then if he knocked it free of the hook, returned to take it in his mouth, Bill tried letting his bait run aft following the strike, thus giving the sail the illusion that he had killed his prey; whereupon the fish promptly swirl-ed about, took it in his mouth, and his troubles began. I would like to have been aboard the day that first sailfish was hooked on rod and reel and won his place for all time to come as a beautiful and spectacular game fish. I can picture the open-mouthed, bug-eyed excitement on that boat when the prick of the hook started those terrific rushes, those wild leaps and tail walks, all foaming against the blue. Here was a fish that could put on the greatest show of them all and try the true skill of the angler as no game of the open sea had done before. True, the leaping tuna of Catalina was a somewhat showy fighter, as was the tarpon of less open waters; but both were, at that time at least, main strength game, and their jumps, at best, were few. In the sailfish, Captain Hatch had found a strenuous and willing fighter, easily accessible, present in good numbers and existing in waters and under skies and climate the most beautiful in the world. So he set himself about the study of the sail and how to hook and play him. He learned the proper interval to allow between the strike and the pick-up. He studied methods of rigging mullet so they would troll in a life-like manner, having seen that a sailfish shies at a bait that looks unnatural to him. He found mullet somewhat short of ideal for sailfishing, since it is soft, wears out quickly, and is ruined at once for further fishing when struck by a sail which fails to pick it up. So he cast about for tougher bait and hit upon strips from the sides of bonito and dolphin and from the bellies of barracuda. They worked. And so began the nearly universal use of cut bait for sailfishing as practiced to this day.

With the use of these cut baits arose the problem of making them fast to hook and leader easily and quickly, in a way to make them troll well. At first the new-fangled bait was held at the forward end of the hook by a wire pin only, and the fish frequently knocked it off the pin in the strike, when it became a shapeless gob which no longer interested the sail. This difficulty was overcome by securing the forward tip of the bait to the leader with thread or fine wire. But this took time and bother when business was brisk, and to overcome this difficulty the safety pin was invented. I have been unable to learn if Captain Hatch was the creator of this device, but its simple ingenuity is like him and I shall believe it was his idea until it can be shown it was the notion of some other man. Anyway, it has continued in use among all guides, varying in shape according to each captain's idea of what constitutes an ideal safety pin, but the principle is the same in all.

Captain Hatch was cagey and kept the results of all his experiments to himself, with the result that he was the only guide to bring in sailfish consistently from 1915 to 1923. He achieved a deservedly great reputation and his services were in high demand. But the climax came in 1925, during the tournament at the Long Key Fishing Camp, when he brought in one hundred and thirteen sailfish, as against one hundred and six racked by the twelve other boats fishing in the contest.

There are dozens of fine guides along the Florida coast, and I have fished with many of them. They all work hard and most of them are good company as well. It is not easy to refrain, right here, from naming a few of them for their knowledge of sailfishing, seamanship and constant attention to the success and comfort of their patrons; but I am confining myself at this time to the one man who discovered and developed the methods that have made the sailfishing charter possible to all of them.

Captain Bill is easily the dean of American charter boatmen and continues to hold his high place in the esteem of his patrons and his fellow pro's. He and his cruiser "Patsy" find themselves booked for the Florida season before the

Captain W. D. ("Bill") Hatch, dean of American charter boatmen.

season begins, and big-game anglers of the country compete for his services during the offshore season in the North.

In the early days of rod and reel sailfishing the tackle was clumsy. The heavy rods, lines and reels are museum pieces now. And the sails were fought with might and main. Hook him and hold him was the order of the day. But no one could hold him so hard that he couldn't jump once or twice in spite of this manhandling, which by no means brought out his possibilities; and the sailfish continued to grow in fame as a grand game fish. In the early 1920's lighter tackle came into vogue among sportsmen who believed the sailfish, like other game fish, would put on a better show if more lightly held, and a sail rig was evolved consisting of a two piece, six-foot-overall rod with a tip not to exceed six ounces in weight and a butt not to exceed fourteen inches in length. The tip was rigged with proper guides and had a hand grip above the base where the tip was inserted into the butt socket which carried the reel seat and had another long grip below. Star drag reels had been made by the Vom Hofes in 1911 and catalogued in 1915 (these dates from Mr. W. B. Fenton, President of Edw. Vom Hofe & Company). These marked a tremendous advance in reels for the big-game angler and came early into general use for sailfishing in the 3/0 and 4/0 sizes with lines of various weights. It was found that standard nine-thread linen line skillfully handled, would put the light restraint on the sailfish which made him fight more desperately and showily to rid himself of the hook and was at the same time strong enough to pump a sounding sulker and to handle well a tired fish in bringing it to the boat. So nine-thread line was adopted as light tackle for sailfish, and the six-ounce-tip, six-foot rod became the famous 6-9 tackle of club and tournament rules of the present day. This rig is plenty heavy enough to manage any sailfish likely to be hooked in the Atlantic.

The game sailfish during the early twenties, grew in popularity by leaps and bounds, the tales of his game qualities began to attract anglers to southern Florida from all the world. As these men came in greater and greater numbers to the various Florida towns accessible to the Gulf Stream, the business of guiding for sails assumed the aspect of a major industry. Boats, tackle, and the quality of fishing captains improved rapidly and various cities began to create fine docking facilities for their fleets of charter boats. Chambers of commerce saw the publicity value of the sailfish for their communities and began to broadcast him in the papers as news and in fine pictures in the rotogravure sections of Sunday editions throughout the land. No real estate development on the east coast of southern Florida during the boom years failed to list the sailfish as an important reason why you should "make your home with us." The railroad and steamship companies urged the public in their folders to buy tickets to the home of the sailfish. Hotels sought the patronage of the sailfish-minded and the sail was, and still is, a never failing topic of conversation among anglers of all walks of life in southern Florida and everywhere else in the Union where offshore sportsmen get together.

The sailfish has done a great deal for southern Florida.

It was bound to follow, with the development of lighter tackle for sails, that some salmon, trout or bass fisherman from the fresh waters, or some man who fished blues or stripers with tender rigs, would try just how far he could go with sailfish. Various stunts were tried with more or less success, until, on January 5, 1929, there appeared in the rod and gun column of the New York *Herald Tribune* the following story:

"L. R. Connett, president of the L. R. Connett Marine Transportation Company of New York, and a member of the Miami and New York Anglers' Clubs, established a new vogue in fishing when he landed two sailfish over fifty pounds on a twelve foot grilse rod with a nine thread line and a 2/o reel. He was fishing with H. U. Birdseye of New York, on board the 'Patsy' commanded by Captain W. D. Hatch.

"The rod is the lightest tackle ever used on a sailfish and is virtually a trout rod. One fish was landed in thirty-nine minutes and gave thirty-seven leaps from the water. The other was landed in nineteen minutes. A six ounce tip and nine thread line is considered light tackle but Mr. Connett's feat showed that a sailfish can be played and landed on the lightest tackle. The party landed three fish, but released two of them, Mr. Birdseye catching the third fish."

Within a couple of years of this date I met both Mr. Connett and Mr. Birdseye and have had the story at first hand from them. The possibility of taking a sail on a grilse rod occurred to Mr. Connett in the summer of 1928, so among his tackle when he went South in December for his winter stay, he included a couple of his salmon rods. These were twelve-foot, three-piece grilse rods, the butt piece having two grips, the assembled rods weighing twelve ounces each. Connett's ambition to fish the stream with the buggy whip was received with smiles and witty comments on Pier 5 in Miami, where the characters and achievements of anglers get plenty of caustic discussion. Even Captain Bill Hatch, that open-minded guide, with whom Connett and his friend Birdseye were going to try the salmon rods, was skeptical about the possibility of setting the hook with so limber a rod or playing a sailfish at all if he managed to get on. However, Connett had his own ideas about all these questions and when a sail was raised and smacked the bait, he dropped back to him in the usual way but instead of setting the hook by coming back with his tip, he pointed his grilse rod straight toward the fish and gave the whole rig a jerk backward for a full arm swing and set the hook with the strength of his line and his thumb pressure on the reel. There ensued a pretty fight and the sixty-pound sailfish was landed easily after a short battle during which he leaped more and fought harder than any sail was ever seen to do before.

Mr. Henry U. Birdseye, then of New York but now of Miami Beach, describes this experiment in a recent letter as follows:

"Now as to the question of fishing for sailfish with fly rods and extremely light tackle. The idea originally started with Lyndon Connett, who about 1928 brought to Miami for a fishing trip with me, some 12 foot salmon rods. These were used and several sailfish landed, but while they were probably the most deadly piece of fishing tackle ever invented for sailfishing, they were found to be impractical because of their extreme length, and the difficulty of getting the fish near enough to the boat for the guide to get hold of the leader. I speak of them as 'deadly' because in the first place the salmon rod is as heavy at the butt as light tackle (6 ounce tip), and the enormous length and springiness of the rod never permitted an inch of slack line to the fish. In other words for 90% of the time the fish was far away from the boat, 50% of the rod went out of action as it was in a straight line with the line, and you have virtually the action of a 6 foot 6 ounce rod."

The success of this Connett experiment excited tremendous interest among anglers and charter boatmen who had always regarded the sailfish as much too powerful for anything lighter or less stiff than the light tackle six-ounce tip. Other anglers began to try light stuff for sails at once. Quoting again from the Birdseye letter:

"The following year (1929) a bet was made by some people who ridiculed the idea of light tackle, — that I could not take a fly-rod and use it in the Gulf Stream for three consecutive fishing days without its being broken. The only fly-rod I had at that time was a 4½ ounce 9 foot rod, and to this I fastened an 8 inch wooden butt because no wrist is strong enough to hold the average fly-rod during a ten or fifteen minute fight with a fish, no fly-rod reel is big enough to hold the required amount of line, no one hand action with a regular fly-rod can get in line fast enough or control the line when fighting with a sailfish. The reel used was a 3-0-Vom Hofe, and 400 yards of 6 thread line. The first sailfish was landed in sixteen minutes and weighed forty pounds. Forty-six leaps were made and the fish literally ran itself to death. Using this same rod, eight sailfish were caught, and probably a hundred other types of fish.

"There was a great disadvantage to the use of this extremely light rod, however, for when a fish of the plunging type (bonito, tuna, etc.) came along and sounded, it was extremely difficult to raise the fish from the bottom and land it. Experiments were therefore conducted to see how light a rod could be produced and yet have lifting capacity. After repeated experiments it was found that a 9 foot rod, weighing 5½ ounces (about the weight of a standard bass rod) would give the desired result, and practically all of the extra ounce was put in the lower part of the rod just above the reel where the strain is naturally the greatest. In order to remedy the defect of detachable handle the rod, however, was increased 12 inches and this extra foot put 3½ ounces onto the butt so that the total weight of the rod was 9 ounces. This rod was manufactured by Heddon, and it is the official rod of the Key Largo anglers' tournament. How successful it has been you know, and no one has ever broken a rod in fair usage."

As I understand it, Mr. Birdseye and Mr. Stewart Miller of Miami collaborated in the experiments which resulted in this salt-water fly-rod as now manufactured by Heddon and called by them the "Stewart Miller Salt Water Fly Rod." I purchased one of these rods from Stewart Miller in 1930 and the following spring used it on sailfish for the first time, getting two sails the first day, one of which weighed sixty-eight pounds, the other fifty-two. Both were strong and willing fighters and put on the most spectacular battles I had ever seen. The length and spring of the rod made it necessary to let the sailfish have their way at all times, and the light drag of the reel and the line in the water made them take to the air dozens of times, wildly plunging and shaking to dislodge that pestiferous thing which was annoying them so. The length and willowy spring of the rod, together with the skillful maneuvering of the boat, gave these fish no instant of slack line and they wore themselves docile in jig

Courtesy of Lynn Bogue Hunt.   *Photo by Parter Varney.*
LANDING THE SAILFISH.

Photo by G. W. Romer, Miami.
LYNN BOGUE HUNT.

Courtesy of Lynn Bogue Hunt.

N. Jerlaw of Chicago with his world's record sail-fish on extremely light tackle at the Long Key Fishing Camp, Long Key, Florida.

Photo by DeLaney & Beers, Miami.

74½ pound sailfish caught in 36 minutes on a Stewart Miller saltwater fly rod by Henry U. Birdseye.

time. The sixty-eight pound sail was in the boat twenty-nine minutes after he was hooked, and the fifty-two pounder lasted exactly eighteen minutes, ten of which were spent in leaps and tail walks. All this with none of the old-time grinding and hauling on the part of the angler. In fact, except for the rapid reeling when the fish were headed toward the boat, and the necessary work in bringing the tired fish up to the captain's reach, I had nothing much to do but watch the fish, and at no time was either fish more than three hundred feet away, due, I believe, to the fact that they took to the air almost at once upon feeling the hook and came out repeatedly after very short runs. I have adopted this rod for my own constant use off Florida, and have easily taken all offshore fish of Florida waters with this salt water fly rod except marlin and I believe it is a wholly adequate rig for any marlin which is likely to be hooked in the waters off Miami or down the Florida Keys. Bimini and Cuba are a different story, as would be the Pacific on sails. This rod is fine for dolphin, bonito, small tuna and barracuda as big as they are likely to come off Florida. I once killed a forty-seven-pound amberjack with it, but for bulldog reef fish the rod is not fair to the rest of the party. The rod is a good one and tough, and will never be broken on fish in the hands of an angler of any skill and experience. All members of the parties at Key Largo Anglers' Club tournaments of December 1932 and 1933 were using these rods for six days on each occasion and no rod was broken, though they took a great many sailfish and several of the party on each trip had never fished for heavy game before. This rod being nine feet long makes it necessary for the angler to move back from the stern as he brings his fish alongside, so the captain may reach the leader, and in a heavy sea this is a bit awkward and constitutes the one objection to the rod on some of the boats that do not have roomy cockpits. It is an ideal rod for use from those boats which have fishing seats aloft, as so many of them are being equipped nowadays.

For those who depend upon the boat to furnish light tackle, the captains are beginning to carry rods of Calcutta cane, another innovation of H. U. Birdseye, and I quote him on this new idea:

"Now as to the development of the solid bamboo rod. Most rods are built from split bamboo which comes from Tonkin, French Indo-China, but recently I discovered here a shipment of what are known as Calcutta canes, and began experimenting with these. The Calcutta is fairly straight, practically solid, and nearly unbreakable. The hole in the interior of the cane, even at the butt, should be no larger than the lead in a lead pencil. I experimented with these rods, — built and gave away a number of fly-rods (10 feet long and made in two pieces, cut in the middle), — just as good today as when made, although it must be admitted that they take a slight 'set' which is easily taken out by bending the rod against the 'set' after the fish is landed. These rods, as I have said before, are practically unbreakable, and I know of only one which has been broken, and that was when a very powerful man tried to set the hook in a large tarpon and splintered his rod in the terrific jerk he gave. There have been several hundred of these Calcutta cane rods built, mostly in the three-six class and here they are ideal. I deliberately tried to break one some time ago on a fifteen-foot shark, and having fought him normally for over an hour, I screwed down the drag to the extreme limit of the 6-thread line and bent the rod practically double, and with this amount of strain only succeeded in breaking the rod after ten minutes of trolling. Any split bamboo rod would have broken in the first thirty seconds. Recently the charter boatmen are buying heavy butt ends and use them for rods which they give to their parties, and in some moving pictures taken of the big marlin at Bimini I noticed that Tommy Gifford was using these rods for his larger fish, and having no difficulty in handling marlin up to three hundred pounds."

The reader will see, in the portrait of Captain Bill Hatch, that he is holding one of these Calcutta bamboo rods.

Some time before the fly rod was perfected, a neat light rig was developed, consisting of a six-foot, six-ounce overall rod, using six-thread line. This outfit is called 3-6 tackle and is a favorite with many sailfish anglers and remarkable fishing stunts have been done with it. I have never used this rig, being entirely devoted to the salt-water fly rod with nine-thread line.

Within very recent years some successful sailfishing has been done with much lighter tackle than any of the above. Notable among the anglers who have been trying to take sails on delicate rigs is Mr. N. Jerlaw of Chicago, who landed in February, 1934, a fifty-five pound sailfish in twelve minutes on a six-thread line and a rod weighing only two and a half ounces overall; the bamboo in the rod weighing just one and a half ounces and the aluminum one ounce. This rod is slightly over five feet long and a small bass reel was used. This is a world's record to date, but Mr. Jerlaw is trying to beat it during this 1935 season. On February 19, 1935, fishing from the Long Key Fishing Camp, he fought a large sailfish for fifty-eight minutes, using his two and a half ounce rod, a small bass reel and a four-thread line as against the six-thread line above. He lost the fish, but the fact that he held a big one for so long on the lightest tackle ever used on sailfish is an achievement in itself and reflects great credit on the extreme skill of the angler.

I have never gone beyond the fly rod and nine-thread line in my fishing for sails. These light tackle stunts are interesting to all anglers but in practice they are for the few and must lose a tremendous number of fish. The salt-water fly rod is plenty sporty and it is a killer of sailfish beyond any I have ever used. I have lost sails on it, but always from kinked leaders or lines parted in any of the ways this can happen in sailfishing; never from any fault of the rod and never in landing the fish. I do not in the least mind losing a fish that has put on a grand show. I take off my hat to the warrior who has proven himself too much for me and my rig or has had the fortune to place any of the many hazards of sailfishing between himself and me. Of course if he is gilled or has swallowed the bait, his chances of freeing himself are small, and in these events he would die of his injuries if he did get free; but if fair hooked and he escapes, no especial harm will come to him. I think the presence of the hook in his mouth will not last long and will in no way interfere with his feeding or any other of the joys of life for a sailfish. I have caught a number of sails that have had extensive injuries from shark, barracuda or what not at some time in their lives but have seemed to be in excellent trim for all that, and I am not willing to believe that a mere hook in his jaw is going to slow a sail so badly that the sharks will get him.

There is always some controversy as to the wisdom of releasing sailfish after they have been played to the boat; the arguments against this being that sharks can easily catch a tired sail or will be attracted to him by the slight discharge of blood from where he was hooked. Long ago I saw a sailfish, which was on its side from exhaustion and ready to be taken aboard, so electrified by the approach of a big barracuda which came up to see what it was all about, that he leaped aboard from a standing start, and it took the captain, the mate and the angler to subdue him in the cockpit. My first 6-9 sailfish was brought to the boat motionless on its side, after forty minutes of strenuous fighting, but the instant the captain touched the leader, that sail jumped so high and so far forward as to poke his bill through a cabin window, screen and all! On another occasion, a sail ready to be brought aboard after thirty minutes' fighting in the green water, was so scared by a huge grouper that he tore away for the Stream and was not brought aboard until twenty minutes later, a half mile out in the blue! I have had sharks kill my sailfish on the line, but not often. Sharks are not particularly bad in Florida waters. I think I have lost a good many sails that from their actions I believed were being chased by sharks, but in each case the line seemed to have been parted by the shark himself when he snapped at the fish, or it was rasped in two on the shark's rough skin. Once the sail is free, I do not believe any shark except possibly a white shark or a mako could catch him. These and many other instances are good evidence to me that a released sail can take care of himself. I have stood by several times to see how soon a tired sail could get going, and a minute or two has always been enough for him to gather way and be off about his affairs. Setting the boat full speed ahead starts a released sail off like a shot. So release your uninjured sail with a clear conscience as to his future.

I am thankful that my sailfishing began with a six-ounce tip. The captains were still carrying very heavy rods and lines for their patrons' use and still do unless they know their man, since all sorts and conditions of anglers who visit Florida want to write home that they have caught the famous sailfish in the Gulf Stream, and very few of the general run are to be trusted with tackle that can be broken. I had fallen in love with a Vom Hofe six-ounce-tip, six-foot rod at Boca Grande where, in my ignorance, I had gone for tarpon in *January*, rigged with a ten-ounce rod and a Meisselbach surf-casting reel. There were no tarpon, and I had to be content with sea trout, spanish mackerel, blue-fish and redfish, with an occasional jack in the passes. With my outfit, this was cruelty to fish, so I blew myself to the Vom Hofe rod which, with one other, I have to this day. They have seen a lot of service and with an annual coat of varnish are still as good as new, though some years have passed since I took them out of the store. I have caught very many sailfish on them, a few marlin, many tuna up to fifty pounds, an amberjack of seventy pounds off Marquesas Keys below Key West (this was the first heavy fish of my career), and all the small stuff that comes between. The amberjack was the victim, also, of my first Edward Vom Hofe 4/o reel, which is still in service and but for a spread spool (my own foolishness in directly reeling and so packing the eighteen-thread line while fighting a boatload of barracuda at Sand Key off Key West), has given splendid service. My one objection to the Vom Hofe reel is the undersized handle, which badly cramps the fingers during a hard fight. For this reason only, my Vom Hofe's have taken second place in my tackle box to the Pflueger Atlapac, which I have in 4/o and 6/o. These reels are a trifle heavy but are sturdily built, have big line capacity and above all are equipped with man-sized crank handles which can be used all day without giving the angler writer's cramp.

All my sailfishing these days is done with the Stewart Miller-Heddon salt-water fly rod on which, because of its lightness and quality, I use a Pflueger Capitol reel of three hundred yards, nine-thread line capacity. This is a very inexpensive reel as compared with Vom Hofe's and the Atlapac, but if kept well oiled and packed with grease, will give perfect satisfaction. On this reel the adjustment of the drag is a little coarse. A very slight turn of the star will tighten the drag too much or give the angler a more free spool than he wants. A few trials will overcome this, but it is a thing to be borne in mind in the excitement of handling an active sail.

I began my sailfishing with eighteen-thread line, went from that to fifteen, then to twelve and finally my mentors in the game, Jack Mahony of Miami and the guide who has always been my favorite, Captain O. L. Schubert of the Floridian Fishing Dock, Miami Beach, decided it was time for the promising pupil to get in the light tackle class and begin using nine-thread. It is a sad story. I bought a nine-thread, of what brand I do not know. The sails began smacking my bait while still in the green water. I had twelve of them on before noon, and every one popped my brand new nine-thread line. The thirteenth, at about three in the afternoon, took my bait while I was letting it run aft, and before I could thumb the spool or throw on the drag, he gave me the backlash of a lifetime, so I quit and headed for the Government Cut. I hadn't much line left anyway, and the mess on my reel finally had to be hacked off with a knife. On the way in, Schuby said to me, "What kind of line was that you were using today?" I told him I couldn't say, since I had put the line on the reel at my hotel and had tossed the spools in the waste basket. "Well," says good old Schuby, "you go yourself around to the tackle stoah tomorrow mawnin and get yourself an Ashaway line, and we'll go outside and catch ourselves a sail. I think that was poah line you had today." I did, and by ten o'clock the next day had my first light tackle sailfish in the cockpit after a hard, forty-minute fight, in which the hook had cut such a slot in the fish's lower jaw that it fell out as he came over the side.

There may be lines as good as those made by the Ashaway Line and Twine Company; I am sure there are no better, and I use nothing else in all my salt-water fishing.

Captain Schubert was my first guide out of Miami and I have fished more with him than with all the others put together. At sailfishing he is preëminent. He is a well-read, entertaining and personable man, works hard for the success and comfort and safety of his patrons, and as an instructor in the art of sailfishing he is perfection. He taught me the technique without my being aware that I was being instructed. He has patience with the beginner's blunders, is always optimistic about the next one, and will start early and stay late if you want him to. Captain Schubert is a particularly good man if there are ladies in the party and gives them all the breaks so far as comfort and easy handling of the fish are concerned. His cruiser is a thirty-eight foot Matthews, appropriately named "Serenade." He uses outriggers if you wish, has fine chairs in the cockpit with racks alongside for glasses and bottles, and atop the cockpit roof has a seat aft on either side, from which the angler can fish with ease, out of the way of the mate in the cockpit, while the captain manoeuvers the boat from a steering wheel and engine controls aloft behind the rods. These seats are ideal from which to fight a sailfish. From this point the angler can watch the sail's approach and see him strike and take the bait; a great advantage.

I have a great personal regard for Captain Schubert and fish with him in preference to all others, but that does not mean that there are no others as good, and I am going to give here a list of those with whom I have fished successfully and the names of some that I know to be fine men but with whom I have never had the good fortune to go to sea. Next to Captain Schubert, I have fished most with Captain Larry Munro aboard his "Warrior," Pier 5 Miami. He is a fine sailfisherman and a hard working and amusing man. Captain Tom Frazure and his cruiser "Fish Hawk," also Pier 5, gave me one of the most exciting days I have ever had with sailfish. More about this later.

I spent two very rough days off Key Largo aboard the "Night Wind," Captain Harry Hill, Pier 5 Miami. He knows sailfish, cuts a fine bait and has a good boat. He is as keen about the game as the angler himself could possibly be. Captain Harry would make a fine artist's model for a swashbuckling pirate,

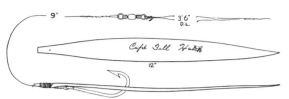

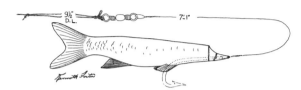

Captain W. D. ("Bill") Hatch. Cruiser "Patsy." Pier 5, Miami City Yacht Basin, Miami, Florida.

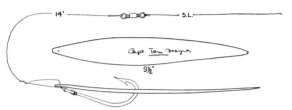

Captain Tom Frazure. Cruiser "Fish Hawk." Pier 5, Miami City Yacht Basin, Miami, Florida.

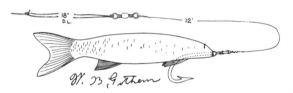

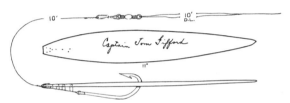

Captain Tommy Gifford. Cruiser "Lady Grace." Pier 5, Miami City Yacht Basin, Miami, Florida.

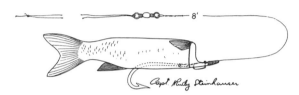

Mullet baits as cut and attached to rigs by Captains Herman Gray, Kenneth Foster, Rudy Steinhauser and W. B. Githens — four famous captains of Palm Beach and West Palm Beach, Florida.

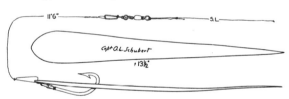

Captain O. L. Schubert. Cruiser "Serenade." Floridian Fishing Dock. Miami Beach, Florida.

All the baits and rigs shown in this series of drawings are from actual baits and rigs sent the author by the captains themselves and all bear their autographs.

Captain Lloyd McNeil. Cruiser "Vairene." Miami City Yacht Basin, Miami, Florida.

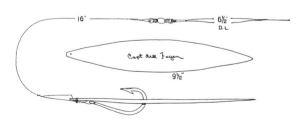

Captain R. W. ("Bill") Fagen, Cruiser "Florida Cracker II." Pier 5, Miami City Yacht Basin and Hotel Flamingo, Miami Beach.

Captain George M. Stevens. Cruiser "Skylark." Chamber of Commerce Fishing Dock. Miami Beach, Florida.

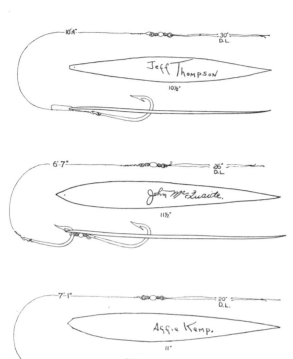

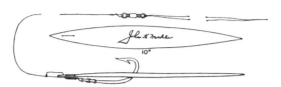

Captain John H. Mickle. Sombrero Lodge (Fishing Camp) Marathon, Key Vaca, Florida.

Strip baits as cut by Captains Jeff Thompson, John McQuaide and Allie Kemp — three famous captains of the Key Largo Anglers' Club, Key Largo, Florida. Also the rigs employed by these men showing the bait in side view as applied to the hook and leader.

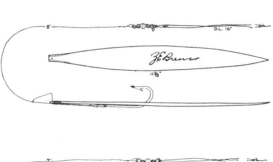

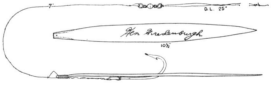

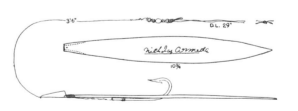

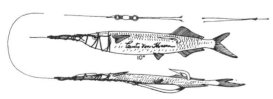

Ballyhoo bait as made by Captain Curtis Von Hoesen. Sombrero Lodge (Fishing Camp) Marathon Key Vaca, Florida.

Strip baits as cut by Captains J. E. Brewer, Kenneth Fredenburgh and Nicholas Armeda — three famous captains of the Long Key Fishing Camp. The dotted lines in the baits show the part folded over in tying the bait to the leader. The rigs used by these captains are also shown in profile with the baits attached.

but is a good tempered and agreeable man in spite of his fierce appearance. Captain Al Kemp of the Key Largo Anglers' Club is a good sailfisherman and has a good boat, the "Ann Farley." Captain Al is a keen sportsman himself and is full of funny stories of his experiences. Captain Lee Brewer and his cruiser "Hoo Hoo," also of the Key Largo Anglers' Club, constitute another good pair to draw to.

Captain Bill Hatch and his cruiser "Patsy" need no recommendation from me. The whole fishing world knows and admires this man. Captain Dick Morgan and his cruiser "Miss Sadie," Pier 5, Miami, are a good pair. I fished only one day with him, which raised no sails, but it was easy to see he is a competent man.

I have never fished with Captain George M. Stevens aboard his splendid boat the "Sky Lark." He is a top-notch man of very wide experience in Atlantic and Pacific waters, a husky, hard-working sailfisherman with whom you cannot go wrong. He sails from the Chamber of Commerce Fishing Docks, Miami Beach.

Captain Tommy Gifford thinks, sleeps, eats and works fish, fish, fish. He has done a tremendous lot to develop big game angling and is, I believe, the first charter boatman to use outriggers, which he has carried to the nth degree. His boat, the "Lady Grace," can be recognized for miles, sweeping the sky with her tremendous outriggers. He is of the best and his "Lady Grace" is equipped with everything that goes to make successful sailfishing. He can be found at Pier 5, Miami.

I once spent several days with Captain Lloyd McNeill aboard his cruiser "Vairene." His is a very comfortable boat and he is ace high as a guide. Captain McNeill knows the sail and marlin fishing games and as a reef fisherman is unsurpassed. It was aboard the "Vairene" that I saw a 25 pound runner put over on the Bimini reef as *live bait!* An eye-opener to the Northerner.

Captain Bill Fagen is another outstanding man with whom I have not had the good fortune to go to sea aboard his famous cruiser "Florida Cracker II," Pier 5, Miami. Captain Fagen is one of the best out of Miami and spends the summer fishing season at Montauk, as do Captains Hatch, Gifford and Herman Gray of Palm Beach fame.

From Key West, Ernest Hemingway in a letter recommends as sailfish guides of high degree Captain Eddie (Bra) Saunders and Begley Filer. Other good guides are Harold (Jakey) Key, Merle Bradley and Darrell Lowe; and adds, "In mentioning their names always include the aliases, as everybody here is located by his nom de guerre." Which is a good practice anywhere down the Coast!

By consulting the autographed drawings of baits and rigs as used by many outstanding sailfish guides, the reader will find several other names of good men who will give the angler his money's worth. This is not to be taken as a list of all the good men. There are dozens of others all the way from Fort Pierce to Key West, but I do not happen to know them and have had no direct recommendation. The angler can size up his man and from his boat and fishing outfits and the care he appears to take of them, get a pretty good idea of his quality as a fishing guide.

Opinion varies among anglers and guides as to the best baits for sailfishing, but they seem to be unanimous in their first choice, and this is a strip cut from the side of the bonito or little tunny. The bright silver of this fish's sides, together with the red color of the flesh side of the cut bait, makes it a skin the sailfish loves to tap. Next in order, in general opinion, is a bait cut from the side of a dolphin with its flashing golden yellow on the skin side and white on the reverse. Both these are tough and will stand a good bit of trolling and some knocking about by the small fry. These two fish are plentiful, normally, in sailfishing waters and strike any bait with a will. A feather bait tailing the teaser will get them, as will a spare hand line trolled short of the sail baits. Both fish hit the sail baits also, and spoil them for further sailfishing, but are royally welcomed aboard, since each one will furnish from two to four fine cuts of lunch for sailfish.

Bonito, you get one or two or three out of a school, but with dolphin several may be taken out of a school by keeping the first one hooked, trailing astern while slowly churning ahead until another takes the bait, and keeping this one in the water until a third is on, meantime chumming with scraps of fish until you have the whole school of beauties under your stern and the slaughter begins. They will notice their brothers and sisters kiteing heavenward after a bit, and quit that dangerous neighborhood in a body; but meantime I have seen nineteen of grand bait size taken from one school and all this while a sixty-eight-pound sailfish was being played on a fly rod.

A generous slice from the belly of a barracuda, including the ventral fins, or, if cut far back, part of the lower half of the tail, or without either of these, according to the taste of the guide, but always with the scales removed (for a reason I could never fathom), makes a fairly good sail bait and except a bait from a whip ray, is certainly the toughest of them all. The fish-belly white of the skin side makes a good show in the water and sails will strike it pretty well.

The ballyhoo, or balao, is one of the natural foods of the sailfish and makes a bait he will go for in a big way, but it is a soft and tender little thing and will not troll long, nor will it stand any mauling from other fish without being ruined. The ballyhoo is a good deal of fuss and bother to put in shape for trolling and is prepared in various ways.

Silver mullet is another of the favorite dishes of the sailfish, and therefore makes a good lure for him, but the mullet again is a tender fish and a messy job to prepare as a bait. Some of the methods are shown in the drawings of baits as used by Palm Beach and Key West charter boatmen.

The whip ray seems to be a last resort, is very tough and is certainly better than nothing.

Cero mackerel, Spanish mackerel and king mackerel will attract sails, but these baits are tender. Whole needlefish make fine baits, are easy to attach, troll beautifully and are among the food fishes of the sailfish. We found sails striking them right and left just outside the red can buoy off Angel Fish, while fishing in the tournament at the Key Largo Anglers' Club in early December, 1933, and needlefish slid out of the gullets of many of the sails when they were hung up for weighing. Needlefish can be taken in fine-mesh seines in favorable waters and by patient fishing with a small hook where they can be chummed close to a dock.

Anyone with a skiff and an outboard who will troll a very small spoon close to the mangroves can, in an hour or two, get a bucket full of about the most killing sail baits I have ever used — small barracuda ten to fifteen inches long. Using half of the 'cuda split like a mullet, it trolls well and the sails surely do like them.

Sailfish are occasionally taken on feather baits when trolling for other fish, but in the very great majority of cases they have been fouled in striking at the feather, which they will do freely. I know of no artificial bait that will work on sailfish.

All these lesser lights among baits, put together, are not worth a half dozen bonito or dolphin, but all sailfishermen have experienced scarcity of bait outside and the makeshifts here given are better than putting to sea with nothing on the ice, depending on bonito, dolphin or barracuda outside that may not be there. Most of the charter boat captains try to keep a supply of salt baits against a day or two of scarcity, and while these will take sails, they fall far short of something nice and fresh on the hook.

It is a pleasure to see a skillful captain prepare a sailfish bait from the side of a bonito. He strips the ten or twelve inch piece from the side of the fish, as shown in black in the drawings of bait fishes; lays it skin side down on his cutting board, and trims the edges carefully to the outline he wants; next, he very tenderly cuts the flesh down to the proper diameter, tapering as he goes both ways from the center, until the three dimensions of the bait are just right. Finally the edges of the bait from head to tail are beveled paper thin, a hole is punched for the safety pin and it is ready for the rig. All this is while watching for sails, keeping an eye on other boats in the neighborhood, and, if he has no mate aboard, regulating his motor and steering the boat!

Captain George M. Stevens of the Chamber of Commerce Dock of Miami Beach has given me such a good paragraph on sail bait cutting from the guide angle, that I am quoting it here:

"Regarding bonito bait, in making the bait the length depends on the size of the bonito, but never should be over 10 to 12 inches long, and approximately from a quarter of an inch to a half inch in thickness. Fish have a grain formation in the meat, and the bait should be cut so that the grain of the meat will troll with the water while in motion. This does away with the bait curling on the sides, also the edges of the bait must be chamfered off allowing it to have the shape of a boat. This is done by shaping the bait first and then drawing the knife down each side at about a 45° angle. After the bait has been fully shaped and cut, the meat side of the bait, to make it still smoother, should be scraped with the cutting edge of the knife, thus smoothing it off so the action of the bait when being trolled will give perfect motion of a fish swimming."

And from a later paragraph:

"All cut baits should be tied ahead of the hook on the leader wire with ordinary sewing twine. Four or five twists will be sufficient. The reason for this being that when a sailfish hits the bait, it quite often tears it loose from the pin on the leader wire if it is not tied on. Therefore spoiling the looks of the

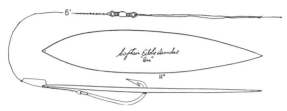

Captain Eddie (Bra) Saunders, Key West and Pirates Cove, Florida.

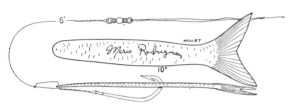

Captain Mario Rodriguez, Key West and Pirates Cove, Florida.

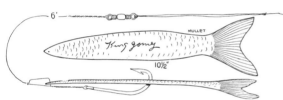

Captain King Gomez, Key West and Pirates Cove, Florida.

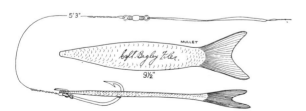

Captain M. P. Bradley, Key West and Pirates Cove, Florida.

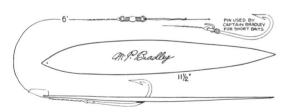

Captain Begley Filer, Key West, Florida.

Spanish mackerel, showing in black how the fish is cut for bait. Pacific Sailfish Club.

Cut mackerel bait from belly of fish to be trolled with point of hook down. Anal fin much cut away.

Cut mackerel bait, shown as trolled with hook down and belly up, with ventral fin much cut away. At the head of the bait a small float is used.

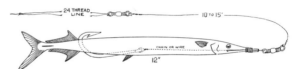

Whole gar fish shown as trolled with point of hook up.

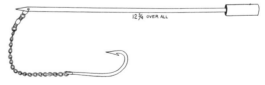

Device used in drawing hook into the body of whole fish. The brass rod is inserted in the fish's mouth and pushed through the belly back of the anal fin. The swivel is then attached to rod and the chain or wire is drawn forward through the fish's mouth, carrying the shank of the hook into the fish's body and bringing the point of the hook through the body and out the back.

These drawings are from sketches by H. J. Wempe, President of the Pacific Sailfish Club, Box 174, Balboa Heights, Canal Zone. They show how baits are cut and rigged by members of that club.

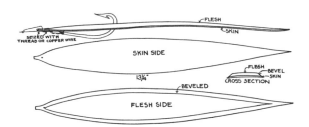

The rigid hook. The leader wire is passed two ways through the eye of the hook and two or three turns are taken around the shank making the hook a part of the leader in effect.

The loose hook. The leader is fastened to the hook by a simple loop of the leader through the eye of the hook leaving it to swing free of the axis of the leader.

The simple tandem hook. The second hook is attached to the leader hook by opening the eye of the second hook enough to pass the barb of the leader hook and then closing the eye of the second to normal.

The swivel tandem hook. The swivel is attached to the second gang hook by opening the eye. This combination is attached to the leader hook by opening the eye and sliding the shank down before closing the eye again.

FOUR WAYS OF RIGGING HOOK AS PRACTISED BY FLORIDA SAILFISH GUIDES IN GENERAL

Time-saving swivel-snap for changing baits quickly. Also a four double line becoming double and method of binding loose ends with fine copper wire to prevent "bubble" in water which frequently causes small fish to cut the sailfish line.

The ideal sailfish bait as designed by John Mahony of Miami, Florida. He is one of the most observant and certainly the most experienced of sailfish anglers of my knowledge, having taken over 400 during his eleven or twelve years as a resident of Southern Florida.

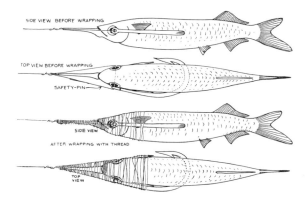

Whole ballyhoo baits as rigged by Captain George M. Stevens for trolling for sailfish from outriggers. Below are Captain Stevens' instructions for the preparation of this bait.

"First pass the pin of the leader wire through the eyes of the Balao. Then pass the hook through the body. Important: Do not remove any of the scales from the Balao. It must remain in its natural state as it will then stand the speed of travel through the water much better. Wrap the body of the Balao with No. 24 thread, starting at the pectoral fins up to the bill on the leader wire, paying particular attention to the closing of the mouth with plenty of thread to keep the water out and the eyes to keep them from protruding. After this is completed, take a fish knife and cut a slight slot at the bend in the hook in the body of the Balao, thus allowing it to lie closer to the body."

bait when it is released by the angler, and then, in case the sailfish does not take the bait on the first drop, the bait being tied on to the leader as mentioned, when the angler reels back it remains the same as when he started.

"At this point another bait is worthy of mention, this bait being known as the balao (ballyhoo). This is a more or less natural bait for many kinds of fish, and when trolled properly, very good results are obtained. The day of the outriggers is here to stay. And balao as a rule are trolled from the outriggers. The advantages of outriggers are very numerous. First: They place the baits from 30 to 40 feet out from the sides of the boat putting them in clear water, keeping them away from the boat. Secondly: The position in the air allows the bait to skip on top of the water giving a jumping motion which causes the fish to become excited when he sees it, increasing the chances of catching him on the first drop, due to the fact that the angler's line is fastened into a clothes pin which releases the bait immediately upon the strike, allowing practically enough drop on the line itself to take care of the requirements. Cut bait can be used very successfully as well on the outriggers. The baits should be trolled approximately from 40 to 60 feet from the stern of the boat; nothing less than a 10/0 hook should be used in the trolling of balao. The pin on the leader wire should be half again as large as the one used on cut bait. The pin passing through the eyes of the balao and then the hook placed from one side to the other of the body. Then sewing twine should be used by wrapping around the body and continue up to the end of the pin of the leader wire lapping its pectoral fins, the eyes, closing the mouth and continuing to the end of the pin. The scales of the balao should be left intact." This from one of the ablest charter men of the Miami region, and his remarks might have come from any of the good captains of the Florida coast.

In trolling, the bait is dropped astern to from forty to seventy-five feet depending on the captain's judgment. It should always be visible to the angler and the captain, and the distance from which it can be seen will depend on the surface you have at the time. The bait is visible much further in a heavy sea. When it rides down the face of the sea, it shows clearly a long way back. The captain, the mate and the angler will watch it constantly to see that it continues to swim as it should and that it remains clear of grass and gulf weed which is present at times in large quantities in the edge of the Stream where the sails congregate. The angler will learn to dodge these nuisances by watching the masses as they pass astern and guiding his bait accordingly, or if a bunch of weed seems unavoidable, he can sometimes keep clear by putting his rod, tip down, over the side in the hope the high-riding weed will pass over the bait. Swinging the bait into the wash of the propeller is a good way to dodge the weed when it is coming in large quantities, but here the angler must watch that he does not foul the teaser or his partner's line. Nothing so provokes hard feelings and profanity as a careless fellow who is constantly in a mess with the teaser or your own rig. Of course it will be impossible to avoid the weed at all times, and when the stuff catches on the rig it should be reeled aboard and cleared at once, for no sail will tap a bait so fouled. When you pick up a small bunch of weed, you get a nearly perfect imitation of a sailfish tap, and unless you are sure it is weed, it is wise to drop back, on the chance it is the real thing.

In fishing over the stern, two or three anglers at a time are the limit of wisdom; one from each chair at the sides and one in the middle. Three good anglers can troll in this way for days on end without messing each other's rigs, the two on the sides holding their rods wide off the beam and the middle man keeping his bait directly aft of one or the other edge of the transom and so clear of the teaser.

When outriggers are used, five can troll at once if the party is that large. With outriggers, the angler's line is swung up to near the outer end of the rigger and held there by a snap clothespin. With this device the bait is trolled about abeam from the stern of the boat, and the rolling progress of the craft gives the bait a fine, skipping, jumping motion which makes the sailfish frantic to get it. If the line is not knocked free of the clothespin by the strike, the angler can free it by a slight jerk of his rod, and the bight of his line affords the ideal drop-back to the sail. Outriggers are very effective and are fun to use, since the fisherman can see the whole show from the rush at the bait to the hooking of the fish.

The beginner will find the tap hard to recognize for what it is, especially if he has fished for species that grab the bait and run. It is hard to overcome the instinct to strike the instant he feels the tug at his bait. This is fatal in sailfishing, for if the bait does not stop in the water when the sail hits it, and more especially if it jumps ahead, he will know there is something wrong and nine times out of ten will quit right there. Many a thousand sailfish have been missed in just this way or by being slow in releasing the drag for the drop-back.

A sailfish strike checks the bait in the water for an instant only. It feels to the angler as though some tiny fish had grabbed his bait and at once let go. On feeling this "tap," which it literally is, since the sailfish kills its food by a smash with its bill, the angler should release his drag as quick as a flash and let his bait sag aft for about ten seconds, then throw on the drag and reel fast.

If the sail has picked up the bait after hitting it, you will know it at once, for engaging the drag, the forward motion of the boat and jerking up of the rod tip as you start reeling, will set the hook and your reel will begin that soft, smooth monotone as the sailfish starts his run. Sails differ as do humans. Some are alert and pick up the struck bait quickly. Others seem to lose track of it after the strike and again, the sail sometimes comes from the side at such speed that he runs beyond after the tap, and it takes him a little time to swirl back to pick up his kill. At any rate, if the sail is not on when you start reeling, keep your bait coming as fast as you can and he will see it moving and rush it again. You may have to do this half a dozen times before you have him on. If the sail happens to be full fed, he will smack your bait for the fun of it, or perhaps he is a born killer and will strike your bait with no intention of taking it in his mouth. Such fish can often be teased or angered into wanting to swallow that bait by jerking it rapidly ahead and letting it sag back with the rod only, not using the reel, or by setting the boat ahead at high speed or by circling rapidly.

Rarely, a sailfish will take the bait in his mouth and run with it, without any preliminary tap. Don't strike this fish until he slows up or stops to swallow the bait, for while he is running he is merely "pinching" the bait with the tip of his lower jaw and is getting off by himself where he can swallow it before it is snapped away by another fish. A certain number of these "pinchers" will drop the bait when they feel the drag of the line in the water, but the above tactics will hook a good many.

The fish is always struck, of course, with enough drag to set the hook firmly in his rather hard mouth. When he starts his fireworks, reduce the drag just enough to enable you to recover line when he runs toward you or gives you slack in any other way. As soon as the sail begins to tire and the danger of quick rushes seems about over, you can screw up the drag a bit and begin gently and easily to work him up to the boat, always being ready, of course, to loosen up if he acts as though a shark or a barracuda were after him or starts a new burst of speed for any other reason. Nine times out of ten, the lighter you hold the sail the quicker he will kill himself and the more spectacular will be his frantic efforts to shake the hook. Of course a sail may be fairly hooked in the upper jaw and yet the hook will sometimes turn back into the eye from the inside, since the eye is very low on the face. Such a fish is not likely to jump much but will get at right angles to your line and slowly sulk along with short rushes and bulldog shakes. This hook in the eye takes most of the fight out of him and he can usually be brought to boat in a hurry by pumping. Another most distressing thing that may happen to a greedy sail, or because the angler dropped back too far, is a hook in the gullet or, having swallowed the bait, a hook in the stomach. Such a fish will fight very feebly and is quickly brought alongside. This is a pitiful thing to see, for the strain of the line promptly pulls him inside out and he dies very quickly. No angler can be blamed for hooking a sail in the eye, but it is rare to hook a sail in the gullet or stomach with a properly timed drop-back. I never free a sail that has been hooked in the eye, and of course one hooked in the gills, throat or stomach is in a dying condition as you bring him close to.

When your fish has been fair hooked and is brought to the boat apparently exhausted, he may still have a dash or two left in him, and it is well to keep your drag on until the instant the captain takes the double line or the leader in his hand. Throw off the drag at once, keeping a thumb on the spool in case of accidents, until the fish has been released or until he has had the "headache stick" and is in the boat if you want to save him.

When your line begins to rise to the surface, the sail is coming out in the air. This is when he shakes the hook as he snaps his whole length as wildly as he knows how. While he is under water, the drag of the line makes it impossible for him to get rid of the hook, but when he comes out, bring the rod tip up and back so he can shake no slack into the line. Otherwise you may have the chagrin of seeing your hook go flying fifty feet away from that fish.

The most skilful sailfishermen with light tackle will lose fish. The hazards of the game are plenty. Bonito, dolphin, mackerel and what not strike at your swivel, or at a bit of weed your sail may be trailing on the line at high speed. Bunches of gulf weed are filled with living things, little crabs, tiny fish and dozens of other kinds, but worst of all, small barnacles with razor edges which will cut your running line. Drifting sticks, cocoanut hulls and logs are in the Stream to some extent, but the sea off Florida is no such mess of crates, broken chairs and garbage as you may find twenty miles offshore from Long Island. Sharks which go after your sail may cut the line or rasp it in two on their rough

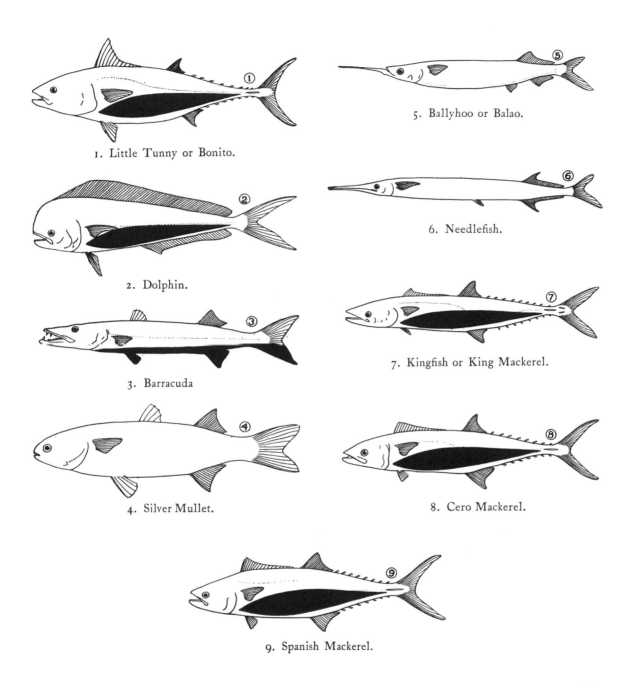

1. Little Tunny or Bonito.

2. Dolphin.

3. Barracuda

4. Silver Mullet.

5. Ballyhoo or Balao.

6. Needlefish.

7. Kingfish or King Mackerel.

8. Cero Mackerel.

9. Spanish Mackerel.

A series of drawings of the various fishes used as baits in sailfishing, numbered in the order of their importance as generally accepted by the charter-boat captains. The black areas show the cut used on those which are good strip bait. Those not showing black areas are used whole or in the full round but trimmed in various ways, or are split lengthwise, thus becoming two baits of a half fish each.

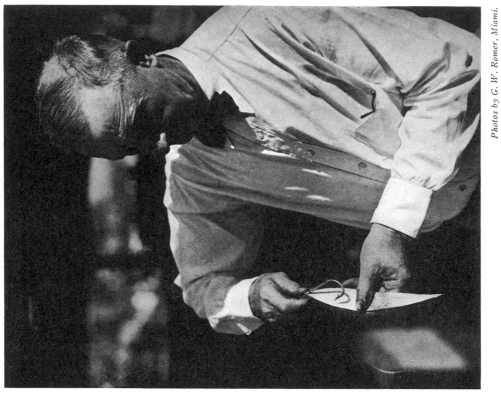

Photos by G. W. Romer, Miami.

Captain Hatch shows a completed bonito bait with the hook about to be inserted.

The capable hands of Captain Bill Hatch trimming a bonito bait.

hides; or your sail may part your line with his own body by getting into the bight of it or by rolling himself in the leader until the tender line is dragging across the fins.

The jumping sail sometimes throws a loop in the leader or makes one by a quick manoeuver in the water. If he pulls this tight when he straightens away again, it is all off, for the instant this tiny bend is opened, the piano wire parts like wet paper. Watch your captain break the wire with his fingers when he has finished a leader, and you will see the one weakness of this tremendously strong stuff.

Sailfishing with consistent success is a matter of experience. Anyone who likes fishing and doesn't get seasick, can become proficient. The sail is a beautiful and active fighter and is tremendously game, but he is not strong. He has not the staying power of a marlin of the same weight. Tuna, tarpon, big marlin and swordfish are all immensely more powerful than sails. A big crevalle jack, grouper or amberjack will work you *hard* on the same tackle that will wear down a sail with ease in half the time. The heavy big-game fish demand plenty of skill in the angler but require brute strength and stamina too. A big sailfish on light tackle is a matter of tenths of an hour, as against hours required for the whipping of really big game. I am speaking of Atlantic sails now. In the Pacific, Indian and Oriental seas, sailfish grow very much larger and probably would do up a nine-thread fly-rod angler on the first run; but from what I have been able to learn of them, they fight exactly like Atlantic sailfish, and I dare say they can be handled with a six-ounce tip and all the fifteen-thread line a 6/o reel will hold, if the angler will let the sailfish have his head. This ought to get a response from somewhere!

Any weather, from a flat calm to all the sea you can stand, is good sailfishing weather if the fish are there and are hungry. When the fish haven't had a period of fasting, I think a good roll on the surface puts them in a sportive mood and sailfish will chase and smack the bait for the fun of it if not hungry, and can easily be made parties to the game by a little teasing. A really hungry sail is going to get that bait no matter what the weather.

John Mahony of Miami is the most experienced and competent sailfish angler of my acquaintance. He has fished them two or three times a week for some years and his faithfully kept log shows over four hundred sailfish brought alongside on his rod, a tremendous record for one man. He releases all uninjured sails, which would seem to be a good thing for the sailfish population off Florida. His log notes all angles of sailfishing and I show here what he has to say about the weather:

"Personally, or at least from my own record, I can't find that the weather makes any difference; extraordinary catches are just as likely to occur in bright, flat calms as on a breezy, overcast day. The only consistent factor I have observed is that the fishing is generally no good for a few days when bad weather is headed this way from a northerly sector, but before we begin to feel the effect.

"On the other hand, Bill Hatch (who is the most competent and careful observer I know) says that the best sailfishing occurs when a fresh breeze is blowing anywhere between NW. and NE. At such times the fish travel south in large schools, 'tailing' along the surface of the western edge of the Stream and moving at a good, fast clip. They are then in a sportive mood, and need no encouragement to take the bait. Whether they are running from cold or unsettled weather, or merely chasing food, is not known.

"When the wind is from the south quadrant, Bill claims that the fish are heading north, are down fairly deep and are mostly scattered rather than schooling. Also that they are more likely to be further off shore in blue water.

"In calm weather, they are where you find them, and one spot is just as likely as another. You can generally depend on finding them under hovering frigate birds or gulls."

The beginner will want to have his first sailfish mounted and the adept may want to save a very big one, so I am giving here a list of taxidermists who do excellent work and are financially sound and reliable. These men are not mere fish-stuffers but are business men and naturalists of intelligence. They use the most modern methods and do work that has permanence. It is impossible to choose among them for quality.

My own work up to the present has been done by Francis West, who has a winter shop at his home at Pompano Beach, Florida, and a summer place at Gay Head, Martha's Vineyard, where he should be addressed at Chilmark, Martha's Vineyard, Massachusetts. Mr. West is a great student of fish, colors his mounts accurately and does a fine job on any fish, from a little Beau Gregory to a gigantic basking shark. He does a great deal of work for the museums of the country. I have known Mr. West a long time and have always gone to him to have my fish mounted.

SAILFISH

At Miami, Mr. Albert Pflueger, of the Pflueger Museum Company, 1156 North Miami Avenue, Miami, Florida, does a tremendous business in the mounting of game fish for sportsmen. He has a competent staff of workers and employs an artist who, when I visited the shop in the summer of 1934, was making the finest color drawings of tropical fish I have ever seen. The Museum is well worth a visit by the angler. There he will see dozens of sailfish, marlin, tarpon, groupers, jacks and what not, in every stage of the process from skins or the whole fish to the completed and nicely painted job hanging on the wall.

Mr. Fred C. N. Parke, of the Parke Marine Museum, North Ocean Boulevard, Palm Beach, Florida, shares with Mr. Pflueger the bulk of the Florida business. I have never visited his museum but have seen his work in many places, and it is fine. Mr. Parke is a naturalist as well as a taxidermist, and both he and Mr. Pflueger have done a great deal to help me make complete my chapter on sailfish in this book.

One day last winter I was invited to the home of Mr. Orton Dale to have a cocktail and take a look at his seven-hour, bluefish-rig, one hundred and four pound marlin, taken last summer off Manasquan, New Jersey. The fish had been mounted by Fred Huber, taxidermist, whose address is State Highway, Belmar, New Jersey, and Mr. Dale wanted my opinion as to the sort of job he had hanging on his wall. This proved to be the smoothest, most alive, mounted fish I have ever seen, and I recommend Mr. Huber to the most fastidious angler in the world. It is good to know of an expert so accessible to the northern fisherman.

Florida sailfishing begins at Fort Pierce. I have never fished there; I understand it is quite a run out to the right waters. I know none of the guides, but believe there are some good ones and good boats. Stuart is the next point south where there is said to be sailfishing. I know no more about this place than about Fort Pierce.

Palm Beach and West Palm Beach are about the best places in Florida for sailfishing. There are plenty of the best guides and boats; the sailfish are just off the beach, and a lot of them. The Gulf Stream comes right ashore here, and it is not uncommon to have a sailfish on within a quarter mile after leaving the inlet. In fact, sails have been hooked within the jetties. Herman Gray, the foremost charter boatman out of Palm Beach, wrote me lately he had a sportsman hook one this winter within the jetties. Captain Gray put his patron ashore and the sail was played and landed from there; a hot number if ever there was one!

BIG GAME FISHING

Between Palm Beach and West Palm Beach the angler can find accommodations to suit the fattest or flattest purse. Boats may be had at the usual rate.

Between Palm Beach and Miami are a number of good spots. Delray, Fort Lauderdale, Pompano, Boca Raton and Hollywood. There are guides and boats to be had and plenty of sailfish not far out.

Miami has the largest and finest fleet of charter boats in the world and her captains are unbeatable anywhere. Most of them are tied up at the very fine Municipal Yacht Basin right on the waterfront in the afternoon shadows of some of the fine hotels on Biscayne Boulevard. At Pier 5, down both sides of which the charter boats lie, between eight and nine in the morning in the winter season, there is a great stir of cars arriving and discharging fishermen and their gear; great running about of mates loaded with customers' rods, tackle boxes and lunch. Bait, ice, cases of beer, kiteing hither and yon, all to the roar of starting motors and the smell of exhausts. Goodbyes, orders and miscellaneous chatter swell the din, and hopes run high as one by one the cruisers pull out for the Stream. An inspiring hour and scene. The boats begin drifting back at about five in the afternoon, and from then until dusk Pier 5 is one of the sights of Miami. It seems like half the world is there to watch the boats as they are skillfully jockeyed into their berths, and to stand big-eyed and silent as the strange creatures from the sea are tossed out of the fish boxes. Dolphin, bonito, barracuda, wahoo, kingfish, jacks, groupers, tuna, are pitched by the dozen to the depressed walks beside the pier, while the proud anglers get their final dividend on the day as they bask in the admiring glances of the crowd. "Would y' lookit the sailfish?" says someone, and there is a stampede down the pier to the boat, where the wide tail of one of these champions sticks up out of the fish box or a mate is hoisting one on to the walk. More sails come ashore and more as the boats back in, until a fresh stir in the crowd announces "Some guy's got a marlin. Geez, look at that fish — bet he weighs a hundred," and they are off again. Here comes the photographer. The folks back home are going to have real proof now. The captain and the mate slam the catch on the spiky racks. The proud fishermen from Kankakee and Keokuk take their places on each side; the crew crouch below the fish. The photographer squeezes the bulb, and the big day is over.

Pier 5 is for the tourist and winter crowd, but plenty of blasé dyed-in-the-wool sportsmen sail from there too. Miami has hotels to fit any pocketbook. The rates for the boats are the same as elsewhere.

SAILFISH

At Miami Beach fine guides and boats sail from the Floridian Fishing Dock and from the Chamber of Commerce Fishing Dock, both situated at the eastern end of the County Causeway. Miami Beach is a beautiful place, with numbers of the finest hotels in the world. These are expensive stopping places during the winter months but there are a few places for the less well-to-do at this season. In the late spring and during the summer, some of the very fine places open their doors to visitors at rates within the reach of very modest incomes. Miami and Miami Beach should be known to the world as cool and altogether delightful summer resorts with day after day of sunshine and dry breeze while northern cities are sweltering with heat and humidity. The sailfish are off-shore there too all summer, in large numbers, as are all the other game fish but marlin and kingfish. Across the Gulf Stream forty-five miles away are the great fishing grounds of Bimini. There are some sailfish there, but the great game is the marlin, which is to be found all summer in those waters. Giant tuna are there in the spring.

Below Miami, the first good sailfishing station is the Key Largo Anglers' Club, a feature of the Florida Year Round Clubs. This is a delightful spot with good boats and guides, and one of the best hosts of my experience, Captain D. A. Curtis. There is a central lodge and dining room. The sleeping quarters are rustic cabins, fitted with up-to-date plumbing, and beds that are hard to leave. The food and service are excellent, as they would have to be under Captain Curtis. This is one of the best places in Florida for sailfishing, and I have caught more sails off the reef, out from Angel Fish Creek between Carysfort Light and Pacific Reef, to the north, in day after day fishing, than have ever fallen to my lot elsewhere.

Below Key Largo is Sombrero Lodge Fishing Camp. A new and very fine resort for anglers, beautifully situated at Marathon on Vaca Key. Fine quarters, good food, good boats and captains and lots of sailfish. I understand that one must be recommended, to be accepted as a guest at this camp.

The oldest, most extensive and perhaps the best of the Florida fishing camps is the Long Key Fishing Camp on Long Key about half way between Miami and Key West. This camp was created several years ago and on an unprecedented scale by the Florida East Coast Railway and under the genial and capable management of George G. Schutt, has maintained first place as a resort for sportsmen and their families who want comfort, pleasant surroundings, good food and, above all, good fishing, especially for sailfish. The Camp's list of guests over the years reads like a Who's Who of sportsmen, business men, artists, writers and the socially elect of the country. It is one of the most delightful spots in the world. The Camp has a central lodge and dining room. There are many cottages for the guests, with boardwalks over the sand between them. This is the only camp down the Keys that has a good bathing beach; a fine feature, in my estimation. The boat dock is a short walk away from the main camp on the Gulf side of the Key, and the Camp provides boats and guides of the best quality, at prevailing rates. One steps directly from his pullman car into the midst of this little paradise. The Camp cannot control the fish, of course, but no guest there will ever be disappointed in the comfort and joy of being in this ideal tropical spot. Long Key Fishing Camp shows a long and impressive list of sailfish caught over a period of years and among them some very big ones. It is one of the best places in Florida for sailfishing.

Next to the Long Key Camp in point of age and size is Pirates Cove Fishing Camp. This place has the same pleasing quality as the larger camp and lies between Long Key and Key West. There are plenty of sails offshore from here and an abundance of reef and bay fishing. Pirates Cove is owned and operated by Mrs. Edith Wright, a very fine person, who took over the Camp and its management after the recent death of her husband, who founded the Camp. There are good boats and guides there and the patron can be sure of the best of everything. I recommend Pirates Cove highly.

Key West is the last of the good sailfishing places on the map of Florida. There are two hotels, the Casa Marina, a very fine place owned and operated by the Florida East Coast Railway and managed by Mr. Peter Schutt. The Casa Marina stands directly on the ocean side of the city of Key West. In the town of Key West is another less pretentious but good hotel, La Concha, in the heart of the city and near to the piers where the guides tie up. Key West is a West Indian town in the United States and I call it a most interesting and picturesque place. Certainly the sailfishing there is all that can be desired. The largest sailfish ever taken in Atlantic waters was landed there by Ernest Hemingway and T. J. S. McGrath one day last spring. Some of the best guides fish out of Key West, and I recommend the port highly to the angler.

You will want to take photographs and movies of your sailfishing. The light is very strong in sailfishing regions off Florida, so much more powerful than in

Cottages at the Long Key Fishing Camp.

Photos courtesy of Lynn Bogue Hunt.

The boat dock, Key Largo Anglers' Club, Key Largo, Florida.

The Rendezvous. The Lodge at Pirates Cove Fishing Camp, Florida.

Photo by Cox Studios, Inc., Miami Beach.

The Lodge, Key Largo Anglers' Club, Key Largo, Florida.

northern sunny weather, you will over-expose every negative and foot of film if you use the same aperture you would on the same kind of a day at sea in the North. I use a 2X filter on all three lenses of my Victor Cine camera and expose through these with the same aperture I would use in the North without filters. Remember, you are only a hundred miles from the Tropic of Cancer when you are fishing from Miami south, and the actinic rays are abundant and lively. At Bimini the light is much stronger than on the Florida side, due, I think, to the immense Bahama Bank where the bottom is mostly white sand, the water is shoal and the reflection terrific; so much so that this green light is reflected to the clouds and you behold a phenomenon of nature it is better to tell to the elect only — clouds soaring overhead that are tinged a soft emerald green beneath. The white terns flying over the Bank and over the reef are green as green underneath and by contrast the white of the wing edges and flanks exposed to the sun are beautiful pale orange — a thing I have seen many times but would not dare to paint for the laity. So watch your light carefully and in the Bahamas cut down your aperture one more stop with 2X filters or three stops without.

One of the best places to get advice on the use of cameras in southern Florida is the Miami Photo Supply Company at 37 S. E. First Avenue, Miami. The proprietor, Mr. W. C. Brown, is a genial man and knows his stuff.

The same strong sun will burn the skin like the mischief in about a quarter of the time the same thing would happen at midsummer in the North. Many a northerner has acquired a burn in an hour that made him miserable for days. Take it easy with the sun for a few days, exposing yourself for a few minutes at a time for a day or two. In this way, you can gradually acquire a fine coat of tan without undue suffering, and you may find yourself, at the end of a week, able to fish stripped to the waist, as I like to do. I have to wear a hat, except for short intervals, as this tropical sun gets me quickly without one. I have always been impressed by the fact that commercial and professional fishermen never go bareheaded. I found the reason some years ago by fishing in the Stream off Key West for about two hours without a hat. I was put out of business for the rest of the morning, and it was forty-eight hours before my head was any good again.

The light at sea down there is hard on the eyes, too. I wear sun glasses part of the day and use those of a pale orchid color. The usual yellow ones give the sky and sea a sickly hue that is very disagreeable to me.

For sunburn and the prevention of it I have found nothing so good as a liberal use of cocoanut oil. Smear it on well and let it soak in for at least a half hour before exposure and then *take it easy*. I cannot put too much emphasis on the power of the Florida sun to broil the newcomer to a turn in a half hour. Bad sunburn, next to seasickness, is the killjoy of sailfishing.

My first sailfish was caught on a day when, from my hotel window on Miami Beach, the sea looked pretty white. A lively east-northeaster was blowing and very few boats were leaving Pier 5 that morning, but Captain Schubert is a good seaman and values his life at least as much as I do mine, so we went. It was about the meanest sea of my experience but the sails were there and willing. My fishing partner and myself were covered with bruises before the day was over but we hooked four sails and a marlin and brought in the marlin and three of the sails, the hook having pulled out of the fourth right alongside as the boat rolled away from him.

The biggest sea I ever fished in was a tremendous ground swell running south against the Stream. It was a bright day and a ten-mile breeze out of the northeast was rippling the faces of those solemn swells. When we were at the bottom of the trough, we were alone in the world with blue walls of water towering around us. Only the birds and the topmasts of the tankers going south in the green water were visible. When we rode over the crest it was like looking down into a football bowl, and the other boats fishing around us were slowly poking their mast heads above the seas or sinking out of sight beyond the next one. The ocean was alive with flying fish; bonito were ripping about; and schools of dolphin were bounding over the surface in their greyhound fashion out of pure joy of the lifting seas. The sails were hitting well. I have forgotten how many we hooked, but I well remember one that tail-walked up the face of the sea from the bottom of the trough where we were, and went into the air against the sky as he reached the top of the wall. The sight of the day was a marlin that appeared over the top and came sliding down behind my bait. He looked like a long bronze minnow against the wall of that great sea. He struck while he was in the trough and we were riding like a surfboard down the face of the next one. He came out of the crest we had just left like a flying fish, heading east at sixty miles. "Easy with that one," said Schuby. "Not many marlin are brought in on nine-thread." We saw him again as he came out of the crest of the following sea, and then he was gone. The strain of those great rollers, the action of the boat and the power of the fish were too much for me and my nine-thread line.

One day my partner and I had three double-headers in a tumbling sea and managed to land five of the six fish. There were lively times aboard, what with four of us in the cockpit of an Elco Cruisette — the two anglers crawling about each other from port to starboard and back again, trying to keep our tender lines apart as the wildly fighting doubles crossed and recrossed during the battles. It is something to do to land a double-header in a sea. Three at a time must be a circus. I have never seen it but I know it has happened.

My most exciting day with a sailfish was during the Anglers' Tournament at the Key Largo Anglers' Club in early December, 1933. Sailfish were plentiful and the weather ideal. Bob Davis and Hi Phillips, of the party of notables, had fished together the previous day and hadn't so much as seen a sailfish. "I think sailfishing is the bunk," said Hi that night in the Club lounge; "I think it is just another one of those things people blow about but don't do." He had never fished for sails before and the Captain told me privately that both his sports had been muffing them all day without seeing a fish. So, on this day I went to sea with Hi as his mentor. We had just rounded the light on Pacific Reef, when the two of us had sail strikes, bang, bang — like that. I had been preaching to Hi all the way out to the Stream and out of the corner of my eye I saw him go through the ritual all regular, and hook his sail. Meantime, mine had grabbed the bait about forty feet astern as I reeled in after the tap to show the big brute where was the meal he had so neatly killed a moment before. This was the biggest sail I have ever seen. When the hook went home, he reared out of the water and towered in the air like a sponson canoe on end and looked as big as one as he hung there. Down he went in a white smother of foam and tore away for fifty feet to another skyscraping jump under which I could see the horizon. The next time he came out was at right angles to his run, and as he turned completely head over tail and I could see him throw a loop in the bright leader as he threw his tail aloft. His next run pulled the loop tight and his next leap straightened out the kink and he was gone; the only sailfish I ever really regretted losing. He was so big! Hi's fish was still on but he was hanging in the air horizontally and exhibiting all the reluctance to go back in the water that a sailfish does when a shark is after him, and sure enough, the line was parted then and there and Hi had lost his first sailfish, through no fault of his own.

We raised ten sails that day, hooked eight and brought in only one. All our fishing was in green water, and the sharks were bad. I think pursuing sharks lost us every sail we had on, that day, by rasping or biting the line. And those fish certainly hated to be in the water while we had them on. None of them was killed on the line and every one probably escaped the shark with ease as soon as the line was parted. The boat that day, was the "Sea Hawk," and Captain Tom Frazure and his mate, Vivien Rutherford, worked very hard and with great skill all day. The fact that we saved one fish, late in the day, was due solely to the captain's manoeuvers in keeping close to him and taking him aboard while he was still very lively, getting himself a good wetting in the process.

I like to do my Florida sailfishing out of Miami, and in the spring or summer, when the weather is reliable and the winter jam of tourists and what not have gone North. Now you find Florida at its very best. Hotel rates are low on Miami Beach. Take up your quarters there, preferably right on the water, and be assured of coolness in the tropics; a paradoxical thing but true of the east coast along the beaches. It gets pretty hot during the day, back in Miami City and on the beach just before dawn in early summer the trade wind drops to nothing and real tropical heat pervades your bedroom, until you awaken soaked with perspiration in the atmosphere of an oven. You crawl out of bed and go to your east window and there behold, away over beyond the Bahamas, the beginning of a day in such a halo of glory as you will never see in any other place. Great piles of clouds rise and rise to the zenith, changing form with slow majesty, and all shot through with the pearl and rose and blue of a rare shell. In this latitude the sun is quick about bringing broad day, for the Tropic of Cancer is not much over a hundred miles to the south and at noon in summer your shadow is no bigger than your hat. With the sun clear of the horizon, making a glowing furnace of these wonderful clouds, the good cooling "trade" comes rippling, all silver, across the dark ribbon of the Gulf Stream away out there beyond the bright green water of the reef, and a few minutes later is swaying the drapes of your room and clicking the fronds of the cocos and palmettos outside. Mocking birds are mewing and trilling all over the place, and the tiny beach pigeons are darting about their morning affairs on coppery wings.

This is something to get up to day after day, and sunrise is like this nearly always, in southern Florida. It may be varied with rain squalls drifting, gray and sombre, across the blazing east and etching flaws over the calm sea, but it is nearly always windless and is eternally worth getting out of bed early to see.

But if this lifts your soul when seen from your bedroom window, imagine being in it and part of it on a cruiser on the very edge of the Stream itself when the "trade" begins to make a sparkling undulation of all the vast ocean to the east and the clouds start their daily race across the sky to nowhere, casting wide shadows over the sea. With the breeze come the fish. Terns wheel and pitch at the small fry driven to the surface by the dolphin and bonito and graceful frigate birds swing slowly overhead, watching for the flying fish to take the air ahead of the hungry killers, or, corsairs that they are, swoop at the terns to rob them of their hard-earned morning meals. Oily slicks and ripply flaws show schools of fish here and there. A wide foamy flash of silver means a cloud of ballyhoo bursting into the air like the crest of a breaking sea. Flying fish, on ghostly wings, tear out of the water and soar away from the death that pursues them below.

As the breeze rises, that puzzling chop begins to dance where green and blue waters meet. The Stream, swinging its eternal way to the north, sets up a swirling eddy against the motionless green of the reef and the freshening trade whips the swirl into a cauldron of unbelievable color where blues run from ultramarine to pale turquoise, which becomes the most liquid emerald and all so intense it seems impossible they are not giving off light of themselves. It is in and about this riot of color and motion that the game fish hunt their prey, and it is there you cruise in the rip, out in the blue, back in the green, north and south, waiting for a strike from sailfish, marlin, dolphin, tuna, cero mackerel, kingfish, bonito, grouper, barracuda, amberjack and a dozen others, all fighters in the measure of their powers.

If you begin just before dawn and stay in the green for a while, you are likely to have a good day's work in an hour, with the brutes of the reef. Amberjack which strike like a sledge run up to seventy pounds out here. Long fast runs and sullen pulling like a wild bull tells their story. One amberjack in a lifetime would be my choice, and that only for the sake of having done it. A heavy jack is too much labor and strain on the tackle for a chap who won't show until he is licked. He is a waste of time when the showy ones are possible. The groupers are sullen lads too, who take the bait with plenty of dash and then make for a hole in the coral, from which it takes too much valuable time and patience to dislodge them; but if you are on the reef in early morning you have to take what comes, and once a fish is on, you get him in time or he parts the tackle some-where. If you see a long, slim, silver arrow bounding over the water like a grey-hound, that will be a cero and well worth your while for his pounds, and a grand broiled fillet when you get him home. A big barracuda strikes with a smash and puts on a fast and dogged battle. He may give you a grand jump or two, and when he comes over the side, snapping those wicked jaws, you will resolve to be careful about going in the water where a barracuda might be, especially if you have seen how he can slash and chop some fish which was helpless on your line. Jacks, runners, yellowtail, and what not, do their best for you until about nine o'clock when they stop feeding and you have had all you want of that fish-ing for the rest of your days. The trade has now kicked up the proper chop for sailfish and the sun is high enough to make basking attractive for all the surface fighters.

Now the choicest baits come off the ice and are trimmed by your captain with a nicety and skill that it is a pleasure to behold. All rigged with bait safety-pinned to the ten-foot wire leader and pricked through by the hook in exactly the right place, you swing out into the blue for a run in the Stream alongside the rip. Anything can happen now. It may be the little tap you feel or you may see the sail himself as he swings in or rises from below, or, from the alert captain "Watch that one boss, off the weather," and you see a bronze torpedo tearing in from a hundred feet away, sword and dorsal ripping a white line of froth in the blue as he rides down the sea to smash the bait. Off goes the drag. The bait sags back a few seconds while your sail makes the sea boil in his swirl to pick up the little fish he thinks he has killed. On with the drag, and reel for dear life. If he has picked up the bait, you set the hook and instantly, back there, a tower of purple, blue and silver tears out of the sea, all foaming, and shaking his supple length like a mad thing. Back into the water in a smother of white, he rips the line off your reel at express speed. Now you hear that soft *wheeee* of sibilant smoothness that pays you principal and interest at once on the high cost of good reels. You watch your line as it gets lower on the spool, and the captain swings the cruiser into the sailfish's run; the line begins to rise further and further away from the boat. "Watch out now, boss, he's coming up. Don't let him get slack when he breaks," and away out there, one hundred, two hundred, three hundred feet off the weather bow, not at all in the direction your line enters the water, out he comes again, wide-mouthed, shaking furiously as he opens a white trough in the blue sea in a long run with only his tail in the water, such is his power. Back down again in a column of spray. Out again and in on his back. Run, run, run, now under the surface, now with his sword and head and shoulders out, tearing the sea white again in his terrific speed. Reel and recover line when you can. Let him run when he will, but recover your line. His runs are getting shorter now and his leaps not so high. Thirty minutes have gone by. Sweat runs down your neck, your muscles are tired. Forty minutes! And it looks as though you are going to win. Your sail's runs are short now and for leaps the best he can do is to raise his forward third and forlornly wave his dark and shining sword toward the sky. Closer and closer in you bring him, until at last you behold your warrior, two seas away, all bronze and silvery green, tiredly trying to keep his head turned from the pull that is slowly working him up to the boat. The double line starts up from the water, then the swivel and now the bright wire of the leader rises inch by inch while you reel and back away from your chair and you release your drag as the captain grasps the wire in his gloved hand. Easy now, captain, as you lead him to the boat. Gently, as you raise that grand head to grip the sword, and gently, too, when his thrashing flurry is quiet, reach down and slip out the hook and turn him loose. "Ah, sailfish, you're much too grand a fighter to be killed!" And slowly his bronze back and sides of moonlight green drift down and away in freedom, his purple sail weaving and twisting as he gathers way.

No sailfish angler needs to be told of the lifting glory of a day in the Stream. If you have never done it and have an appreciation of beauty and a love of fast fishing, try it. You will treasure the experience long after the cost and the sunburn have been forgotten.

SAILFISH RECORDS FROM FLORIDA, GULF OF PANAMA AND COCOS ISLAND, PACIFIC OCEAN, SO FAR AS AVAILABLE TO THE AUTHOR.

The largest sailfish ever taken in the Atlantic was caught in the spring of 1934. This is an extraordinary sail for these waters and it is a record that will probably never be beaten. The following extract from a letter about the fish from Ernest Hemingway to the author tells the story in the graphic Hemingway manner.

"The big sailfish was caught on May 23, 1934, about 8 miles from Key

West on what is called the 10 fathom bar just off the Western Dry Rocks. Thomas J. S. McGrath was fishing with me and we left the docks at 2:30 P.M. Inside of an hour he was hooked into a good sailfish on light tackle which a shark took from him after about forty-five minutes and fifteen jumps. I had an amberjack and grouper outfit 16 oz. Hardy tip, old style Pflueger Templar reel and 21 thread baited, and as I was handling the boat, etc. myself told him to slack this out while we put on another bait. The big sailfish smashed the bait almost as soon as it was out. McGrath shouted for me to take him, that his arm was still cramped from the other fish and that he couldn't deal with him. I told him to stay with him, that I would handle the boat for him and that he would find his arm would clear up. But his arm was really bad and after a few minutes he insisted that I take the fish. He had been ill with arthritis and was in no condition to fish or would certainly have caught the fish. I took the fish over with no idea how big he was and was amazed at how he could pull. I promptly announced that he was foul hooked because no sailfish could pull that hard on 21 thread line. I treated him as though he were foul hooked and worked him very hard, standing up with him out on the stern. Brought him to gaff pretty quickly, saw how big he was, told the amateur gaffer to gaff him in the head; he pricked him somewhere toward the tail and we had fireworks. There was nobody to handle the wheel who had ever been on the boat before and I had less than two hundred yards of line. Fought him on the spring of the rod like a salmon with the lever drag off (you know how that old style Templar works) using my fingers for the braking. Was afraid to let him get out far for fear he would make a run and pop the line. Holding him close and bringing him up to easy gaffing six times with the citizen missing him each time, passed the rod, reel and all under the stern, under the propeller and rudder each time he went under the boat. He finally gaffed him and we took him on board 43 minutes after he was hooked. At no time, after I took him over, did he have more than sixty yards out. Most of the time he was about twenty yards out; but strong. He pulled like an amberjack; jumped clear eleven times. We weighed him on a tested scale before eight witnesses including Charles P. Thompson of this city, Darrell Lowe, Al Dudek, and others and he was 119½ pounds. With a steel tape measured 9 feet ¾ inch and girth 35 inches. Thomas J. S. McGrath of Shreveport, La., has all the measurements, length of bill, etc. The fish has been mounted and is in Key West for anybody to see. I would of course not send him in as a record since I did not hook him and McGrath would not because he did not land him. It was a female fish and was very beautifully built. Was caught on a flood tide around four-thirty in the afternoon in ten fathoms of water with a heavy, dark stream on strip mullet bait."

RECORDS FROM THE PACIFIC SAILFISH CLUB

These records have been furnished the writer by Mr. H. J. Wempe, Secretary-Treasurer of the Pacific Sailfish Club of Balboa, Canal Zone. This club was organized on May 1, 1932, and by March 9, 1933, had a membership of twenty-nine. Practically all members are employees of the Panama Canal who run their own boats. To quote Mr. Wempe: "We have no licensed guides but some members often act as guides and take out visitors from the United States and other countries." The fishing season for sailfish runs from April to December, with July apparently being the best month. For those who wish to try the Pacific sailfish, the region of Panama Bay is easily reached by steamer from New York or New Orleans, on the ships of the United Fruit Company; or if in a hurry by Pan-American planes from Miami.

1932

First club prize won by 118 pound sailfish. Second prize by 110 pound and third prize by 100 pound fish. Only a few sails were caught during this year.

1933

Month	Number	Average Weight	Largest Sailfish
January	0	. . . . . .	. . . . . .
February	0	. . . . . .	. . . . . .
March	0	. . . . . .	. . . . . .
April	1	127 lbs.	127 lbs.
May	5	101½ lbs.	130 lbs.
June	14	105½ lbs.	128 lbs.
July	17	106 lbs.	146 lbs.
August	15	106 lbs.	120 lbs.
September	7	108 lbs.	131 lbs.
October	8	99½ lbs.	149 lbs.
November	8	100 lbs.	136 lbs.
December	1	100 lbs.	100 lbs.

1934

Records were kept for the months of May and June only. Over 100 sailfish were landed. All the smaller fish were released.

May	17	104 lbs.	140 lbs.
June	16	. . . . . .	150 lbs.

RECORDS FROM LONG KEY FISHING CAMP, LONG KEY, FLORIDA

1925-26

Total — 294.

Dec. 28, 1925
Wm. Glazier, N. Y. City... 7' 64 lbs.
Jan. 18, 1926
Dr. G. D. Rosengarten, Phila. 7'8" 67 lbs.
Jan. 19, 1926
T. D. M. Cardeza, Phila.... 8'1" 74½ lbs.
Jan. 24, 1926
T. D. M. Cardeza, Phila..... 7'2" 66½ lbs.
Feb. 4, 1926
C. A. Caldwell, N. Y. City... 7'7½" 65 lbs.
Feb. 5, 1926
A. Reybein, N. Y. City...... 7'10" 76 lbs.
Feb. 5, 1926
Mrs. A. Petzer, N. Y. City... 7'10" 66½ lbs.
Feb. 12, 1926
E. Bartlett Hayward,
Annapolis, Md.......... 8'3" 78 lbs.
Feb. 14, 1926
Fred K. Burnhans,
Martinez, Calif. .... 7'3" 68 lbs.
Mar. 5, 1926
Rollin H. Mills, Cleveland.. 7'7" 62 lbs.

1926-27

Total — 410.

Dec. 26, 1926
F. Emmett, New York City. 7'10" 64 lbs.
Jan. 20, 1927
H. Rathbone, Lincoln, Neb... 7'11" 62 lbs.
Jan. 26, 1927
C. W. Barron, Boston, Mass... 7'11" 68 lbs.
Jan. 27, 1927
Mrs. W. G. Gomez,
Buffalo, N. Y.......... 7'7" 60 lbs.
Feb. 5, 1927
R. Weingart, New York City. 7'2" 66 lbs.
Feb. 11, 1927
C. C. Robinson, N. Y. City.. 8'1" 87 lbs.
Feb. 20, 1927
C. B. Smith, N. Y. City.... 7' 62 lbs.

Feb. 24, 1927
  Judge A. J. Butler, Phila, Pa.. 7'5½" 71 lbs.
Feb. 25, 1927
  Harlan Kelsey, East
    Boxford, Mass. .... 7'6" 71½ lbs.
*Mar. 1, 1927
  T. D. M. Cardeza, Phila., Pa. 7'8" 93 lbs.
Mar. 1, 1927
  C. F. Warfield, New York... 7'4" 60 lbs.
Mar. 8, 1927
  W. W. Smith, New York.... 7'9" 79 lbs.
Mar. 11, 1927
  J. B. Stevens, New York..... 7'4" 62 lbs.
Mar. 11, 1927
  C. W. Barron, Boston, Mass... 7'2" 60 lbs.
Mar. 11, 1927
  Mrs. S. C. Badger, New York. 7'7" 68½ lbs.
Mar. 18, 1927
  Dr. W. A. Fisher, Balt., Md.. 7'7½" 69 lbs.
Mar. 20, 1927
  J. S. Starling, Wash., D.C.... 7'1" 67 lbs.

* Record for Camp; taken on 6-ounce tip,
  12-thread line.

1927-28
Total — 515.

Jan. 1, 1928
  Harold S. Graeb,
    Bellerose, L. I. .... 7'4½" 60 lbs.
Jan. 14, 1928
  Col. E. M. Chance, Phila., Pa. 7'2" 60 lbs.
Jan. 17, 1928
  T. A. Whitehead, N. Y. City. 8' 84 lbs.
Jan. 31, 1928
  J. O. Roberts, N. Y. City.... 7'9" 84 lbs.
Feb. 1, 1928
  E. E. Durant, Worcester, Mass. 6'9" 65 lbs.
Feb. 1, 1928
  B. Christoffers .... 7'3" 68 lbs.
Feb. 4, 1928
  Herbert Haase, Chicago, Ill... 7'8" 70 lbs.
Feb. 4, 1928
  Chas. Miller, New York City 7'6" 66 lbs.
Feb. 9, 1928
  Robert King, Ft. Myers, Fla.. 7'7" 66 lbs.
Feb. 10, 1928
  Dr. John A. Gaines,
    Tampa, Fla. .... 6'10" 63 lbs.
Feb. 11, 1928
  Mrs. John T. Dorrance,
    Camden, N. J. .... 7'10" 71 lbs.
Feb. 12, 1928
  Mrs. M. M. Stevens....... .... 64 lbs.

Feb. 23, 1928
  Fred Fletcher, N. Y. City.... .... 70½ lbs.
Mar. 23, 1928
  W. C. Ladd .... 7'5" 66 lbs.

1928-29
Total — 407.

Jan. 16, 1929
  Mrs. Wm. G. Gomez,
    Buffalo, N. Y. .... 7'8" 67 lbs.
Jan. 21, 1929
  Mr. Andrews .... 7'3½" 65 lbs.
Jan. 31, 1928
  B. W. Crowninshield,
    Boston, Mass. .... 7'9" 67 lbs.
Feb. 20, 1929
  Col. Henry C. Barthman,
    New York City .... 7'4½" 65 lbs.

1929-30
Total — 190.

Feb. 6, 1930
  W. J. Metzger, Detroit, Mich. 7'8" 61½ lbs.
Feb. 11, 1930
  Thos. F. Cooke .... 6'11" 63 lbs.
Feb. 12, 1929
  Mrs. C. R. Wykoff,
    Buffalo, N. Y. .... 7'7" 61½ lbs.
Feb. 12, 1929
  Mrs. Harlan F. Stone,
    Washington, D. C. ...... 7'9" 66 lbs.
Feb. 13, 1929
  Dr. Kellogg .... 7'5" 64 lbs.

1930-31
Total — 64.

Dec. 29, 1930
  G. B. Buchanan, N. Y. City.. 7'9" 73 lbs.
Feb. 25, 1931
  Col. Henry C. Barthman,
    New York City .... 7' 66 lbs.

1931-32
Total — 100.

Feb. 20, 1932
  Miss Jane Erdmann, N. Y. C. 7'7" 67 lbs.
Feb. 21, 1932
  Col. Henry C. Barthman,
    New York City .... 7'6" 67 lbs.

SAILFISH

1932-33

Total — 49.

Feb. 2, 1933
    R. A. Passmore, N. Y. City .. 7′8″   60 lbs.
Feb. 15, 1933
    Col. Henry C. Barthman,
    New York City .... 7′1¾″   63 lbs.

1933-34

Total — 102.

Dec. 20, 1933
    G. B. Buchanan, N. Y. City. 7′7″   60 lbs.

MIAMI BEACH ROD AND REEL CLUB

Mar. 1929
    Capt. Charles Pease using 12 oz. tip,
    24 th. Line .... 82 lbs.
May 30, 1932
    Mr. Henry U. Birdseye using fly rod 76 lbs.
Mar. 25, 1933
    Mr. E. C. Roby using 3/6 tackle.. 58½ lbs.
May 12, 1934
    Mr. Julio Sanchez, 12 th. 6 oz. tip. 74 lbs. 11 oz.
May 22, 1934
    Mr. Julio Sanchez, . 9 th. 4 oz. tip. 60 lbs. 1 oz.

Only the largest fish are brought in by members of this club, all others are released; so the above represent but a small part of the numbers caught by members. Several larger than those shown have been disqualified for infractions of the club rules. The average weight of all those brought in since 1929 has been 52 pounds and the Chairman of the Prize and Contest Committee, Mr. Don McCarthy, estimates the average weight of all sailfish hooked by members would be around 43 pounds.

Mr. McCarthy reports one sailfish of 92 pounds from the Miami vicinity, caught by Mr. Gus E. Kroth, (not a member of the club), date unknown. Mr. Albert Pflueger of Miami reports what seems likely is this same fish which won first prize, Miami Angler's Club. Mr. Pflueger gives no dates but makes the weight 92 pounds and length, 7 feet. He also reports a sail of 87 pounds, length 7 feet 6 inches caught by Mr. Ray Adams, President of the Miami Beach Rod and Reel Club, but gives no date.

COCOS ISLAND, PACIFIC OCEAN

Reported by Mr. Al Pflueger, Miami, Fla., from records by Captain Bob Byrnes.
"Largest 11′8″ long, 165 lbs., by Miss Peggy Hardwick, Cocos Island, Pacific, Sept. 1931.
Smallest, 65 lbs., 9′6″ long, by Mrs. Kathryn Hoyt, July, 1934, Cocos Island.
1934, the party of six caught over two ton of sailfish, averaging 135 lbs. each, 10 feet long.
On each trip to Cocos Islands, Capt. Byrnes; not less than 25 fish caught, and as high as 40 fish."

This island is reasonably accessible from the United States by way of Southern California or Panama.

TAHITI, SOUTH PACIFIC

September 28, 1931
    Eastham Guild .... 160 lbs.

RECORDS FROM PALM BEACH, FLORIDA

Giving an idea of the great concentration of sailfish in those waters. These figures furnished by Mr. Fred C. N. Parke through Captain Herman Gray.

Record of sailfish catches at Palm Beach, 1934 and 1935:

December, 1933	113
January, 1934	269
February, 1934	394
March, 1934	260
April, 1934	129
	1165
December, 1934	317
January, 1935	538
February 1 to 19, 1935	131

Largest number in one day, 1934—53
Largest number in one day, 1935—89

[53]

From a painting by Lynn Bogue Hunt   *Courtesy of the Artist*

WHITE MARLIN
The artist handling the rod aboard the "Pacific" off North Bimini.

CHAPTER II.

MARLIN OFF CUBA

BY

ERNEST HEMINGWAY

ARLIN and broadbill swordfish have been caught by commercial fishermen off the north Cuban coast for more than seventy years. Commercial fishing for marlin and broadbill was introduced by men from Manila in the Philippine Islands who brought the method of drifting with the current of the Gulf Stream in small but very seaworthy skiffs fishing a dead bait with from four to six heavy handlines at depths varying from seventy-five to one hundred and fifty fathoms. The Cuban fishermen — there are as many as seventy boats fishing marlin regularly within a distance of thirty miles each way along the coast from Havana — set out each morning during the season two or three hours before daylight and drift with the current of the Stream to eastward. When the northeast trade wind rises about ten o'clock in the summer mornings, they row their skiffs into the wind to keep their lines straight down from the limber sticks to which they are looped and which by their sudden dipping will show a fish taking the bait.

Marlin and broadbill, when they are swimming deep, take the bait in much the same manner, first, perhaps, picking off a few of the sardines with which the point of the hook is covered, then seizing the whole fish used as bait between their jaws to crush it a moment before swallowing it. When the fishermen feel the weight of the fish solidly on the line, they strike hard on the handline, double handing it in as fast as possible to take up the slack. The fight the marlin or broadbill puts up depends on whether it is a male or female fish and how it has been hooked. Sometimes a marlin will jump as many as forty times and will tow the skiff behind him while he jumps with as much as two hundred and forty fathoms of heavy handline out. A fish putting up this type of fight will be a heavy male fish that has been hooked in the mouth or through the bill. Again, you will see a blue marlin of more than four hundred pounds pulled up to the skiff in less than ten minutes, making no runs and only breaching feebly, his whole stomach hanging out of his mouth when he has been hooked deep. I have seen a female broadbill, weighing more than three hundred pounds, from which forty-three pounds of roe were removed when she was butchered out, caught in six minutes on a handline, and I know of a male broadbill that weighed more than six hundred pounds that four men, working in relays on the same sort of handline, fought for five hours before he was landed. Once a fish is brought close to the boat, it is invariably harpooned before being gaffed.

Because commercial fishermen have been taking these fish for so long off the Cuban coast with hook and line, more is known there of their feeding habits and fighting ability than perhaps anywhere else. I first heard of the Cuban marlin fishing seven years ago when, on a trip after big kingfish at the Dry Tortugas, I met Carlos Gutierrez then in command of a fishing smack which had put into Tortugas to catch bait. Carlos went smack fishing in the winter months and fished marlin, and broadbill, for there are always a few mixed in with the marlin run, from mid-April until the first northers of October ended the hurricane season and sent the smacks out again to the red-snapper grounds.

He told me how the Cubans fished for marlin, described the different fish and the time of their runs, and said he was sure we could catch them trolling, as the fish which feed deep in the early morning come to the top when the trade wind blows. The commercial fishermen, he told us, hoisted a sail on their skiffs and ran in when it became too rough for them to fish, and it was then they would see the marlin travelling to the westward, riding the swells. He had frequently hooked these fish trolling with a handline.

It was not until 1932 that we were able to put in a season after marlin in Cuba, but since April twentieth of that year we have fished two hundred and eighty days for them in the period of their run off the Cuban coast and have taken one hundred and one fish. Off Cuba the marlin travel from east to west against the current of the Gulf Stream. No one has ever seen them working in the other direction, although the current of the Gulf Stream is not stable; sometimes, just before the new moon, it is quite slack, and at others it has a westerly set as far as forty miles out from Havana. You will sometimes see marlin circling on the surface when they are feeding or when they are breeding, but you never see them travelling other than to the westward. Marlin will bite when the current has a westerly set, but they do not cruise or travel on the surface, and they never feed as well as when there is a heavy current to the eastward and a fresh east or northeast breeze. At such a time they come to the top and cruise with the wind, the scythe tail, a light, steely lavender, cutting the swells as it projects and goes under; the big fish, yellow looking in the water, swimming two or three feet under the surface, the huge pectoral fins tucked close to the flanks, the dorsal fin down, the fish looking a round, fast moving log in the water except for the erect curve of that slicing tail.

The heavier the current is running to the eastward, the more marlin you will see travelling along the edge of the dark, swirling current from a quarter of a mile to four miles off shore; all going in the same direction; seeming to travel at a uniform speed of six to eight miles an hour. We have been fighting a fish, on a day when they were running well, and seen six others pass close to the boat in half an hour. Some idea of how plentiful they are in a good year is shown by the official report of the Havana central market, which showed eleven thousand small marlin, i.e., fish that dressed out under one hundred and twenty-five pounds, and one hundred and fifty large marlin as brought to market by the fishermen of Santa Cruz del Norte, Jaruco, Guanaboa, Cojimar, Havana, La Chorrera, Marianao, Jaimanitas, Baracoa, Bañes, Mariel and Cabañas during a period between the middle of March and the eighteenth of July of 1933. All of these fish were taken by hook and line. Between the tenth of April and the eighteenth of July of that same year we caught fifty-two marlin and two sailfish trolling with rod and reel. The largest black marlin we caught was 468 pounds, a long, thin fish, 12 feet 8 inches long; the largest striped marlin weighed 343 pounds and was 10 feet 5 inches long. The biggest white marlin weighed 87 pounds and was 7 feet 8 inches in length. On the twentieth of May of that year I caught seven white marlin and we saw twenty-six fish. It was a wonderful year for fish.

The white marlin run first in late March, April and May; then come the immature striped marlin with brilliant stripes which fade after the fish dies. These are most plentiful in May and run on into June, and both are marvelous light and medium tackle fish. After these smaller fish are gone comes the run of striped and black marlin together. The biggest run of striped marlin is usually in July and as they get scarce the very biggest black marlin run during August and September and until the first northers come in October. A few very large striped marlin come early in the season with the white marlin, but if they appear they are gone in a day or two; but the possibility of encountering them complicates the tackle problem. The so-called blue marlin, too, are liable to appear at any time during the spring and summer.

There is no definite time when the fish appear each year. The white marlin may be running heavily in late March of one year and another not appear until toward the end of April. Everything seems to depend on the amount of current in the Gulf Stream. When there is much current off the Cuban coast, fish will be plentiful as long as the current lasts; when the current slackens fishing is invariably poor. The west wind puts the fish down just as the east wind brings them to the surface. They will also bite on a north wind unless it is a backing wind. On a backing wind the fish seem to stop feeding altogether. No fish feed off the north coast of Cuba with a south wind blowing. Few of the commercial fishermen will even go out with a south wind. I believed this might be superstition or due to the difficulty of sailing in with a land breeze blowing, because south and southeast winds are sometimes excellent biting winds for fish in the Gulf Stream off Key West, although the southwest is the worst fishing wind there; but no matter how strong the current, or how well the marlin had been running, we never caught any marlin with the south wind blowing. But after a south wind, with the start of the trade wind again, fish would start feeding at once.

As regards the moon, marlin seem to feed best after the first quarter on through the full moon and to drop off during the last quarter. They usually drop off in feeding for a day or so when the moon is full. We have never caught many fish during the last quarter of the moon, or on a new moon, although in the 1934 season, when least expected, there was a heavy run of blue marlin during early September on the last quarter of the moon and on the new moon. I missed the run, having left to attend to some work, positive that the fish would not run

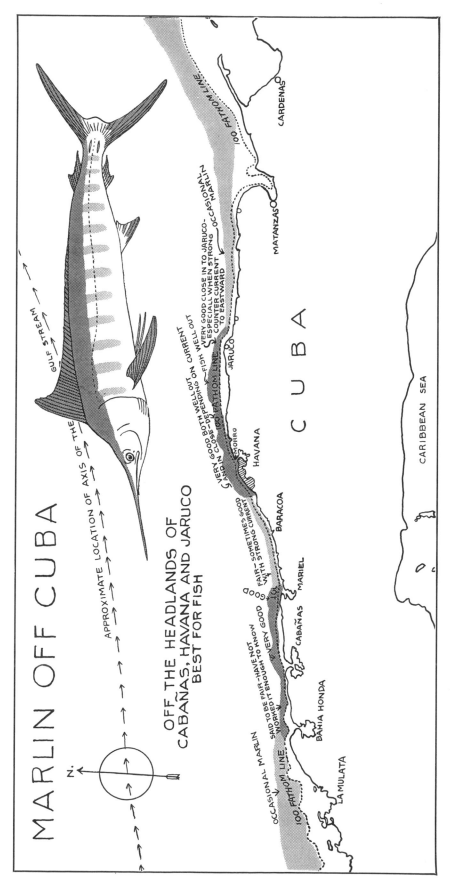

MARLIN OFF CUBA

N.

APPROXIMATE LOCATION OF AXIS OF THE

GULF STREAM

OFF THE HEADLANDS OF
CABAÑAS, HAVANA AND JARUCO
BEST FOR FISH

OCCASIONAL MARLIN
100 FATHOM LINE
SAID TO BE FAIR—HAVE NOT
WORKED IT ENOUGH TO KNOW
VERY GOOD
GOOD
FAIR—SOMETIMES GOOD
WITH STRONG CURRENT

LA MULATA
BAHIA HONDA
CABAÑAS
MARIEL
BARACOA
HAVANA
MORRO
VERY GOOD BOTH WELL OUT AND IN CLOSE—DEPENDING ON CURRENT
FISH WELL OUT
VERY GOOD CLOSE IN TO JARUCO—
ESPECIALLY WHEN STRONG
COUNTER CURRENT
TO EASTWARD
OCCASIONAL MARLIN
JARUCO
100 FATHOM LINE
100 FATHOM LINE
100
MATANZAS
CARDENAS

C U B A

CARIBBEAN SEA

Drawn by Lynn Bogue Hunt from information supplied by Ernest Hemingway.

during that phase of the moon; and thus learned not to put too much confidence in lunar data.

Anyone wanting light tackle fishing for white marlin, which are one of the most spectacular of all sporting fish, should plan to fish Cuba in late April or in May when these fish are usually the thickest. Because of the heavy sea that often comes up in the afternoon when the trade wind is blowing against the current, and the possibility of having to work a fish in really heavy, breaking sea, I do not believe in using any line lighter than 15 thread. With 15 thread line, an 8½ or 9 ounce tip and a reel large enough to hold enough of the line so that if you hook a really big fish you will have time to turn the boat to go with him before he strips the reel, you have tackle that will permit any small marlin to make a brilliant fight and yet enable you to deal with a moderate sized fish in rough weather, and a big fish if there is no sea running. I do not believe it is sensible ever to use any reel smaller than a 9/0 in the Gulf Stream off Cuba as you can never be sure that you will not hook a very large fish. It is about twenty to one that the fish you will hook in May will be a white marlin and that you will hook no fish larger than 125 pounds. But on the always present chance of a big fish, you should have enough line to give you time to get around and head into the northwest when the big fish makes his first run and, since you are fishing in deep water, you must have enough line to handle the big fish when he sounds.

In June, when the first of the big striped marlin are due, you can use standard heavy tackle. June is not a month of much current usually, therefore it is not so rough and you can handle a really big fish on 24 thread line. June, with its heavy rains and possible slack current, is the marlin month to be least recommended. But in July, August and September, when you will only see a white marlin by accident and the fish will be running from 250 to over 1000 pounds in weight, you need 500 or 600 yards of 36 or 39 thread line, and a good big reel whose working you are absolutely familiar with, the drag of which can be loosened instantly no matter what pressure is on it, and a husky but limber tip of eighteen to twenty ounces.

For white marlin we use 10/0 Sobey or O'Shaughnessy hooks, which will also deal with any marlin up to around 250 pounds. They both have advantages and disadvantages. The Sobey is stronger, cannot open and will hook better in the tough part of the upper jaw, but its sharp, triangular cutting point keeps on cutting after the fish is hooked and is jumping, and I believe many fish throw the hook because the Sobey hook set in the juncture of the bill and the roof of the mouth often cuts such a long gash that it is flung loose by a leaping fish. Many times you will bring a fish to gaff and have the hook fall out when the fish is lifted aboard. The O'Shaughnessy is thinner, lighter in a strip bait so that the fish does not feel the metal and jump to throw it as you are slacking to him before he is struck, as white marlin will often do with the heavier Sobey. But they are so thin that in a long fight with a heavy fish, and a marlin has terrific strength in his jaws, they may either open or be broken. Fishing for large fish with a big bait such as a whole cero mackerel, bonito, barracuda or kingfish, we use a 14/0 Pflueger Sobey, 13/0 Pflueger Zane Grey or 14/0 Vom Hofe Grinnell swordfish hook. I have had very good luck with the Hardy Zane Grey swordfish hook. It is a wonderful hook, not too thick in the shank for driving it in as the Grinnell hook sometimes seems, yet strong enough never to have broken on big fish, and it is slightly offset, a great aid in hooking a fish. Being offset, though, it has a tendency to make a bait spin in the water so we only use it on a very big bait which is skipped along the surface. For white marlin we use any sort of strip bait; dolphin, bonito, mullet or whole mullet, goggle-eye, pilchards hooked in tandem, small mackerel, or a small fish called a guaguancho.

For white marlin we use number 13 tinned wire as supplied by Vom Hofe in quarter pound coils, 94 feet to a coil, retailing at $.45 a coil. The stainless wire is not as strong as the ordinary and it is best to make leaders new every day. We use a fourteen foot leader with Hardy number one, "sildur" swivel. This same wire will hold any size marlin and in three seasons of fishing we have never broken a leader; when fishing for big marlin you can use steel cable wire of 500 or 750 pound test, and feel safer since there is little likelihood of this size cable catching around the marlin's bill when you are slacking the bait to the fish. Light cable wire of the 220 or 150 pound test variety, suitable in size for white marlin and small striped marlin, and admirable to fight them once they are hooked, is absolutely unsuited to hooking the fish as at least fifty per cent of the time, in our experience, it will coil around the bill when the fish takes the bait and make it impossible to set the hook properly. This is the explanation of the great part of the marlin which jump free after a few frantic leaps. A white marlin when he takes a bait does *not* go down head first. His head comes up and his tail drops and if you can observe him from a high enough place on the boat you will see that he seems almost to be standing on his tail, straight up and down in the water. It is at this moment when the line is being slacked to enable the fish to get the bait well into his mouth that the very flexible cable, when slacked, will coil and loop around the bill. The fish feels the wire on his bill and starts off to one side or another, the wire comes taut, wound around his narrow bill like a coiled spring and the fish goes into the air to try to get rid of it. He may jump as many as twenty times and on a taut line the wire will hold; but on a slack line he will throw it, or when he sounds and changes his direction, or circles, he will get rid of it. Usually he throws it in the first few jumps. Fishing early in the 1933 season we once lost twelve marlin in two days using the cable, all of them after from three to twelve jumps. Figuring out what the trouble was, we shifted back to the old style piano wire and hooked and landed six out of the next eight fish that struck. This, of course, is an abnormally high average of hooked fish to strikes. On a strip bait marlin are easy to hook, but on a whole bait to hook one out of three fish that strike is a very good average.

Of course one cannot say that all marlin go tail down and head up to take a bait in; sometimes they come from the side and take the bait off sideways in their mouth and you cannot see how they take it in when you slack off. But one thing I can say—that I have never seen or felt a marlin tap a bait. Since their upper jaw is immovable, when they come behind a bait to take it they must shove their bill and upper jaw out of water to seize the bait with their lower jaw. Swimming with tail deep in this awkward position, their heads wobble from side to side and the bill wags and can easily be entangled in the leader when you slack the bait into their open mouth. Fish that see the bait when they are swimming deep often surge their whole length out of the water when they smash at it. Sometimes their rush takes them so far that they seem to lose the bait or they feel that they have missed the bait and do not come back after it again. It may be difficult, too, for them to see the bait when they have to go into the sun for it. We have also found that when we have a strike while going to the eastward with the current and miss the marlin, if we turn at once and head to the westward over the same piece of water, we will often hook the fish.

Marlin hit a trolled bait in four different ways. First, with hunger; again, in anger; thirdly, simply playfully, last, with indifference. Anyone can hook a hungry fish who orders the boat stopped when the fish seizes the bait, gives him enough line to get the bait well into his mouth, orders the boat put ahead, as the marlin is moving off with the bait, screws down hard on the drag and sets the hook with four or five good hard strikes. If the fish moves off slowly, strike him again three or four times, as the hook may not be set yet. If you pull it out of his mouth, reel in and speed up the boat and the marlin, if he is hungry, will usually smash at it again.

A white marlin will usually jump immediately when he feels the hook and may make his run in any direction. A striped marlin, too, will usually jump instantly when hooked and may run in two or three directions before heading for the northwest. A big black marlin may jump at once if he is hooked in a tender place, but if he is not being caused any particular pain he will move slowly and heavily, almost like a big shark, circling deep or even swimming toward the boat, and you can often bring him close to the boat before he realizes he is being led or even, possibly, that he is hooked at all. But when he does realize it he heads straight out for the northwest like an under-water speed boat. He may fight an hour or more before jumping or he may jump early in the fight. A blue marlin is so voracious that he will often swallow the bait; then he will jump, showering blood, his stomach will hang out of his mouth after two or three jumps; he will circle stupidly, wagging his bill out of water in agony, try to sound but give it up if you hold him, and you should make every effort to work him as fast as is humanly possible without smashing tackle to get him in to gaff before the blood calls up sharks. Until we had a run of blue marlin off Cuba in 1934, I had never hooked a marlin in the belly or even in the gullet. Out of four blue marlin we caught last season, three were hooked in the belly while trolling. They swallow a bait as fast as a jewfish, whereas striped or white marlin will go into the air the minute they feel either hook or leader in their mouth. They go into the air the first time deliberately to throw out the bait and often you will see the bait thrown and a shower of flying fish come out of the marlin's mouth at the same time. The white and striped marlin are dainty feeders with electric quick reflexes; the blue marlin, at least off Cuba, is a voracious feeder which takes a bait in like a shark; and where the white and striped marlin are so fast that you can hardly follow their movements in the water when they are unhooked and at speed, the blue marlin seems comparatively slow and logy. I have no great respect for black marlin in comparison to the striped fish, except for their size, but I believe no fish could possibly give an angler greater sport than the white and striped marlin.

To return to the way in which marlin hit a bait, the really hungry marlin smashes at the bait, if he comes from the side, with bill, hump, dorsal fin and tail out of water. If you pull the bait out of his mouth he will come for it again as long as there is any bait on the hook. The fact that the hook may prick him does not seem to upset him if he is hungry. Remember that he is used to swallowing fish with spiny fins whole. If he is a black marlin and you have two baits he will sometimes take one and then come after the other. We had one fish hit one bait, slam back to take the other and with two baits in his mouth, come into the wake of the boat after the teaser. Luckily one of the leaders was caught around his bill, and wagging his bill he threw the bait and a few seconds later the leader came loose, so that when he went into the air for his first jump, he was on only one of the rods. But I can still see that fish charging back and forth at the baits, bill, fin and tail out, and then coming toward the boat after teasers, paying no attention to the fact that he was hooked until he felt the pull of the leader on his bill as we were both pumping line on him and striking.

"I've got him," said Joe Russell.

"Hell, no, I've got him."

"We've each got one."

"No, we've both got the same one. Look at him. He's big as a horse!"

Then Joe's reel going zing! zing! zing! as the marlin wagged his bill out of water.

"He's going to jump," Joe shouted as the lines slanted out and straightened, then rose. "He's off," Joe yelled.

"I've got him," you yelled and you remember how he nearly jerked you forward out of the chair as he rose full length clear of the water on a tight line, not thirty yards astern, you loosening the drag, the fish long, purple-black and making a splash like a horse falling off a cliff when he hit the water to come out again and again and again and then go down deep to head for the northwest.

The angry fish strike puzzled us for a long time. He would come from below and hit the bait with a smash. But when you slacked line to him he dropped the bait. Screw down the drag and race the bait in and he would slam it again and drop it. The only way to hook a fish that strikes that way is to screw down on the drag and hit him hard when he smashes. Speed up the boat and strike back at him when he hits the bait. There is too, an outside chance of foul hooking him. That sort of fish will hit the bait to kill it as long as it seems to be alive. I believe they are male fish in breeding season who kill any small fish they see.

The playful marlin, possibly a fish that has fed well, will come behind a bait with his fin high, shove his bill out of water and take the bait lightly between his bill and pointed lower jaw. No matter how fresh the bait may be he drops it. Speeding the boat up may make him take the bait better but you should hit him as soon as he turns with the bait for he is almost certain to drop it. The instant you see it go into his mouth, hit him. If you jerk it away from him it may make him take it harder the next time.

The indifferent fish will sometimes follow the boat, if you are going to the westward, for as many as three or four miles. Looking the bait over, sheering away, coming back to swim deep down below them and follow, indifferent to the bait as food, yet curious. If such a fish swims with his pectoral fins tucked close to his sides, he will not bite. He is cruising and you are on his course. That is all. The instant a marlin sees the bait if he is going to strike or even play with it he raises his dorsal fin and spreads his wide, blue pectorals so that he looks like some great, under-sea bird in the water as he follows.

The black marlin is a stupid fish. He is immensely powerful, can jump wonderfully if you have not hooked him in the belly, and he can ruin your back sounding but he has not the speed or the stamina of the striped marlin, nor his intelligence. I believe the black marlin are old female fish past their prime and that it is age and sexual change that gives them that black color. When they are younger they are much bluer in color and the meat, too, is whiter and of better quality. The meat of the very big old black fish is almost uneatable. If you fight them fast without resting, never letting up on them, you can kill them quicker than you can kill a striped marlin of half their size. Their great strength makes them very dangerous for the first forty minutes. I mean dangerous to tackle; no fish is dangerous to a man in a launch. But if you can take what they give and keep working on them, they will tire quicker than any striped marlin. The 468 pounder was hooked in the roof of the mouth, was in no way tangled in the leader, jumped eight times completely clear, towed the boat stern first when held tight, sounded four times, but was brought to gaff, fin and tail out, in sixty-five minutes. But if I had not lost a much larger striped marlin the day before after two hours and fifty minutes, and fought another the day before for forty-five, I would not have been in shape to work him so hard.

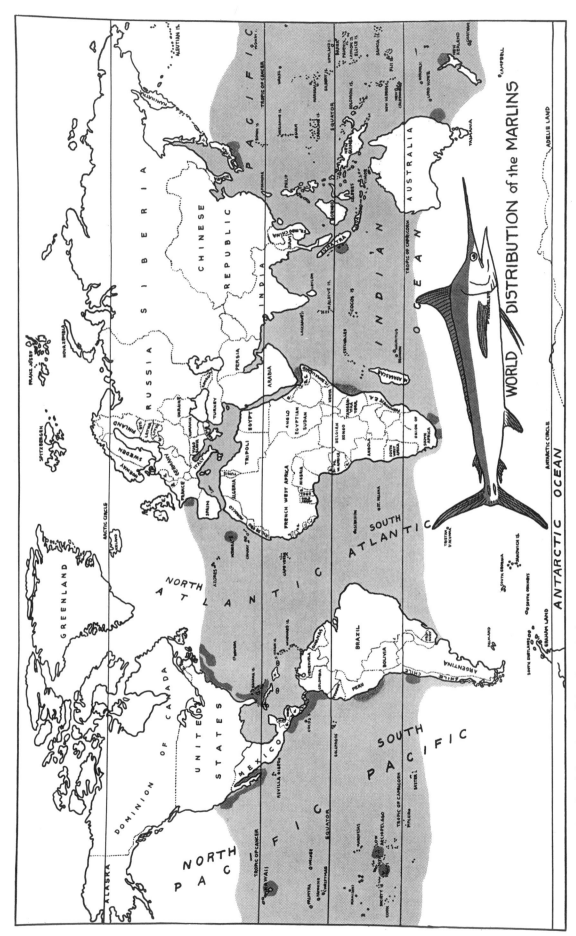

Drawn by Lynn Bogue Hunt from information supplied by Ernest Hemingway.

Fishing in a five-mile-an-hour current, where a hooked fish will always swim at least part of the fight against the current, where the water is from 400 to 700 fathoms deep, there is much to learn about tactics in fighting big fish. But one myth that can be dissipated is the old one that the water pressure at one thousand feet will kill the fish. A marlin dies at the bottom only if he has been hooked in the belly. These fish are used to going to the bottom. They often feed there for we find bottom fish in their bellies. They are not built like bottom fish which always live at the same depth but are built to be able to go up and down in any depth. I have had a marlin sound four hundred yards straight down, all the rod under water over the side, bend double with the weight going down, down, down, watching the line go, putting on all pressure possible on the reel to check him, him going down and down until you are sure every inch of the line will go. Suddenly he stops sounding and you straighten up, get on to your feet, back into the chair, get the butt in the socket, and work him up slowly and heavily, but steadily. Finally you have the double line on the reel and think he is whipped and will be coming to gaff, and then the line begins to rip out as he hooks up and heads off just under the surface to see him come out in ten long, clean jumps. This after an hour and half of fight; then to sound again.

The 343 pound striped marlin jumped 44 times. Every one has a fish in favor of whose qualities he is prejudiced. I am frankly prejudiced in favor of the striped marlin as we meet him off the Cuban coast. All marlin have stripes and as yet the various marlin have not been properly classified by scientists, so I will not put in my theories on them here. But what is called a striped marlin off Cuba is a marlin that runs in weight from 125 to more than a thousand pounds, with a small, depressed head, long, finely shaped bill, bright silver coloring when the fish dies, and broad violet stripes from one and a half to nearly three inches wide which remain clearly visible after the fish is dead many hours. A true striped marlin is never plum-colored as the blue marlin shows in the water and when he jumps the broad stripes are clearly visible. The female counterpart of this fish is the silver marlin, shaped the same, bright as a freshly minted dollar and with very pale stripes which fade out entirely. This is also a wonderful fighting fish. The commercial fishermen who handle them on handlines and know how they pull will catch a 400 pound blue marlin, hooked deep, in a quarter of an hour or less. A striped marlin of the same size, hooked in the same way, will often take the same man three or four hours to bring alongside his skiff. The striped marlin fights with his mouth tight shut on the leader and nearly always after the first jump, when he vomits what is in his belly or in the top of his belly, jumps with his mouth tightly shut, while the blue or black marlin almost invariably jumps with his mouth wide open. The commercial fishermen say the only fish that will outpull the striped marlin is the male broadbill and that no fish can out-jump him. They say the fastest thing in the water is the first run of a big tuna or a hundred pound wahoo. But they claim that on a handline, once a tuna's head is turned, when he is towing a skiff, he is whipped and will only circle. The wahoo makes one great run at the start and another excellent run when you get him up to the boat and the market fisherman's lines are really too heavy for him to show how fast he is. But no one can say what will happen with a big male broadbill or a big striped marlin. These same fishermen call the blue and black marlin "bobos," or fools. They swallow the bait, get rattled and sometimes quit, and their main problem is to keep them from going down deep to die. Of course, to a rod and reel fisherman who has not line strong enough to deal with the weight of the fish, or is inexperienced in handling heavy fish, the mere size of blue and black marlin can make them a problem. But as a sporting fish they can never, at least in waters where I have fished them, rank with the striped marlin. Although, if hooked in the mouth, they can put up spectacular fights before they tire.

The mako shark is caught off Cuba all through the marlin run. They are as strong as a broadbill, can leap marvelously, but have no heart. They will sometimes make a terrific fight for a short time, but when they find they are still hooked, will come to gaff docilely with all their strength intact. But when you gaff them, look out. And when you take them in the boat afterwards, look out. I believe they are the only fish in the sea that will deliberately attack a man while they are hooked. I know of numerous cases of this among the commercial fishermen and was lucky enough to get a cinema picture of a mako jumping twice at a fisherman in a skiff who was playing him on a handline. Of course, what really makes a spectacular fight in a fish, if we do not try to deceive ourselves, is panic. A mako has no panic. He probably feels little pain from the hook, too, and that is why he comes in so easily sometimes.

Considering the size the fish attain, the present Atlantic records on marlin taken with rod and reel are ridiculous. The largest fish we have taken weighed 468 pounds. The largest taken in Atlantic waters on rod and reel, the taking of which is doubtless described in the Bimini chapter of this book, weighed 502. Yet the commercial fishermen of Cuba do not consider a marlin which dresses out 750 pounds of salable meat with the head, guts, flanks and tail removed, a phenomenal fish. The largest marlin ever caught by commercial fishermen dressed out 1,175 pounds of salable meat; several have been caught which dressed out over a thousand pounds of meat. The head, guts, flanks, blood, hump, fins and tail, which are cut away before the fish is sold, will weigh from a quarter to a third of the weight of the whole fish.

The difficulty is to have the tackle and the knowledge of the fish to handle such a one when he is hooked. To catch a really huge marlin a man must be prepared to spend several entire seasons in the Gulf Stream. Some years exceptionally big fish run, in others there seems to be a top limit of four hundred to five hundred pound fish, as there was in 1934, and no giant marlin running. I caught the biggest fish I had a strike from in 1934, a 420 pounder, so I have no apologies for that season, but in 1933 through lack of experience, unsuitable tackle and some bad luck, we lost marlin whose size I would not dare to estimate in print. The next year we had more experience and the proper tackle and the biggest fish were not running. Happily, in fishing, there is always a season ahead.

Tactics, as I see them now, with very big fish consist in this; first be certain you have really hooked the fish. It would not be exaggerating to strike firmly and solidly at least a dozen times on a really big marlin with all the strain the tackle can stand. His mouth is very hard and, at the start, he may have his jaws shut tight on the leader so that you cannot set the hook.

When the fish is first hooked if he fights deeply and slowly, work him as hard and as fast as you can. The slower he works the faster you should work. The faster he works the easier you must take him. When he is slow never give him an inch of line unless your refusal to let him have it would break it. It is the ability to work always close to the breaking point of your tackle and never break it that makes a real fisherman with heavy tackle. You cannot do this with a drag alone as you cannot feel the strain you put on accurately enough. You must use your hands on the reel to know what drag you are safe in applying. When the fish is jumping have a very light drag on, stand up if you can, and hold your rod high to get the belly of the line out of the water and have the boat follow the fish, keeping him on the quarter and watching for a shift in his direction when he goes down. As soon as the fish goes down, tighten up on your drag and get every bit of line back that you can. When you have run up on the fish, try to lift him by pumping. Any time you can hold him you can get line on him. If he is sounding straight down you must put every bit of pressure possible on the line without breaking it. Make him bend the rod as far as it will go without breaking it, and start raising him instantly the moment he stops. Don't let him rest or have time to make any plans.

Try to take the play away from him at all times and never simply defend yourself against the fish. More big fish are dominated and convinced by heavy tackle and led to gaff than ever are killed by the tackle. It is better to convince him than to try to kill him. The ceaseless bend of the rod putting the utmost strain on him to lead him is what convinces him. When you get him coming, work as hard as you can to keep him coming and you may be able to bring him alongside on that course without having him start circling. If he starts to circle, as most tired fish will do, first try to turn him by holding him as hard as you can with the spring of the rod. If you cannot hold him, keep the boat well ahead of him and be content to let him take out line each time on the circle but try to get a little more back than he takes out each time he turns toward you. When you have shortened his circle, try to turn him again. The first time you turn him try to bring him alongside on the course he is on. As soon as the boatman takes hold of the leader, stand up and loosen your drag and watch one thing — that your rod tip is clear at all times and that there is no loose line to catch around the guides or anywhere else in case the boatman cannot hold him to the gaff and has to turn him loose. Make your boatman understand beforehand that he is only to gaff the marlin in the head and that he is not to try to gaff him unless he is absolutely certain that he can reach him. In gaffing always reach over the fish, see the particular part on the head that you are aiming for, and then bring the gaff toward you with plenty of force. Unless you gaff for a definite place it is like trying to hit a quail by shooting at the covey. When the fish is gaffed, let the boatman hand the gaff to the huskiest man on board to hold while he grabs the fish's bill with a gloved hand, pulls upward on it and clubs the fish between the eyes until his color changes and you know that he is dead. You can put a line through his gills and shift him astern and using the gaff and his bill to lift, get him over the roller on the stern and bring him aboard head first.

The essence of tactics — after the fireworks over which you have no control are over and the work commences — seems to me to be to know that the fish, down deep, wants to go either one direction or another and to handle your boat accordingly. This is not to fight him with the boat but rather to avoid fighting the weight of the boat against the fish. The ideal to be achieved is to have the boat a neutral yet mobile point from which to work the fish. No angler can match a big marlin in strength when he is going away from you, against the current, so if you pull against him with the boat thrown out he must take line until you will have to run up on him again to get the line back. It is for this reason that you have to manoeuver the boat. Discover which way he wants to go and then keep a little ahead of him. As long as he is strong he will usually want to go to the north-west, i.e., out to sea and against the current. When you get him rattled he will change his course. When he begins to tire he will usually go with the current. If you cannot bring him up one way try to make him turn and often he will come up steadily and easily in the opposite direction. Put the boat ahead enough to get him astern, then throw out the clutch while you try to raise him. Try never to put any strain on him with the boat. If he is coming toward the boat you will have to get ahead of him again. Usually you will have to do this a great many times.

When there is a heavy current, remember that if you fight a fish with your clutch out and the fish heads into the current, that current will be carrying your boat, which weighs several tons, away from the fish at the rate of four to five miles an hour if the fish only maintains his position. Of course if you are in a light boat you can shut down on the drag and let him tow the boat. But if you do not work him to get him up and keep him up, the chances are he will go down deep to die. They always try to go down, and you must hold them.

Remember that what you want to do with a big fish is pull his head side-ways and upwards. If you work him so that he is going straight away it is as big an advantage to him as for a man to be able to pull on a line over his shoulder. Remember the more a big marlin jumps at the start the better chance you have of landing him, if he is still on after he jumps. Repeated jumping, that is twenty or more jumps, tires the fish greatly and also fills the sacks along his backbone, which take the place of an air bladder, with air which prevents him from sounding deeply. If he jumps enough he cannot sound at all. He will try to, but the air will hold him at a certain depth. If you fight him fast there is no time for his pressure apparatus to adjust itself, if it is ever able to adjust itself after such effort. If you see a marlin, after the very first part of the fight waggle his bill out of water, it means he is hooked deep and is a whipped fish. You should put on all pressure and work him as fast as possible. At the end of a fight, if a fish begins to jump wildly it is almost certain that sharks are after him. Stand up, loosen your drag while he is jumping and if he is on a very short line ride with the jumps with your rod, that is dip to them, to keep the line taut and at the same time keep from smashing the tackle. The instant he goes down, tighten up your drag, sit down and see how fast you can bring him in.

A twenty foot bamboo pole with a sharpened file on the end is the best thing I have found for keeping sharks off a fish when he is in close. Shooting at them with a rifle is useless. Try to hit them in the head with your lance, but hit them. Have a line on the pole so you can retrieve it if one carries it off.

As I see big-game fishing with rod and reel it is a sport in which a man or woman seeks to kill or capture a fish by the means which will afford the fisherman the greatest pleasure and best demonstrate the speed, strength and leaping ability of the fish in question; at the same time killing or capturing the fish in the shortest time possible and never for the sake of flattering the fisherman's vanity, using tackle unsuitable to the prompt capture of the fish. I believe that it is as bad to lose fish by breaking unsuitable tackle in an attempt to make a light-tackle record as it is to allow animals to escape wounded in an attempt to get a record bag or a record head.

Talk of giving the fish a sporting chance on excessively fragile tackle seems nonsense when one realizes that the sporting chance offered the fish is that of breaking the line and going off to die. The sporting thing is to kill your fish as promptly as possible on suitable tackle which does not prevent him running, pulling or jumping to the best of his ability, while you fight him as rapidly as possible to kill him as quickly and as mercifully as possible.

Any good heavy-tackle fisherman who would be willing to fish drifting for three or four seasons off the Cuban coast would undoubtedly, by hooking fish in the belly so they could not fight, be almost certain sooner or later of breaking the world record for marlin. But all he would demonstrate would be that there are huge marlin to be caught off Cuba by drifting and letting them swallow the bait, and the commercial fishermen have been demonstrating that for seventy years. There are also huge fish to be caught there trolling — just as big as have been caught drifting — and that is something that interests a sportsman to prove.

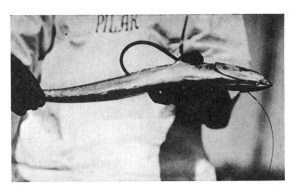

(1) Hook is inserted in mouth of fish and brought out a little behind pectoral fin.

(2) Hook is drawn out until only eye is left in bait. Then hook is turned and point is re-inserted into bait and pushed through to other side. A slit is cut along line of the shank so that shank of hook lies parallel with backbone and eye of hook is well drawn inside mackerel's gullet.

(3) Shows how hook projects after it has been brought out through mackerel the second time.

(4) A strip is now cut along back of mackerel from tail to back of head and along belly from tail to throat. These strips have attractive movement for game fish when bait is trolled and also act as rudders to prevent spinning. The mackerel jaws are tied shut on the leader and bait is tied fast to leader so it cannot be pulled down.

(5) The bait is now tied around belly and around gills.

(6) Completed baits. A mackerel on left; a guaguancho or small barracuda-like fish on right.

PREPARING MACKEREL BAIT FOR TROLLING FOR MARLIN

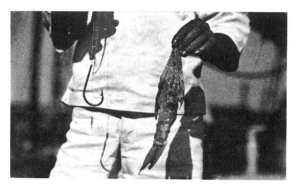

Strip mullet bait with two side trolling fins. Hardy Zane Grey hook. No. 13 piano wire leader rigged with safety pin fastening for strip bait trolling.

Carlos Gutierrez who prepared all the baits on this page, holding a strip bait hooked and tied on.

A cero mackerel.

Preparing a guaguancho or barracuda for trolling. Showing how the belly of a guaguancho is slit to give a trolling strip. Any of these baits can be put on complete in from three to five minutes.

The only difference in preparing a sharp snouted fish with long gill openings is that the original insertion of the hook may be made just behind the gill opening instead of through the mouth.

Left to right: Strip bait on safety pin rig, strip bait tied, mackerel, guaguancho and mackerel baits.

When there is little current in the stream and no east breeze so that the fish do not come to the top, marlin may still be caught drifting. In this form of fishing a whole cero mackerel or a kingfish is put on the hook, head downward, the hook being introduced into the body of the fish at the tail, while the fish is held curved in the hand, and run along the backbone until the point is brought out through the skin a little behind the gill opening; shank of hook and leader being inside the mackerel which hangs head down with the curve of the hook and the barb projecting. The tail of the fish is then tied fast to the leader so it cannot be pulled down; another thread is tied around the fish where the hook projects and all the projecting part of the hook is covered with sardines or pilchards hooked onto the projecting curve and barb by passing the point of the hook through both their eyes. This bait is lowered over the side and allowed to sink with its own weight and that of the leader to a depth of from seventy-five to a hundred and twenty-five fathoms. Usually four baits are put out on four different rods at seventy-five, ninety, one hundred, and one hundred and twenty-five fathoms. The baits float deep with the current and the engine is manoeuvered occasionally to keep the lines as perpendicular as possible. A strike is signalled by line running off the reel, perhaps slowly at first in a series of jerks, then steadily and rapidly when the fish has taken the bait in his mouth or swallowed it. As the fish moves off he will usually hook himself against the pull of four to six hundred feet of line moving through the deep water.

Occasionally a white marlin will come to the top and jump with the bait before the fisherman's rod or reel give intimation of a strike. He has taken it from below and come straight up with it. As soon as the fisherman knows he has a fish on, the boat is headed toward the northwest and the fisherman reels and pumps while the boat is going ahead to straighten out the deep belly in the line. Once he has a taut line on the fish, if the fish has been hooked in the mouth, the problem is then the same as with a fish hooked trolling except that as a big fish always heads out against the current, the boat has the advantage of heading out with the fish from the start without the necessity of making a turn while the fish is making his run, as would be necessary when hooking a fish while trolling against the current. This eliminates the most difficult and most exciting manoeuver in trolling. Striped marlin and white marlin are sometimes hooked in the mouth when drifting, but blue and black marlin are almost invariably hooked in the gullet or stomach.

To me it is a method of fishing to be employed by a sportsman only when the fish can be taken no other way due to a lack of breeze or current, or when, due to there being a great quantity of feed in the lower strata of the current, marlin keep down and will not come to the top; or when the expenditure of gasoline for trolling is a dominant consideration. A fish hooked in the mouth while drifting can put up as good a fight as one hooked trolling, but you miss the excitement of the strike and you have a definite advantage over the fish from the start.

Mr. H. L. Woodward, whom we met in 1933 and who is a pioneer rod and reel fisherman for big marlin off Cuba, does not agree with me on drifting. We have had many discussions about it during the times we have had the pleasure of him fishing with us in the 1934 season. In a letter he writes: "I shall give you such pertinent information as I can regarding my fishing, but it is the sport that counts and not the individual. Therefore, *where not absolutely necessary*, please leave my name out of the text of the article. Now for the information.

"I began my salt water fishing in 1915. I have been fishing for marlin since 1921. I cannot tell you how many marlin I have caught because I have not made it a practice to record in writing any fish except large ones. Last season I caught 8. Probably 6 or 7 per season would be a fair average. The largest marlin I have caught was the 459 pound fish, photograph enclosed, showing Mr. Hugo Lippmann and Mr. C. H. Ford with fish. Photograph was taken of myself with fish but turned out very poor. The largest fish I ever caught in the Gulf Stream was a 522 pound mackerel shark.

"The best fighting fish that I have ever hooked and landed in the Gulf Stream was a 360 pound striped marlin. This fish was hooked while drifting, the hook being set well forward in the mouth, just under the eye. This fish fought for one hour and fifty minutes and was at no time over 200 feet deep. The 324 pound marlin which was hooked by Dr. Hernandez, fought for two and a half hours by myself and landed by you on your boat, was one of the best fighting fish that I have ever hooked on the surface. The unfortunate part was that this fish fouled the leader with his tail within the first hour. He made a very spectacular fight for the first forty minutes on the surface and moved so fast that at times we had a double bag in the line.

"You and I have never agreed about 'drifting' and fishing between 450 and 700 feet down. As I have done a great deal of it, I think my opinion is more valuable than yours. Unusual care has to be exercised in striking fish early so that they are hooked in the mouth. If that precaution is taken, fish hooked in this fashion will come to the top immediately and put up just as good a fight as fish hooked on the surface. The 459 pound blue marlin caught in 1934 was hooked at about 550 feet down. However this fish, like all of that species, put up a very poor fight. It is true that I gave this fish a little more time than I usually do when I felt it take the bait. This resulted in the fish being hooked in the back of the mouth. However, my experience coincided with your own when it comes to the ordinary large-headed blue marlin. They are stupid, generally slow in action, and put up a very poor fight.

"Havana men who fish each summer for marlin in the Gulf Stream are: Esmond Brownson who has caught eleven and Thorvald Sanchez who has caught twenty-four, Frank D. Mahoney has caught a number of small and medium sized marlin. Mario Mendoza used to be a great peto (wahoo) fisherman and also caught a few marlin. There are a number of other Cubans and Americans who have been trying their hand for the last one or two seasons. Nearly everybody is handicapped by lack of proper equipment. Boats are not adapted and the beginner generally starts with cheap and ineffective tackle.

"Now about broadbill swordfish. The large ones do not get this far south. In all the time that I have fished the Gulf Stream I have only seen one very large broadbill and I have only caught two small ones. One weighed 262 pounds and the other weighed 212 pounds.

"I will close this letter by saying that from my own personal experience in fishing here and elsewhere, and from all that I have read, I think that no place in the western hemisphere can equal the marlin fishing in the Gulf Stream along the north coast of Cuba during the summer and early fall months. Your own experience in 1933 corroborates my own idea. Eventually the men who love this sport will acquire the habit and come here each year. The local people do nothing of consequence properly to advertise this marlin fishing."

The 324 pound fish Mr. Woodward refers to was hooked by Dr. Hernandez in a small launch without a fishing chair, was fought under impossible conditions by Woodward until, as it was getting rough and the sun was going down, our boat which had been standing by in case they would be caught out in the dark with the fish, took both anglers on board to let them work the fish from a proper chair. The fish was finally brought up, dead, tail tangled in the leader, from a depth of 500 yards. At least there were five hundred yards of 30 thread line out, straight down, when the doctor, whose first marlin it was, suggested that a third angler have a try at the fish. The bringing-up process took one hour and three-quarters. It was interesting to see that a dead 324 pound fish could be raised from that depth on 30 thread line, but it is an experience the repetition of which is to be avoided.

If a fish tangles his tail in the leader jumping he will have to die at whatever depth he is at the time as, if you hold him, pulling his gills open against the water as you try to lift him, will drown him. You can use the currents to lift him by heading against the current for a little, while you try to have it start him lifting. Then go with the current and try to keep the fish coming, even if it is only a quarter of an inch at a time. If you can raise him a quarter of an inch you can get him up. Thirty-six and thirty-nine thread line will take an unbelievable strain when it is wet, and a good twenty ounce tip, when your chair is high enough so you can brace your feet and pull, acts like a derrick.

A fish that is hooked in the belly will go deep to die if allowed to; but he should not be allowed to. Such a fish, once he comes to the top, should be fought on as short a line as possible; try to get him on the double line as soon as you can, hold him hard when he starts to go down and gaff him at the first chance. Many people have gotten into trouble with heavy marlin by being afraid the fish was too fresh to gaff when they brought him close early in the fight. A fish is never too fresh to gaff if you gaff him in the head. If you cannot gaff him in the head, do not gaff him.

As to the advisability of using outriggers to skip bait for marlin I am not competent to judge. When marlin were on the surface feeding, we were always able to get as many strikes as we could handle without them. Fishing without outriggers we have had strikes from seventeen marlin in a single day. A hungry marlin will come right into the wash of a propeller after a bait and one of the greatest pleasures in fishing, to me, is seeing the fish come and feeling him first take hold of the bait. Also, when marlin are plentiful and striking well I should imagine outriggers would be a nuisance.

Thorvald Sanchez, who is a fine sportsman and very faithful fisherman of the Gulf Stream, always uses outriggers and several days last season when fish were scarce he had marlin strikes when we raised no fish. On other days we would raise fish when he would have a blank day. But I believe that out of an

324 pound marlin taken by Dr. Hernandez and Mr. H. L. Woodward.

Photos by courtesy of Ernest Hemingway.

Striped marlin showing shape of head, fins and stripes.

420 pound marlin, July 1934. Ernest Hemingway and Sidney Franklin.

459 pound marlin caught by Mr. H. L. Woodward off Havana, September 1934. Standing with the fish are Mr. Hugo Lippmann and Mr. C. H. Ford.

A 343 pound striped marlin.

equal number of days fished he raised more marlin with the outriggers than we did without them. We intend to give them a thorough trial this season (1935). There is no doubt but that they save much fatigue, but there is no better training for using a big rod and heavy reel than holding that same outfit day after day.

In the winter months when marlin are absent, the Cuban sportsmen fish for wahoo, locally called *peto*, which run to a great size off Cuba. Mario Mendoza with his brothers Raul and Adrian Mendoza, I believe hold the record for having caught the greatest number of wahoo in one day with 14. Their largest on rod and reel weighed 75 pounds. Adrian Mendoza has also taken a white marlin of 136, the Cuban rod and reel record. Dr. Jorge Muniz, one of the first rod and reel fishermen in Cuba, and Julio Cadenas are other Cuban sportsmen who have caught marlin and for many years specialized in wahoo. There are many other excellent Cuban fishermen whose names I do not know, but Julio Sanchez and his brother Emilio have caught many big marlin at Bimini.

Wahoo are trolled for along the hundred fathom curve either way from Havana harbor with Tarp-orenos, heavy metal Tarp-orenos, feather jigs or strip baits. Running to as big as 140 pounds, they are a marvelous sporting fish on medium tackle. They have wonderful speed as well as strength, and making a very slashing fight they do everything but jump. There are certain patches of bottom like the so-called tuna holes of Tahiti, which they frequent and these are known to all the local fishermen. Just off Cojimar, to the eastward of Havana, off Bacuranao in the same direction, straight out from the Morro Castle, and off Jaimanitas to the westward are all famous wahoo spots. I believe the record for one man in a day is held by Julio Hidalgo with nine taken trolling with a handline. The largest I have ever seen weighed 105 pounds, but they have been caught weighing 125 pounds by the commercial fishermen and are said to run much heavier. They have great strength when they are really big, with no loss of speed, and they smash much tackle.

In the summer they live in the cool deep water and do not come to the surface unless the wind should shift into the north when you are liable to get a strike from one at any time. They ruin many big marlin baits, cutting them off as sharply as with a knife just behind the hook. You do not know it is a wahoo so you slack when you feel the strike; then when you reel in there is the bait chopped in two. We catch them by fishing a feather on a light rod and long line between the two big baits. This feather makes a good teaser for big marlin.

Anyone fishing it is instructed to strike hard if they feel anything hit and if they do not hook the fish to race the feather in.

Frequently a marlin will chase it in and then switch to one of the baits which are usually fished about forty feet astern. With the baits we use two teasers; one green or blue, the other white. These you can make yourself in any size. We have found one about twice the size of Pflueger Zane Grey teaser painted green with a red head to be very effective at raising big fish. To keep it from breaking off the line, it should be fitted with a heavy swivel in the head. Teasers get water-logged with constant fishing and need to be replaced and dried out or, when their line happens to break or be cut away by a wahoo or other fish, they will sink and be lost. When a fish charges the teasers never pull them all the way out of the water or he will go down. But keep them dancing out of the water and pull them away from him until you can pass him a bait. The minute the bait is into him or slacked out to him and he turns toward it, jerk the teaser aboard. Always have the teasers tied so some one can reach them instantly if a fish shows behind them.

Lines if fished every day are much better not dried, but when first put on should be wet their entire length and then reeled back on without the boat going ahead very much while you are reeling, so the line will not be packed on so tightly that later on the heat may rot it altogether. Reels need lots of oil and grease. Any time after fighting a big fish, oil your reel again before putting out another bait.

The principal points about a boat are that the larger and heavier it is the better it must be able to be manoeuvered if you are not to break fish off; that the stern must be low enough so that you can get a big fish aboard; that the man at the wheel must have an unobstructed view of the line in the water when a fish is hooked, and the fishing chair must fit the fisherman so that he can brace his feet and pull when the fish is astern, broadside, or on the quarter. The chair too, should be high enough so that when a fish sounds straight down the bent rod will not strike the gunwale. Twelve to fourteen miles is as fast as a fishing boat needs to go with marlin, but you should always be able to get forward with the rod and up into the bow if necessary to chase a jumping fish. When he sounds you can get back into the stern again.

White marlin breed off Cuba in May. They breed in the same way that the grouper does, except that as they are a fish of the current they breed in the current instead of on a reef. The female marlin heads into the current while the male heads in the opposite direction, and while they are side by side the female expels the eggs and the male the milt; the male then catches the eggs in the basket-like opening of his gill covers and lets them pass out through his mouth. We hope, if the fish run well next year, to find the young marlin in the sargasso weed where it would seem logical that they would take refuge along with the young fish of so many other species. The broadbill too must breed off Cuba for the fish are often taken in pairs full of milt and spawn and I have seen female broadbill so full of roe that the eggs would be expelled in the boat when the fish was moved.

The fishermen say that the striped and black marlin breed during July and August but that the very big fish that appear in September and October are usually without fully developed roe or milt and must have spawned some time before. Marlin when they are paired seem very devoted. The fishermen claim the male fish always hangs back until the female fish has taken a bait, but since the male is often only a fraction of the size of the female this may not be pure altruism. I know that we have frequently hooked the female fish of a pair and had the male fish swim around all during the fight, staying close to the female until she was gaffed. I will tell an incident that anyone is at perfect liberty to doubt but which will be vouched for by Captain Joe Russell and Norberg Thompson of Key West who were on the "Anita" at the time when we hooked one fish out of a pair of white marlin. The other fish took a bait a few seconds later but was not hooked. The hooked fish was brought promptly to gaff and the unhooked marlin stayed close beside it, refusing a bait that was passed to it. When the hooked fish was gaffed the unhooked fish swam close beside the boat and when the hooked marlin was lifted in over the gunwale, the unhooked fish jumped high in the air close beside the boat as though to look and see where the hooked fish had gone. It then went down. I swear that this is true but you are quite at liberty to disbelieve it. The hooked fish was a female full of roe.

At another time in the 1933 season my wife caught a 74 pound white marlin which was followed by three other marlin all through the fight. These three refused bait but stayed with the female fish until she was gaffed and brought aboard. Then they went down.

I have never caught a really small marlin but I have seen them jump in the summertime looking not much longer than three feet, and have had strikes from them when we were fishing the big baits, looking not much bigger than a good sized garfish. All marlin seem to suffer much from sucker-fish which sometimes get into their gill openings and get as white and bloated as toads in a well. The native fishermen say that a marlin that follows the baits sometimes and will not strike, is afraid to open his mouth because the position of the sucker-fish worries him so that he is afraid that if he opens his mouth they will get into his gill openings. I believe the sucker-fish must eat a vast quantity of eggs during the spawning season. They should always be killed rather than thrown back into the water.

Aside from their breeding movements, and it is quite possible that they return to the same part of the coast where they were bred as salmon do, marlins' migratory movements may be controlled by the movements of their feed which, in turn, must follow the movement of the plankton. It may be that the blue marlin follow the squid which could fatten and coarsen them and give them the darker color. Again, the striped marlin and the white marlin may move with the flying fish which might account for their greater speed. Marlin, during their run, sometimes stay several days in the same place. Off the monastery down the coast between Havana and Cojimar, where there is a great tide swirl when the current is strong, we several times raised what appeared to be the same fish in the same spot. Carlos Gutierrez told me that when drifting he had once seen a huge marlin in the same place for four different days, recognizable by a harpoon scar on his head. This fish was either circling, or holding himself steady in the current.

Another possible theory on the blue marlin is that they are from the spawn of the degenerated old black fish, while the striped and silver marlin are bred from fish in their prime. But this is all conjecture and is only put in to start more sportsmen wondering where their fish come from and how and where they go. We know very little about them yet; the sea is one of the last places left for a man to explore; and there is wonderful exploring yet for any fisherman who will travel and live for months on the ocean current in a small boat.

Excellent fishing guides with whom I have fished and whom I can recommend as putting on first-rate bait and understanding our methods of fishing even though they do not speak any English, though being thoroughly trained by Captain Joe Russell of Key West and myself, are Carlos Gutierrez of Vives

Ernest Hemingway with a 420 pound marlin, July 1934. Sidney Franklin, U. S. bull fighter on the right.

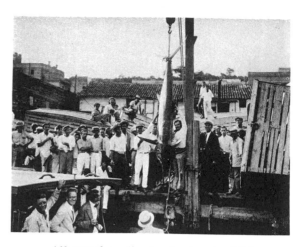

468 pound marlin showing length of fish.

Capt. Joe Russell and C. P. Thompson of Key West with 68 and 87 pound white marlin caught off Cuba on our 1932 trip.

Small striped marlin, 138 pounds.

Big marlin coming out to jump.

Photos by courtesy of Ernest Hemingway.

Tail and fin of a big marlin showing as he is being brought to gaff.

31, Havana, and Angel Prado, known as "Bolo," of San Ignacio, 24. Highly recommended men with whom I have not fished personally are Jorge Cuni who can be reached through the Havana Yacht Club, care of Julio Cadenas for whom he works but who, if he was not fishing, might cede his services; Justo Gallardo, San Ignacio, 24; Raimundo Quinto of Cuarteles No. 1; and Manuel Paredes, also of San Ignacio, 24. These last three are recommended by Carlos who vouches for them, but I do not know how much rod and reel experience they have had. If he recommends them they are good fishermen.

The usual arrangement is to pay a fixed sum, say $2.00 a day, to the guide and have him buy your bait for you. If you catch a marlin let him dispose of it so that it will not be wasted, and if he sells it let him buy the bait himself the next day and share the remaining money among the crew who worked on the fish — in gaffing, handling the wheel, taking him aboard and later cutting him up. You will also soon have a great many people to whom you will have promised fish whether you know it or not; but always see your principal fisherman gets some for himself. They are all keen and conscientious and get up at three or four o'clock to get bait at the market, but a little blood money freshens anyone up.

Launches available for fishing are the "Caiman," belonging to Dr. Charles Roca, a very keen fisherman and good guide himself, address Cero 597 or care of the Havana Yacht Club. The "Caiman" is not fast but can be fished from successfully and has excellent chairs. She is something over 30 feet and you sit in the open under the sun. On the other hand, Charley Roca is a marvelous amateur cook and can mix very good drinks.

The "Corsario," owned by a very enthusiastic fisherman and yachtsman, Claudio Fernandez de Velasco, who can be reached from 12 to 6 o'clock at A8028 and in the evening at U6326, is a fairly fast cabin cruiser that has been fitted up by her owner as a party boat. When we are not fishing in Cuba he will probably have Carlos Gutierrez as guide.

Julio Hidalgo of the Port Pilots, reached at their office in the Calle Caballeria, has a small boat the "Eva" built especially for marlin fishing. A very big fish could be handled from her easily as she is only 24 feet, is light and at the same time seaworthy. You could cut her engine out and let a hooked fish tow her. If Julio had installed a proper chair, she would be a good boat for anyone willing to fish in the sun and her lightness would simplify tactics.

Of the following boats I have only Carlos' information that they have been fitted up as charter boats. All these boats should charter for the same rate as boats of equal size in Florida waters although gasoline is nearly ten cents higher a gallon in Cuba.

"Manjuari," owner José Elias Nobo, G and I Vedado; a 38-foot Matthews cruiser, 65 hp. motor, 4 berths. All information from Fernando Panne, pilot of the port. Same address as for Julio Hidalgo.

Launch "Lena," owned by Aurelio Rocha, Calle 27 and Lima, or the Motor Boat Club; Yacht "Cachita," 41 feet, owned by Oscar Lavin, the Fisherman's Club, 24th St. and Lima, telephone F2400; launch "Adela," owned by Luis Coto Leiseca, a 34-foot cabin cruiser, also at the Fisherman's Club, telephone 2400.

Anyone coming to fish in their own boat should bring their card of membership in a recognized yacht club, which is necessary to obtain a 45-day yacht permit enabling you to fish for sport. This is obtained of the Captain of the Port by application through the American Consulate, and should be applied for as soon as the yacht has made entry. It is renewable on application. The best procedure after that is to obtain a local fisherman as guide and make arrangements with him along the lines that I have suggested. If you are only fishing a few days the rates may be a little higher. It is customary to give a tip, say, ten to twenty dollars to the fisherman at the end of the trip.

Fishing is good either way from Havana Harbor, to the eastward as far as Jaruco; to the westward as far as Bahia Honda. Fish the edge of the current. If it is out, go out; if it is in close, you can fish right in to the hundred fathom curve. A few barracuda will bother you, but there are not many. The biggest marlin are as liable to be close into the edge of soundings as to be far out. Often the current will be well out in the morning and in close in the afternoon. You will find plenty of sharks around the garbage that is dumped out in the current from lighters, but the marlin avoid the discolored water. Stay clear of it or you can foul a propeller badly. There are good beaches to swim about twelve miles to the eastward; you can anchor off and swim into the beach. Don't swim in the Gulf Stream. Sharks really will hit you off the north coast of Cuba no matter what you hear. There is very little feed and few small fish in the Stream; that is probably why the marlin come there to spawn; and the sharks are very hungry. We have had them hit feathers and teasers and they will hit a bait even when you are trolling fast. You do not need to troll any faster than just enough to give your teaser a good lively motion.

White marlin are called *aguja blanca*, by the local fishermen; striped marlin are called *casteros* or *aguja de casta*; black marlin are called *pez grande*, or *aguja negra*. Blue marlin are confounded with the black but are called, sometimes *azules* or *aguja bobos*. Dolphin are called *dorado*; wahoo is *peto*; barracuda is *picuba*. Tarpon are called *sabalo*.

The different bait fish are *pintada*, the cero mackerel; *guaguaucho* a pike-like fish; *lisa* or mullet and *chicharros*, goggle-eyes and *machuelos*, pilchards. Bonito, albacore and small tuna are called *bonitos* or *albacoras*. The broadbill is called *imperador* and the mako shark is called *dentuso*. I hope you catch them all.

From a painting by Lynn Bogue Hunt   *Courtesy of the Artist*

TARPON
David Newell handling the rod at Everglades, Florida.

CHAPTER III.

TARPON

BY

DAVID M. NEWELL

NO fish that swims in lake or stream or ocean may be compared to the Silver King as an all-round sportsman. From his infancy he is a warrior, eager to accept your challenge. Would you whip a fly in quiet waters? A fighting little chap — ten inches long — will rise to meet it. Would you shoot a plug out into the tide rip or into a swirl beneath the mangroves? A fifteen pounder will take it savagely. Would you test your strength and skill in the blue-green Gulf? Two hundred pounds of flashing silver will give you battle. The fly rod enthusiast, the bait caster, the big game fisherman, all may find their hearts' desire in the gamest fish that swims the sea.

Little is known of the life history of the tarpon. Apparently it spawns over a very wide range, for small fish are reported from the Canal Zone, from the east coast of Mexico and Texas, from Haiti, Porto Rico, Cuba, and the rivers and lagoons of both Florida Coasts. Some authorities contend that the tarpon spawns in the brackish water far up such Florida rivers as the Myakka, the Caloosahatchee, Shark River, Lostman's River and the Harney River. Other observers insist that spawning takes place in the open Gulf. I am personally of the opinion that both views are correct. I believe that there are a great many tarpon which rarely if ever go out into the salt water. Likewise I believe that there are many tarpon which rarely if ever go very far up into the rivers. I do know that tarpon spawn by the thousands in the open Gulf some ten miles below the town of Venice, Florida. During the latter part of May, through June, and into July, countless numbers of fish make their headquarters along this coast. When they first arrive, early in May, the females are heavy with roe. Toward the end of their stay the ovaries are well spent and the only conclusion must be that the fish have spawned in the shallow water along the beach.

While fully aware of the fact that I am writing of the tarpon as a big game fish, I feel that no résumé of tarpon and tarpon fishing would be complete without at least a few remarks about the smaller members of the family. Thoroughly to understand this great game fish and his many caprices it is necessary to study him under many different conditions. A close observer can learn a great deal by experimenting with the little fellows — two, three, ten, fifteen pounders. And then when the close observer has finished his experiments he will be apt to say that he is farther than ever from a real knowledge of the feeding habits of the tarpon. Perhaps no other fish is as unorthodox about its eating. Times without number I have been on the tarpon grounds when everything *looked* favorable — water, sky, hour, temperature. Take for example a cloudy, murky June morning. The water is warm, daylight is just beginning to break, the water has that oily, fishy look. Everything is exactly right but do the tarpon strike? They do not! After a while the sun comes up, burns away the clouds, a brisk west wind springs up and the fish begin to strike savagely. Next day conditions may be exactly reversed. Some of the best tarpon fishing I have ever had was during a heavy squall, when the rain drove into my face so that I could scarcely watch my fish. The time to fish for tarpon is "when they're bitin'." Choose weather conditions and tides for your own amusement, but you'll await the king's pleasure just the same.

In plug casting or fly fishing, however, for the smaller fish, light conditions play a large part. Ordinarily early morning, late afternoon, or in the moonlight are the best times for artificial bait fishing. Often fish will rise to a fly or a plug all day when the sky is heavily overcast. Just when I had worked out a very nice formula for the bait caster, a friend of mine and myself got into a school of baby tarpon down near Key West. The water was clear as crystal, the sun was bright, the time was high noon. There was not a breath of air stirring. Everything was wrong, from our point of view, but the little tarpon struck avidly for two or three hours! This experience, however, was most unusual and it is safe to say that the fly and plug casters will rarely do well with tarpon when the sun is bright.

So many different kinds of bait are used in tarpon fishing that it is foolish for any one man to attempt to choose a "best" bait. I have taken tarpon on trout flies, bass bugs, spoons, plugs of every sort and shape, crabs, catfish, rockfish, sea robins, pinfish, grunts, spots, live mullet, cut mullet and what not. Not only is there a great difference of opinion as to the best bait but there is much argument as to the best way to hook these baits. All that I can do is to give my own experience for what it is worth after some years of tarpon fishing with many different guides in many different places.

It has been my experience that a small blue crab is the most satisfactory bait. The bony plates in a tarpon's mouth seem to have been made for the purpose of crushing crabs, and there is no doubt but that the blue crab is standard fare. The hook should be carefully worked through the shell as close to the point as possible. (See illus.) I like a small crab, not over three inches in width, and it should be fresh and lively. Crabs should be kept in a pail in the shade while aboard the fishing boat, and there should be little or no water in the pail. The claws, of course, have been removed by the guide and every tarpon fisherman has observed the curious phenomenon of a blue crab shedding its claws when the tip is crushed slightly with a pair of pliers. Never attempt to *break off* the claws or the crab will die. The depth at which the crab is fished and the method of fishing depend entirely on local conditions. In pass fishing such as is done at Boca Grande, the bait is kept deep by means of a sinker. In open Gulf fishing and often in river fishing the crab is allowed to swim without any weight whatever. A float may be used or not as desired.

There are times and places, however, where the fish will not touch a crab but will strike savagely on almost any kind of small live fish. I have found that a small catfish, from eight to twelve inches in length, is a particularly fine bait, partly due to its tenacity of life. Every experienced angler knows the importance of using a lively, active bait and a catfish will stay alive for several hours. A good guide will always clip the spines with his cutting pliers before placing the catfish on the hook. The hook should be passed up through both lips, slightly to one side of the center of the mouth. Much of the credit for the discovery of a catfish as tarpon bait along the west coast of Florida must go to my friend,

Ashby Jones. Mr. Jones has kept a record of his tarpon catches over many years and is one of the most experienced anglers of my acquaintance. He has taken over fifteen hundred tarpon during his lifetime and has landed several which weighed over two hundred pounds.

Some guides prefer to hook their live bait through the back, passing the hook beneath the backbone. I prefer to hook through the lips because the bait will troll better when one is changing location. Rockfish and pinfish are both excellent bait and I have had very fine luck with sea robins, when I could get them. I have been told that a tarpon will strike a live rat, and some day perhaps white rats will be sold as tarpon bait!

In some localities, such as the sheltered water in the Ten Thousand Island country on Florida's lower west coast, cut mullet is used extensively, as well as whole mullet. In using cut bait and fishing on the bottom an entirely different method of hooking is customary. Here the tarpon does not strike savagely as it usually does on a live fish or crab. It picks up the mullet gently and starts away with it slowly, much as a channel bass would do. Instead of striking instantly as he would ordinarily do, the angler allows his line to run out freely, usually from a coil lying in the bottom of the boat. When thirty feet or so of line has run out the fisherman allows the line to tighten and when he feels the fish he strikes. It is assumed that the fish has had time to swallow the bait, and this is generally the case. It has been my experience that fish caught under these conditions will not leap as often or as high due to the fact that the water is usually shallow and that the fish are hooked in the gullet and not in the mouth.

At certain times during the season the fish seem to prefer an artificial lure to almost any sort of live bait and the most popular of these lures are Wilson Spoons, large Creek Chub plugs in either green or white redhead, large Pike-Oreno in similar finish, and the ever-popular Japanese feather bait, known sometimes as "feather duster." I have been unable to understand why the tackle manufacturers do not work out a really dependable tarpon plug. By this I mean a plug which is properly rigged for tarpon fishing. The comparatively small gang hooks, with which all of these big-fish plugs are equipped are quite useless for tarpon fishing and the guide promptly removes them. He then runs his leader through the metal lip of the plug and twists his tarpon hook on in such a way that it swings beneath the plug, well toward the head end — for every one knows that a tarpon seizes his prey from the head end. If you don't believe

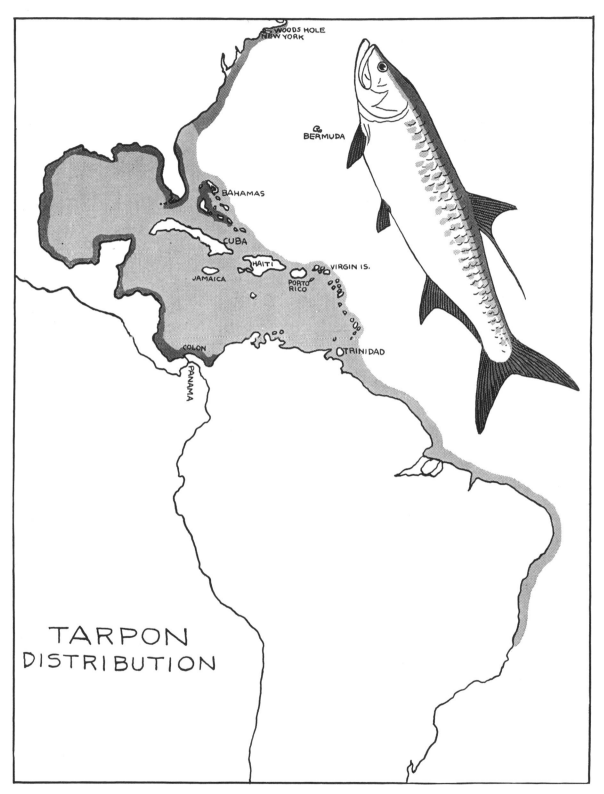

WOODS HOLE
NEW YORK

BERMUDA

BAHAMAS

CUBA

HAITI
JAMAICA
PORTO
RICO
VIRGIN IS.

COLON
PANAMA
TRINIDAD

TARPON
DISTRIBUTION

Drawn by Lynn Bogue Hunt from information supplied by David M. Newell.

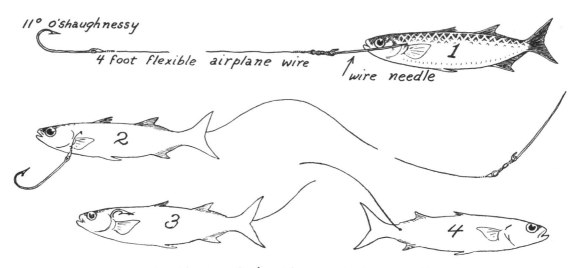

11° O'shaughnessy

4 foot flexible airplane wire

wire needle

1

2

3

4

Method of hooking whole mullet

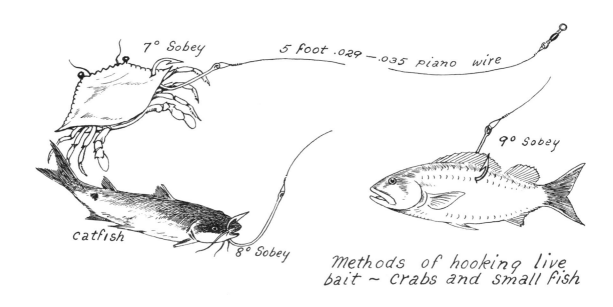

7° Sobey

5 foot .029 — .035 piano wire

9° Sobey

catfish

8° Sobey

Methods of hooking live
bait ~ crabs and small fish

Drawn by David M. Newell.

it look at the kink in your leader just ahead of the bait the next time you have a strike and fail to hook your fish. That bend, three or four inches up the leader, is a sure sign of a tarpon strike.

For live-bait fishing, either with crabs or small fish, I like a number 7/0 Sobey hook, although many anglers prefer a number 8/0 or 9/0. It is a good idea to bend a slight offset into these hooks, and to keep the point needle-sharp at all times. In this type of fishing a five foot piano wire leader is generally used, and should be from .029 to .035 in diameter. It goes without saying that a swivel should be used at the line end of the leader. In fishing with cut mullet or with a whole mullet, flexible airplane wire should be used. The tarpon would immediately feel a stiff piano wire leader and would drop the bait, but the flexible leader allows the fish to swallow the bait. A number 11/0 O'Shaughnessy hook should be used for this type of fishing and when a whole mullet is used the hook should be laced into the mullet as indicated in the drawing. Some guides prefer to draw the leader through the mullet's mouth, follow along the backbone and emerge near the tail. I prefer the method which I have illustrated. A stiff piece of wire is used for a needle, the "eye" of which is merely a closely-bent hook. The needle is hooked into the swivel and the entire leader drawn through the mullet. Entry should be made behind the mullet's head, through the backbone to the opposite side (1). The needle is then run along the backbone until it emerges near the tail on the opposite side from which it entered. (2). The leader is then drawn through until the hook lies in place, (3) and the angler holds his bait from the tail end (4).

In trolling for tarpon with plugs, spoons, cut bait, or feather jigs a very slow rate of speed should be maintained as a general rule. Many anglers insist that additional action is given to the bait by short, sharp jerks of the rod and experience has taught me that this is true. The jerks impart a crazy, darting, dodging action to the bait, which seems to add greatly to its attraction. I have found this to be the case when casting for small tarpon and other salt water fish. A series of sudden, quick darts is much more effective than a steadily retrieved lure. However, it is possible to overdo anything and I have seen a fisherman standing in the stern of his boat, rod under his arm, twisting his whole body furiously as he apparently sought to snap either rod or line with the frenzy of his jerks!

There is a wide difference of opinion on the proper way to set the hook when the tarpon strikes. Of course, when a bait is being trolled there is not much the angler can do — or should do — other than keep his rod tip pointed well toward his lure. When the tarpon hits, it will strike from in front or from the side and the result is a smashing strike that lifts the angler out of his seat. Almost instantly the fish is in the air and either throws the hook or falls back into the water a hooked fish. My personal opinion is that luck plays a very large part in hooking a tarpon. In other words, if the point of the hook happens to engage the bony plates in the fish's mouth, no amount of striking or jerking will do any good. If the point of the hook happens to enter the tough gristle behind or between the "scissors," very little striking is needed, particularly in trolling. In fact many guides insist that no striking is needed, that the fish will hook itself, if it is to be hooked at all. My own experience has been that no actual striking is needed when trolling. The fish will hook itself against the pull of the line. When fishing with live bait, either crabs or small fish, I like to give several short, sharp jerks when I feel my fish, although I have often landed fish which hooked themselves absolutely. One of my largest tarpon hit a rockfish so hard and fast that he took the line right out of the float. I sat there watching my float, wondering why it rode so high and buoyantly! A few seconds later the fish came out, so close to the boat that I thought he was coming aboard. He was thoroughly hooked although I did not even get up all of my slack until he had made his second jump!

In still fishing with cut bait, however, a different technique is necessary. Here the fish picks up the bait gently and goes off with it slowly. The object is to allow him to swallow it. When he has run out a sufficient amount of line, either from a coil in the bottom of the boat, or from a free-running reel, the angler should reach well out, pointing the tip toward the fish. The reel drag should be thrown on and when the line tightens, the angler should strike and strike hard. It is assumed that the fish has swallowed the bait and a hard strike is needed to jerk the hook free of the bait, particularly when a whole mullet has been used. Only years of experience can teach a man how to hook a tarpon and no one can tell him. A "hard strike" might mean one thing to Jack Dempsey and another thing to a one hundred and ten pound book-keeper. And in any event much depends on which way the hook happens to be lying when that bony mouth closes over it.

Tarpon fishing is done in so many different ways and in so many different places that it is impossible to lay down any hard and fast rules for handling a hooked fish. Likewise it is impossible to say that a hooked tarpon will do thus and so. If you say he will do "thus," he is sure to do "so." However, it may safely be stated that a tarpon will go into the air in from three to twenty seconds after he feels the hook, depending, of course, on the depth of the water and the method of fishing. As I have already stated, a fish hooked trolling will leap instantly. On the other hand a fish hooked in the deep water at Boca Grande will take longer to come out. Occasionally a fish will be found, which will not jump for several minutes, and I have taken one fish, which did not jump at all. I once foul hooked a large fish in the back of the head. It jumped once out of astonishment and then settled down to a bulldog battle.

The first jump usually tells the story. Many fish, of course, escape after several leaps, but I maintain that the first jump tells the story. If your fish is still on when he hits the water after that first wild leap, you have a pretty fair chance of bringing him to the release hook. An experienced tarpon fisherman will keep a close watch on his line and when he sees that his fish is coming out he will keep the tip well out toward the fish. Then, when the fish goes into the air, the angler is enabled to take up his slack with his rod and often can throw the fish off balance in the air. I knew an old guide, who was an artist at "smacking them down" and there is no doubt but what it takes a lot of the fight out of a fish to fall flat on the water. In this connection I should like to say that only a hooked tarpon ever jumps clumsily. I have read several accounts of tarpon fishing, in which the statement was made that a tarpon doesn't care how it falls into the water after its leap, and that when leaping for sheer sport, it often falls back into the water on its side or tail with a great splash. This is a mistaken idea. Only a hooked tarpon, thrown off balance by the drag of the line, ever leaps clumsily. I have seen a great many tarpon leap for the pure fun of leaping. I have seen them leap for the purpose of ridding themselves of suckers, and I have seen them leap frenziedly in attempting to escape from sharks. Invariably they described perfect arcs, entering the water nose first without a ripple, and covering a distance of from ten to thirty feet or more. A hooked fish comes out straight up, as a general rule, shaking his head, twisting his body and making every effort to free himself from the hook and dragging line. At such times a tarpon may fall on its side, its tail, or in almost any position. A slow-motion picture, which we secured near Sarasota, Florida, revealed the fact that a tarpon could make three complete revolutions in the air and that it had cleared the surface of the water by at least ten feet!

My own experience has been that a tarpon of about eighty or ninety pounds will furnish more acrobatics than a very large fish. The great attraction of tarpon fishing lies in the beauty of the jumps and when a fish has finished its jumping, most of the sport is over, and the rest of the battle is hard work. For this reason I have given up the idea of light tackle. By light tackle I mean three-six and anything approximating it. I used to be a light tackle enthusiast, and I still like to take tarpon on a fly rod or bait-casting rod. For conventional tarpon fishing, however, where two men are fishing together, I do not advocate light tackle and I shall give my reasons. First, a fish will jump as high and as often on medium-weight tackle as it will on light tackle. Second, when the fish has tired itself by jumping it settles down to sound and sulk, and the angler has a job on his hands with any sort of tackle. The fish must be pumped up, gaffed, or released, and the sooner this is done the better. It can be done in a reasonably short time with medium-weight tackle and a fresh fish can be hooked. Incidentally, the other man in the boat will not have to wait all afternoon for some fun himself. An ideal outfit for such fishing, where a man has had some experience with big fish, would be a nine ounce tip, a 4/o reel, two hundred yards of eighteen thread linen line. For men who are entirely green at the game, I should recommend a twelve to fourteen ounce tip, a 6/o reel, and two hundred yards of twenty-four thread linen line, or even twenty-seven thread.

I do not change the drag on my reel while playing a fish, preferring to set a fairly light drag when I start to fish and to use my thumb as an additional brake, when needed. When the fish has been thoroughly whipped, and he should be *thoroughly* whipped, the angler should stand up and step toward the bow of the boat, allowing the guide to stand in the stern. The drag should be thrown off the reel, so that if the fish should take a sudden run at the feel of the gaff or release hook it will not snap line or rod tip. A releasing hook should always be used where a man does not wish to bring a fish in for mounting or prize entry. Most of the fish released will revive and swim away, although some are killed by sharks. However, the angler should not permit himself any worry in this connection. A big shark can catch a perfectly healthy, free tarpon any time he wants one, all stories to the contrary. I have seen a hammerhead shark go into a school of fish, cut one out of the bunch and chase

LEAPING TARPON.

THE LAST LEAP.

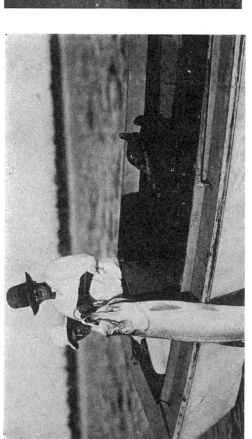

"Uncle George" Rawls, famous coast guide, with a 125 pound fish. Picture shows cockpit of ideal fishing boat.

Who said "The weaker sex?" A woman angler pumping a tarpon.

OUT AND IN AGAIN.

HIGH, WIDE AND HANDSOME.

IN A HALO OF SPRAY.

FLAT DIVE.

BACK JACK-KNIFE.

THIS ONE ALMOST WENT INTO THE TREES.

The above photographs were taken by Van Campen Heilner on the Rio Encantado in Cuba. In the taking, incidentally, the world's record for tarpon was broken. 104 tarpon hooked and released in *one day*, to say nothing of the week's score of 354 fish, is surely a mark that has probably never been exceeded by anglers anywhere at any time. With the exception of five fish which were hooked in such a manner that it was necessary to kill them in order to extract the lure, all tarpon were returned alive to the water.

The stream fished is unmarked on any map and was absolutely virgin water. Mr. Heilner and

LUCKILY RIGHT IN THE CENTER.

TAIL TO.

UP AND OVER.

THREE IT WAS IMPOSSIBLE TO RELEASE.

THE SILVER KING IN A CUBAN SETTING.

PEPE AND A SABALO.

friends were the first anglers ever to wet a line there, not even the natives knowing of the thousands of tarpon or "sabalo" which literally boiled throughout the entire length of the river. 9 thread line and Trix-oreno and Tarp-oreno lures were used.

The angling possibilities of Cuba are little known but undoubtedly it is a fisherman's paradise. The Rio Encantado was accidentally discovered by Mr. Heilner on one of his exploration trips for the American Museum of Natural History and there must be many other streams like it.

Photographs copyright 1935, by Van Campen Heilner.

Dry point by W. J. Schaldach

LEAPING TARPON

it down. Sometimes the tarpon would make five or six wild leaps, but eventually the shark got him. I have read the statement that man is the tarpon's only enemy, proven by the fact that sharks and tarpon have lived together in the same water for ages. This proves nothing. Deer and cougar have lived together also for ages, but a cougar catches a deer whenever it wants one. In the same way a big shark catches a tarpon whenever it wants one. Of course, a sick fish or a hooked fish is an easier prey and in some localities, the sharks make fishing almost impossible. I have myself lost three fish to sharks in one morning's fishing.

There are those who will contend that a tarpon can swim faster than a shark and that consequently the tarpon should escape. This is theoretically correct, but the tarpon does not use its speed to good advantage when pursued by a shark. It gets right up on top of the water and seems to go crazy with fear, making high, wild leaps. In the same way a deer will often be so crazed by fear that it can be ridden down by a good horseman. Like the tarpon, it wastes its strength by high leaps, and wastes its speed by pursuing a zig-zag course.

The presence of a big shark seems to terrify an entire school of tarpon, and at such times there is little or no chance of securing a strike. I remember seeing a giant hammerhead, perhaps eighteen feet in length, go into a school of fish in the shallow water close to the beach, just north of Sarasota, Florida. He got his tarpon, all right, and for thirty minutes the rest of the school milled around in a small circle, each fish apparently trying to work its way into the center of the circle. It is such panic-stricken actions, which make things easy for the sharks. While fish are uneasy over the presence of a big shark, it is next to impossible to secure a strike. After awhile they will settle down and resume their feeding, but the angler is wasting his time when the fish are either scared or travelling.

Travelling fish will never strike — and I have used the word *never* in spite of myself. It is not a safe word to use in describing the habits of game or fish! My *own* experience has been that travelling fish will not strike, and by travelling fish, I mean a school, which is showing regularly on the surface and is moving rapidly. At times it seems that a man could walk on the backs of the silvery beauties, as they roll gracefully close to the boat, so great is their number. I know of nothing more exasperating than to follow travelling fish in a vain endeavor to secure a strike. I have done it countless times and shall probably do it many times again, although I know better. However, a man cannot resist the temptation to drop a bait right into the middle of *hundreds* of fish when these fish are within a few feet of his boat! Again and again I have had tarpon roll all over my line, against my float, against my bait — without paying me and my contrivances the slightest bit of attention.

The wise angler will follow travelling fish, particularly if they are going ashore. (I am speaking now of open Gulf fishing such as is found along the west coast of Florida.) He will not attempt to get a bait into these fish until they have settled. Feeding fish do not show a great deal, unless striking in a school of bait on top of the water. Personally, I like to find fish that are rolling lazily over a considerable area, one here, one there. Usually when fish are behaving in this manner, it is not hard to coax them to strike. But again let me say that no fish is more unorthodox in its habits of feeding. The only way to catch tarpon is to stay with them, morning, noon and night.

Night fishing for the Silver King is a glorious sport, either in the light of a mellow, tropic moon or the velvety dark when every move is a glow of fire. A cool breeze blows in from the west and there is no sound but the unmistakable gurgle as a big tarpon takes a breath. On still nights it is often possible to locate the fish for some distance by this tell-tale "blubbering," as the guides call it. Ordinarily one never fishes for tarpon until they have been sighted, although there are exceptions also to this rule. When one considers the fact that tarpon fishing is done in rivers, in bays, in the open Gulf, in the ocean, in deep water, in shallow water, in swift water, in stagnant water, it becomes evident that no one may do more than give his own experience. Only recently I discovered a man who was catching large-mouth black bass with cut mullet, fishing on the bottom, and he informed me that this was the best way to catch black bass. He may be right. I know he was right in his own fishing ground, for I tried his method. Therefore it is wise to listen to the other fellow when he tells you how to fish — especially when you are fishing in his territory.

It is customary to recommend certain guides, fishing grounds, boats and tackle, but I shall not do this. John Smith may have been a very good tarpon guide and given me exceptionally fine service, but there may have been — and probably were — several other equally competent guides at the same dock. Just because John Smith happened to fish with me and because I happen to be a writer is no reason that the other guides should be left out of a volume of this sort, and unfortunately I don't know their names. I have yet to find a tarpon guide, who did not work hard to get my fish, although some were wiser in the ways of tarpon than others. When I reflect on the fact that I have not yet begun to cover the tarpon fishing grounds, even in Florida, I am impressed by the number of good guides I *don't* know, and I want to be fair to them. In the same way I shall not choose a favorite fishing ground. I have had rare sport in many of them — Shark River, alongside the viaduct at Bahia Honda, Marco Channel, Captiva, Boca Grande, Stump Pass, Manasota, Point o' Rocks, and with the little fellows in the Tamiami canal and the mangrove channels around Key West. It's all fun, be it Texas, Florida, Cuba, or wherever the Silver King abounds.

When it comes to boats I like a skiff better than anything else, when a skiff may be safely used, and as a matter of fact a skiff can take almost any sort of weather when it is handled by a competent guide. There is no finer sport than taking fifteen and twenty pound tarpon on a fly rod from a skiff which is manned by a guide who is interested and onto his job. Also a large fish may be handled very comfortably with regulation tackle from a good, sea-worthy skiff. The ideal fishing boat, however, is a fast, open boat of about twenty-six to thirty feet in length and with plenty of beam. She should contain a live well, and should be equipped with a spray hood, umbrella, and two swivel chairs. Some anglers insist on butt rests being built into the chairs but I prefer a rod belt. Of course an open boat will not be as comfortable as a cabin boat, but on the other hand a fish is more easily handled from an open boat. A good guide, however, can keep his stern to the fish in almost any sort of a boat, so comfort may well be considered. Tackle is purely a matter of choice, provided of course that the proper weight is used, and there are several firms which manufacture rods, reels, and lines of equal merit.

As I have already indicated I am opposed to the use of very light tackle, especially when there are two fishing. It is extremely annoying to watch another man spend two hours pumping in a sulky fish which is too tired to jump. "Uncle George" Rawls broke me of this business some years ago. I was fighting a one hundred pound fish on three-six tackle. After a while old George grunted:

"Better land that fish. I seen the leader when he rolled up that time, and it's beginnin' to get kinda rusty!"

Several minutes passed before he spoke again. This time it was:

[93]

"Well, we'll have to get more bait. These is all growin' up to grouper size — too big to use."

The final straw came when the fish rolled to the surface about sixty yards from the boat.

"Look yonder! That fish has gone to feedin' again!" This was too much. I never carried that rod again where George could see me!

I am assuming that anyone interested in reading a book on salt water fishing will be acquainted with the rudiments of the sport and it is only necessary to say that the fundamentals apply in tarpon fishing as well as in any other form of big game fishing. The line should be allowed to troll behind the boat prior to fastening on the leader and hook. When the wet line is reeled in against its own pull there will be a tight, even spool and very little danger of the line's burying itself as often happens in a loosely wound spool. Also, a wet line is stronger than a dry line and does not burn one's thumb as the dry line does. There are many methods of fastening one's line to the swivel. Perhaps an elaborate system is necessary and advisable, but I have found that a plain double loop is sufficient and far less trouble. Simply pass the double line through the eye of the swivel, pass the hook through this loop, draw it tight, and that's all there is to it.

The smallest tarpon which I have ever seen was four and one half inches long and weighed less than one half an ounce. The largest I have seen weighed one hundred and ninety pounds and was six feet, eleven and three-quarter inches long. The girth was forty-three and one-half inches. Two hundred pound fish are comparatively rare, although many of that weight have been taken since tarpon fishing became a sport. The world's record is held at this date by Mr. W. A. McLaren. Mr. McLaren's fish was taken in the Panuco River, Mexico, and was recorded as follows:

Length — 7 feet 8 inches, girth — 47 inches, weight — 232 pounds.
Other record fish are:
223 pounds—Dr. Howe, Tampico, Mexico.
213 pounds—N. M. George, Bahia Honda, Florida.
210 pounds—Edward Vom Hofe, Captiva Pass, Florida.
210 pounds—Mrs. W. Ashby Jones, Caloosahatchee River, Florida.
　　　　　(This fish is the record catch for women.)
205 pounds—P. P. Schutt, Caloosahatchee River, Florida.

TARPON

A tarpon was reported from the Hillsboro River which was estimated at 350 pounds. Its length was 8 feet 2 inches and it was netted by commercial fishermen. Therefore we may conclude that the maximum weight for tarpon must be in the neighborhood of three hundred pounds, that a two hundred pound fish is an unusual catch, that a one hundred and seventy-five pound fish is a good fish, that one hundred pounders are nearer the average, that a fifty pound fish on a bait-casting rod is the last word in sport, that a ten pounder on a fly rod is even better, that any fish which has a fighting weight of from one pound to three hundred pounds is a gentleman and a sportsman. We must conclude that the tarpon offers a wider variety of sport to a greater number of people in more different places than any other fish that swims. Those of us who have seen him, flashing bronze and blue and silver in the sun, and those of us who have felt his mighty rushes — we know whereof we speak. Long live the Silver King!

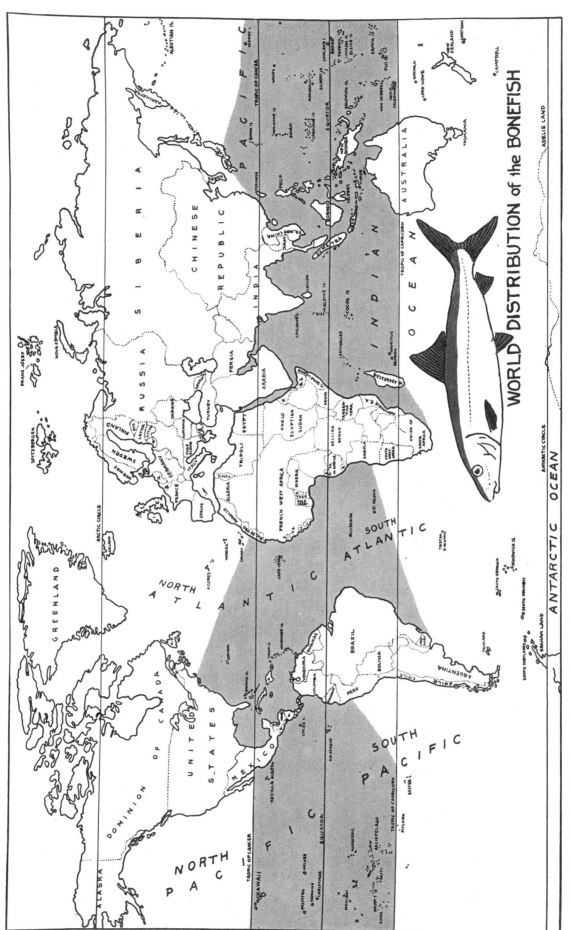

WORLD DISTRIBUTION of the BONEFISH

Drawn by Lynn Bogue Hunt from information supplied by Van Campen Heilner.

CHAPTER IV.

BONEFISH

BY

VAN CAMPEN HEILNER

F all the fish for which I have had the pleasure and sport of pursuing, and this includes a lifetime of angling for everything from brook trout to swordfish, my favorite is the bonefish. From my personal experience I can say he is the gamest fish for which I ever wet a line.

I started my angling experience in fresh water. Trout, salmon, black bass, muskies, pike and a host of others were old stories to me before I caught my first bonefish. For twenty years I have averaged a month a year surf fishing for channel bass and stripers. For seven years straight I trolled the waters off Catalina for swordfish, and caught them. With the late William Scheer, whose son contributes one of the chapters of this book, we fought the great tuna off the Jersey Coast out of Seabright dories nearly twenty years ago. Then they were known as horse-mackerel and despised by the fishermen. When the Overseas Railroad had but recently crossed from the mainland of Florida to Key West, I wrestled with the great leaping tarpon along the viaducts and the fresh water rivers of the West Coast. Yet to none of these will I yield the palm of fighting fury possessed by the bonefish. Each of the above deserves a niche in the Piscatorial Hall of Fame. But in the center, on a pedestal all his own belongs the one and incomparable, before whom all good anglers should uncover — the bonefish.

[97]

Without doubt my brother anglers will look upon these statements with amusement. "He must be a nut," I can hear you say. Well, I am. I admit it. But fortunately I am not alone and all those, including many of my friends, who have concentrated on bonefish over a period of years are just as "nutty" as I. We belong to a select fraternity of maniacs who get a tremendous kick and thrill out of their insanity, and if the rest of the angling fraternity choose to regard us as demented, we are perfectly satisfied. We *know why* we are insane.

For the past fifteen years I have had a fishing camp on the island of North Bimini in the Bahamas and here I have had an unusually excellent chance to fish for and study the elusive bonefish. With some of the world's finest marlin, tuna, and reef fishing at my door I have concentrated on the bonefish almost exclusively.

The bonefish, or banana fish, or to give him his Latin name, *Albula vulpes*, which translated means "white fox," is one of the most widely distributed fishes in the world. As can be seen from the accompanying chart, he occurs in warm seas all over the world. In any part of the tropics from one side of the earth to the other you are almost sure to run across bonefish. As to his life history not a great deal is known. In Florida and the Bahamas he has been angled for extensively and it is from these records and experiences that most of our knowledge is derived.

In appearance he is sort of a cross between a brook sucker and a grayling. His head is sharp and mean looking. His color is silvery white shading to greenish blue on the back. His dorsal fin looks like a shark's as it cuts the water and the upper lobe of his caudal sticks from the water almost as high. In size he runs from a pound to fourteen or fifteen pounds. At this writing, the world's record fish stands at thirteen and three-quarter pounds and was taken by B. F. Peek at Bimini in the Bahamas. The mounted fish may be seen in the American Museum of Natural History in New York.

When the bonefish are small — from one to three pounds — they run in large schools, and as they grow older they seem to break up into pairs or even become solitary. The largest fish I have ever caught, or seen caught, were without exception alone or part of a pair. I have seen bonefish within an oar's length of my boat in clear, still water where I could observe them closely, which I am positive would run fifteen pounds or possibly larger.

Frequently large schools of small bonefish will gang up and form what is known as a "mud," a large patch of discolored water in the center of which the fish are feeding. If the angler can locate a "mud" and get ahead of it, as the fish move slowly with the tide, he can catch bonefish as fast as he throws out his bait. If no undue noise is made the fish do not take alarm and the "mud" can be followed for long distances, similar to following a school of bluefish on the surface.

Bonefish are great lovers of shallow water. As soon as they feel the first thrust of the incoming tide they start to move in over the banks searching here and there for the tiny "ghost" crabs or other succulent bait hidden in the grassy bottom. They will force themselves into such shallow water that they can navigate only with the greatest difficulty and I have frequently seen them struggling with half their backs out of water to pass over some particularly shallow piece of bank.

As the tide continues to flow they work further and further in until at high water they are scattered all about among the mangroves and sometimes way up in the heads of creeks which are dry at low water.

As the tide starts to fall off, they start to come off the banks, though at this stage they do not seem so hungry as before. Sometimes they will pass right over your bait without noticing it or merely pick it up to drop it immediately. However, there are no set rules for bonefish because they will never act the way you expect them to.

They continue to back off the banks as the tide drops lower and lower until at dead low water you will find them settled off in deep holes or in the channels waiting for the never-ending cycle of tides to repeat.

Bonefish average from two to five pounds. From six to eight pounds is a large fish; from nine to twelve pounds is a monster. The ten to twelve pounders are not common. At my camp we celebrate on anything over nine pounds. I expect however to live to see a fourteen and one-half pound bonefish caught and I am convinced that they reach a weight of sixteen pounds.

Now that we know something of the appearance and habits of this wily "white fox" let us see how we go about catching him. While not an absolute necessity, as I shall explain later, our first requisite should be a good boat. This should not be over twelve to fourteen feet long and should be light and extremely flat on the bottom. It may frequently be necessary to drag it by main force over practically dry ground.

It should be equipped with oars, two sharp pointed stakes for fastening its bow and stern, an anchor and an outboard engine. The latter can be of your own choosing. I have two, one more powerful than the other, which I use when the bonefish grounds I wish to visit lie some distance from my camp.

Next are your rods. After considerable years of experimentation we evolved a rod which James Heddon's Sons make for us and which roughly compares with the standard for the 3/6 class of the Tuna Club. It is approximately six feet over all and weighs about six ounces. An important factor is a rather long butt which, when you are fighting a fish single handed, extends well down under your elbow and gives you considerable leverage. This should have about four guides in addition to the tip as a seven pound bonefish can put a considerable bend in your rod. All our rods are made of split bamboo and well varnished. This is a description of the rod which we have found most satisfactory for our use, but any light rod similar to that known as a "bay rod" will serve the purpose.

Next comes the reel. We have found a 1/0 reel filled to the brim with six thread line to be just about right. A bonefish can run off an astonishing amount of line on his first rush and it is well to be prepared. If you are fishing in a locality, as frequently occurs, where there are lots of little mangrove shoots sticking out of the water, it is better to use a nine thread line, as the bonefish will occasionally run around one of these and cause a severe sawing strain on the line. As a rule, however, a six thread line will suffice. The matter of a star drag is optional. Not in order to keep a strain on the line, as this should be done with a thumbstall, but more to keep your knuckles from being skinned up when the fish makes one of its sudden rushes. If you are adept at letting go of the reel handle without injury, then do not use a star drag—otherwise use one, but maintain the lightest of drags.

As to hooks, everyone has his specialty. The writer uses a 4/0 Harrison Sproat which has proved highly satisfactory. This is fastened directly to the line without a leader. Sometimes, however, we have used a 4/0 hook without a gut snell and fastened to this a short piece of leader made out of wire gimp. This has proved advisable on account of the numerous "bonefish sharks" which are frequently about and which, unless the leader is unusually strong, will cut it in a trice.

A small casting dipsey completes your rig but in recent years when fishing in very shallow water and "stalking" bonefish on foot, we have found it is better to use no sinker at all, and to depend on the weight of the bait to cast out the line.

When bonefish are in very shallow water, with part of their backs out, the "plunk" of a sinker scares them though they be a distance of several feet away. In deep water, however, or where there is any tide, a sinker should of course be used. A long-handled landing net, a meat grinder for grinding up "chum," a hatchet for breaking up conchs, a woolen thumb stall and you are all set.

The first thing is to procure bait. If you have a guide or "boy," he has attended to this by the time you have finished your breakfast. On the Florida coast the favorite bait seems to be hermit crab. In the Bahamas, although we have plenty of hermit crabs, we use conch almost exclusively. Sometimes we tip this off with a piece of ordinary blue-clawed crab, sometimes with a piece of crawfish. Conch is easiest to procure, stays on best, and makes good chum. If an occasional crab is drawn aboard while fishing, he is broken up and used along with the conch.

I shall not attempt to describe how to extract a conch from its shell. This is an art which requires considerable practice and can be done with dexterity by your native guide. A hatchet will help him considerably, but if none is available, he can do it by striking one conch against another and through the hole in the top thus made insert his knife with surprising results. I once saw a slightly inebriated gentleman give a conch a drink of whisky which brought him forth from his shell practically instanter.

After a great many of these large shells have been "de-conched," the animal procured from them is then pounded furiously with a stick until it is pliable enough to go on your hook. Sufficient pieces are cut up for bait and the balance is run through the grinding machine into a box or pail to be used for chum. There is no special way of baiting the hook; the writer uses as large and as tempting a piece as he can get on it.

With plenty of bait aboard, rods and extra hooks and sinkers, you shove off from the dock just before low water.

It will take you one or two days to locate just where the fish are feeding, but once this has been done, you head for your favorite spot at once. When you get there, it may be absolutely dry. In this case you can do one of two things; get as near to it as you can and anchor, or drag your boat where you wish to have it and sit down and wait for the tide to come in. Generally you do not have so very long to wait. For as soon as you notice that the tide has started up you will commence to see bonefish.

Perhaps your first glimpse of them will be but a ruffled bit of surface. But if you are used to it you will spot it a long way off. Or it may be a fin cleaving the surface or a whole procession of tails flicking out of water. "Here they come!" you whisper. Your guide commences to cast chum out in the general direction of the oncoming bonefish and you place your bait as nearly as you can in the middle of it. Pretty soon they are up with it and you can see the bonefish tails working around your bait. "Dere dey is, Boss, all about picking up de chum," says your dusky guide and you wait, nerves tense, hardly daring to breathe. Suddenly comes a sly tug on the end of your line, just a quick little pull, no more. It comes so quickly and so easily that it has come and gone before you realize it. But it is in that split second that you must hook your bonefish. If you don't you will reel in your line to find your hook cleaned and the bonefish departed.

If you've been quick enough and have hooked him, you are in for some of the fastest moments of your angling career. The line actually flies through the water with a ripping sound that scares you. Your reel has become but a blur and the speed is so great that your thumbstall has become red hot. Four hundred feet away the bonefish suddenly breaks water, turns and rushes at you as fast as he went from you. You reel until your wrist aches but you can't get in the slack. The bonefish shoots past one end of your boat, kicking up the spray as he goes and a great belly sags in your line. You have never experienced anything like this before and you begin to wonder if you are playing a fish or a fish is playing you.

He's off again but this time the run isn't quite so long as the first one. Two hundred feet away he stops, and for the first time you can get your breath. You pump and you gain—pump and gain again. Now you can see him, cruising in a great semi-circle — blackish green he looks in the water. But he sees you and the boat at the same time and the effect is as if he had been shot through with a high-voltage current. He's gone again and half your line with him. Wow! What a fish! He's run out more line in five minutes than any other fish could in five hours. And it looks as if he was never going to quit. But you keep working on him and this time it looks like the end. You get him almost to the boat and he starts a slow circling. Round the boat he goes and 'round again, nearer and nearer each time. Next time, now. Get the net, Benjie. When I bring him 'round this time, gather him in. All right. Seven pounds? He felt like fifty!

You sit back, light your pipe and crack open a bottle of beer. A warm glow of pride and self-satisfaction suffuses your countenance. You've done a good

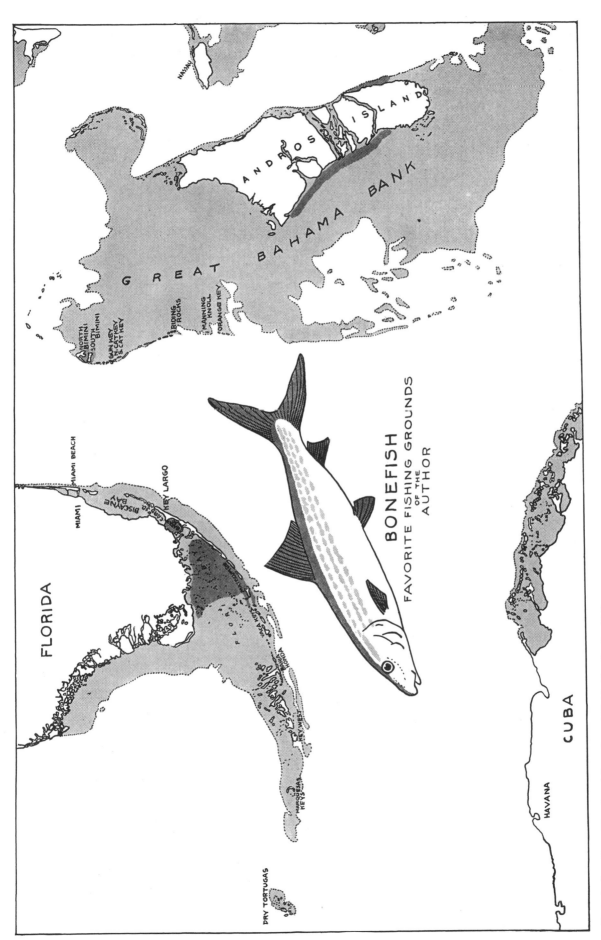

BONEFISH

FAVORITE FISHING GROUNDS
OF THE
AUTHOR

FLORIDA

MIAMI

MIAMI BEACH

BISCAYNE BAY

KEY LARGO

MARQUESAS
KEYS

DRY TORTUGAS

CUBA

HAVANA

NASSAU

ANDROS ISLAND

GREAT BAHAMA BANK

NORTH
BIMINI
SOUTH
BIMINI
GUN KEY
N. CAT KEY
S. CAT KEY
RIDING
ROCKS
MANNING
KNOLL
ORANGE KEY

Drawn by Lynn Bogue Hunt from information supplied by Van Campen Heilner.

TYPICAL BONEFISH COUNTRY.

A PAIR OF NICE ONES.

Photos by courtesy of Van Campen Heilner.

PLAYING A BONEFISH FROM THE BOAT.

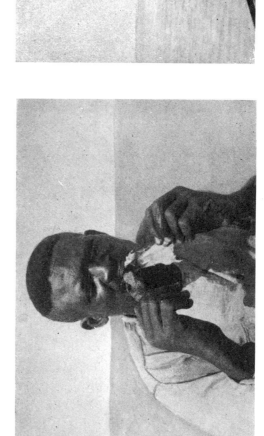

IF NO BAIT GRINDER IS HANDY, YOUR GUIDE WILL DO.

day's work and so far as you are concerned you're willing to call it quits. Not so your guide.

"Great gawd! Lookadere, Boss! Nudder bonefish. Big fellah! See 'im! See him dere!" You look, and sure enough. The excitement is contagious. You cast and wait again.

This bonefish bites in an entirely different manner. The first thing you know he's grabbed the bait and rushed off with it at breakneck speed. No tug. No pull. Just one awful snatch and zow! he's half way to Nassau. This one is a horse of a different color. He just *doesn't* stop. Your thumbstall is burned clean through and your finger hurts. You thrust the reel and rod — the whole works — under water to cool it off. But it doesn't cool the ardour of your bonefish. Smaller and smaller dwindles the line on your spool. "Pull up the anchor! Pull up the stake! He's taking all my line!"

Benjie struggles to obey. But he falls down in the boat and he can't get the stake up; it's jabbed down too far in the marl. You curse, you plead. Too late. The line comes to an end; there's one awful moment, then it snaps and flicks through the air like a wisp of smoke. Bonefish and 600 feet of line have vanished into the blue.

You pick up and start sorrowfully back for camp. You say nothing. Benjie looks as if he were going to cry. You'd promised him five dollars for a ten pound fish. "Awful big bonefish, Boss," he finally says, "awful big!" And that's that.

The next day or the following one you return to your favorite spot but the fish are not there. You wait patiently, but as the tide creeps higher and higher and no bonefish appear you decide to go look for them. You stand in the bow, your rod couchant like a lance and your guide poles you slowly across the banks. Hullo! What's that? A hundred yards or so ahead you see some shadows against the white bottom. Are they bonefish or are they patches of grass? You shove a little closer. A tail flicks the surface. Bonefish! And working your way! You quickly stop the boat, gently lower the anchor and cast out your bait. Perhaps the cast scares them and they break in all directions like a flock of frightened quail. Perhaps they pass you by and pay no attention to either your bait or the chum. Or perhaps you are lucky and it is a day to be remembered. In any case it is bonefishing.

Up early, out all day, poling across the flats for miles. One day you decide to "still hunt" them. You strap a bait box on your belt, roll up your trousers, step overboard, and set out alone across the miles of flats to get a bonefish "on your own." No boat, no net, no chum, nothing but an extra hook in your pocket and you and your rod. To me this is one of the most fascinating and one of the sportiest ways to seek the king of game fishes.

For half an hour you trudge on through the ankle-deep water without a sign of game. You're not in the bay now, you're on the outside flats. If you see a bonefish he will be a big one and probably alone. Just then you do see one, but he's traveling pretty fast. He looks as big as a barracuda. Perhaps he is. No, no question about it now. He's a bone and an old soaker. You wade as fast as you can but unless he stops you'll never catch up with him. But hold on! He's "settled" in a hole. What a stroke of luck! You tip-toe slowly forward.

The hole he is in is about a hundred feet long. And it must be two feet deep. When he's at the far end of it you can hardly see him. Up and down the length of it he swims, turning at each end like a tiger in its cage. But he can leave it any time he wants to. He must have found something there that he likes. You wait until he has reached the far end again and softly cast your sinkerless bait almost to the middle. Back he comes. He's going past it. No he isn't. He's stopped with a little swirl of sand that's plainly visible from where you are. He turns and noses head down for the bait. The lobe of his tail breaks water. There is a swift pull and you've hooked him!

Look at him go! Was there *ever* such a fish! If the hook doesn't come out he *can't* get away this time. You'll run all the way to Haiti after him if necessary. But fortunately it isn't necessary. His first run was magnificent, but you've turned him at last and the conclusion of each rush brings him closer and closer to your feet. Now he sees you and starts to circle. You pivot slowly like a ringmaster in a circus, your rod nodding and swaying a graceful beat in time to his swift plunges. But he's weakening. This time now. You hold the rod high in air with your right hand, bend down and slip the fingers of your left through his gills. A ten pounder! Your boat must be three-quarters of a mile away. You hold up the fish and yell as loud as you can, "A ten pounder! A TEN POUND-ER!" Ah! it's good to be alive!

In all my years of bonefishing there are one or two incidents that stand out in my mind above all others. In my early days in the Bahamas, before we got it down to a science, we used the native sailboats for our fishing excursions; even to going outside on the reef and in the Stream. If you've never trolled out of a sailboat you've missed a lot of fun. You can go right through schools of fish without bothering them at all. Try it some time.

Well, on one bonefishing trip, things were pretty slow. It was about three in the afternoon and the sun was as hot as Tophet. My companion reclined in the stern, his hat pulled over his eyes, his rod resting across his knees. The omnipotent Benjie slumbered peacefully in the bilge. The sight of my two companions and the effect of two bottles of beer was too much for me, so I curled up in the furled sail, one leg over the boom, for a little concentrated sleeping. It was almost dead low water and we were anchored "off in the deep" on the edge of the channel whither bonefish generally go at that time of tide.

A confused babble of sound gradually seeped through to my bemused brain. "Come on, Van, get up! Get up! Wake up! Got a big one on! Big bonefish!" I struggled mightily and dragged myself down from my perch in the sail. Harry was fighting a big fish, sure enough. The fish had out a lot of line and then turning, headed straight for an old stake protruding from the water a hundred yards away.

At this point Benjie distinguished himself with an act of quick thinking that has been a marvel to us ever since. We had a small canoe tied astern, and leaping into this, he paddled towards that stake as if his very life depended on it; reached it two strokes ahead of the bonefish, and pulled it up. Harry netted his fish, a nine pounder.

Another time I remember: my companion and I had pushed our skiff as far inshore as the tide would permit. We then got overboard and waded along the flats looking for bonefish on the incoming tide. For a long time we saw nothing. Then, as if by magic, bonefish tails were everywhere. Hundreds of them, thousands of them. I have never seen such a sight. No matter in which direction we looked, we could see schools of bonefish. Tails, fins, tails, working in across the flats. We cast and we cast. And before we were through we had brought to our feet and released fourteen bonefish. It was just one of those sights and one of those times that comes about once in an angler's lifetime.

Then, perhaps, one of the most memorable times of all. A night of the full moon. Supper over, someone suggested we go out for a try at bonefish. We crossed the bay to the far side, in quite close to the mangroves. The tide was almost full and the water must have been nearly four feet deep. It was as bright as day. Every object on the ocean floor was plainly discernible. For a long time nothing happened. We fished and smoked and looked at the palm trees, tipped with silver in the moonlight. Then I caught a five pounder. And then one of my companions had a strike.

This was one of those fish that just grabbed it and ran. And kept on running. The wet line showered tiny drops of silver onto the shimmering water. A heron croaked dismally over in the mangroves. No one said a word, and my friend fought a silent fight. On the Point, the beacon flashed in time to the bending rod. It was wild and beautiful.

At last we saw the bonefish, big and ghostlike in the crystal clear water. He was a whopper. Round and 'round the boat and then down with the net and into it head first he went. Ten and one-half pounds! The record for that year! Those few hours on the moonlit flats, the palms rustling in the night wind, the big bonefish gasping away his life in the bottom of the skiff; there is a picture I can never forget.

Burning tropic sun, miles of flats glistening on the low water, fins and tails working in with the tide, a lone man-of-war bird circling high in the blue; moonlit nights with the dark shadows of the mangroves stretching toward your boat, the singing reel and the bending rod; these are my memories of days and nights spent in pursuit of that truly king of all game fishes, the bonefish, the sportiest thing with fins.

ADDENDA
The How's and What's of Bonefishing at a Glance

SCIENTIFIC NAME — *Albula vulpes*, bonefish, banana fish, macabi.

DISTRIBUTION — All warm tropic and semi-tropic seas.

FAVORITE GROUNDS — Shallow banks among the Florida Keys and the Bahama Islands.

TACKLE — 3/6 Tackle is about right. 1/0 or 2/0 reel filled with 6 thread line (9 thread if fishing near snags), 4/0 hook, small casting dipsey, thumb-stall and landing net.

BAIT — Crabs of any and all species. Conch and crawfish. By all means chum if possible to do so.

BOATS — A small skiff or canoe as flat on the bottom as possible, with an anchor for the bow and a stake to keep the stern from swinging. And an outboard motor.

BONEFISH

HOOKING, PLAYING, LANDING — Here we have a difference of opinion on which no two anglers will agree. It must be learned from actual experience. To the novice I should say strike at once until you learn just *what* to do. Don't give the fish slack line and don't hold him. Don't bring him into the net until he's absolutely all in.

WEATHER, TIDES — Weather doesn't seem to make much difference. Perhaps a cloudy day is best as the fish cannot see you so well; but neither can you see them. A friend of mine caught nine bonefish in a howling "norther" with the water as cloudy as milk.

Go out just before low water, find a likely place and wait for the bonefish to come in with the tide. On the falling tide, drop off to the edge of the channel and wait for them to drop off and settle.

WHERE TO GO — If you have an outboard motor, it doesn't make much difference. Hire a rowboat or skiff, put on your outboard engine and you are all set. Any of the fishing camps or inns among the Florida Keys, any of the islands in the Bahamas where there is a settlement. All island people have boats.

RECORD FISH — Bonefish will average 2 to 5 pounds. Anything nine pounds or over is a whopper. Ten and twelve pound fish are rare but not improbable. The official world's record in 1935 stood at 13 ¾ lbs., was caught by Burton F. Peek of Moline, Ill. at Bimini in the Bahama Islands on March 9th, 1919, and is mounted in the Game Fish Hall of the American Museum of Natural History in New York City. Fish of 16 lbs. weight have been reported from Andros Island in the Bahamas and the writer believes they reach that weight. Jordan and Evermann state 36 inches as the maximum length. But records fall every year, and perhaps you will be the lucky one; who knows?

Whom the gods would destroy
They first make a bonefisherman.

BIMINI LOOKING TOWARD HARBOR MOUTH.

Bonefish flats on left, Gulf Stream on right, Dower House at second dock from harbor mouth.

CHAPTER V.

FISHING AT BIMINI

BY

S. KIP FARRINGTON, JR.

OARD a Pan-American Airways giant clipper ship at Miami and forty minutes later, after flying due east for 55 miles across the Gulf Stream, or if you prefer a five-hour trip on your fishing boat, you will sight a group of islands. Bimini, South Bimini, Turtle and Pickett's Rocks, named after the pirate who used it as a lookout, Gun Cay, the site of one of the most powerful lighthouses in his Imperial Majesty's service, Cat Cay, the beautiful island home of Mr. Louis R. Wasey, South Cat and the Victory Keys stretching in the order named for twenty miles from north to south. Memorize the names now as you will often hear more of them in the years to come, particularly if you are a fisherman. These islands comprise the outer edge of the great Bahama bank and lie only a few hundred yards from the Gulf Stream which on this side has a depth of water from two to five thousand feet. On the inside there are many miles of shoal water stretching almost to Andros Island and the Jolter Keys, which you will fly over before crossing the Tongue of the Ocean, if continuing on to Nassau, the capital of the Bahamas 110 miles away.

Between these Keys there are cuts and channels; some very shoal and full of coral rocks, others wide and deep enough for large yachts to get through and it is my belief that one of the chief reasons for the great accumulation of many kinds of large game fish on this side, is the constant source of food supply which is swimming through these passes into the Gulf Stream. Besides that the Stream is usually running like a mill race and that, coupled with the great depth of water which is the most important thing, comprise the factors why this stretch of water is the outstanding fishing center of the Atlantic Ocean.

It is practically a virgin field and this is only the third season it has been fished at all. When you stop to realize what the results have been up to this time, not to mention the giant marlin and tuna that have been hooked and lost by different anglers, I venture to predict there will be more record fish taken out of these waters in the next ten years than any place else in the world.

The season begins late in December with a small showing of white or common marlin, many sailfish, a few wahoo and, of course, plenty of fine large dolphin and small southern tuna, kingfish, bonito and the usual abundance of giant reef-fish, barracuda, amberjack, all of the grouper family, African pompano and whopping big jewfish, which are all there the year round. Inside the flats you have his royal highness, the incomparable bonefish which is delightfully described in another chapter in this book. In the early weeks of February the grand-daddy of all Gulf Stream fish begins to make his appearance — the blue marlin. Some people prefer to still call it black but I have seen too many to believe they are not a little bit different from their gigantic and marvelous half-brothers. The white marlin are now very abundant and the sailfish thin out a trifle, but nobody ever misses them or gives one a thought in these waters. The same conditions prevail along through March and April and then by the middle of May the lid blows off and you never know what size fish you may raise.

Instead of jumping one giant blue marlin of 500 pounds and upwards in a month you are liable to see three or four a week. The white marlin are so numerous, and ridiculous as it sounds to admit it, they become a nuisance. I would much rather catch a wahoo. There is hardly a dolphin brought in weighing under 25 pounds and plenty of tarpon are taken which tip the scales up to 100 pounds in the Bimini harbor mouth. But now last, but far from least, comes the torpedo of the Atlantic migrating on the way north to the herring grounds off Maine and Nova Scotia, the great albacore of the banks, horse mackerel of New Jersey and bluefin tuna the world over. You will meet them all headed north riding the swells like race horses, chasing schools of blue runners and bonito almost into Gun Cay Cut.

Acting entirely different in these waters than they do in other localities, 80 percent of them will strike at any bait from the smallest feather to a ten pound cero mackerel and what a sight when they go after it. The ocean opens up as if a safe had been dropped in and from a mile away it looks like a shell explosion on the water. While it is tragic to have to say it, none of these magnificent fish have ever been boated near Bimini unmarked by sharks and most of those hooked have made their get away on account of the heaviest airplane wire leaders, your swivels or lines being bitten in two by other fish in the school. We have taped our swivels and done away with them entirely, using the ends of the leaders soldered into loops, and eliminated double lines by using 54 thread which is perfectly fair in that depth of water with so many sharks around. In fact many fine marlin have also been lost in these waters by lines being cut by other fish. Just a ripple in the water, a bubble, some slight movement and then follows a smashing strike and a tragedy occurs which you never forget. That I well know from experience. By the fourth of July the tuna have all passed by, the white marlin have followed and there is nothing left but blue marlin and there are plenty of them. From August on comes the hurricane season and not many have fished this side of the Stream in late Fall on that account and what fish are there at that time I could not venture to say.

Please do not think from my following remarks about extra heavy tackle that I approve of its use in hardly any other waters of the world. On the contrary I fish with nothing heavier than a 3-6 outfit for marlin and sailfish on the Florida side and hope some day to be able to try my luck with the finest light-tackle fishermen in the world, members of the celebrated Catalina Tuna Club, whose exploits are mentioned with respect by most of us on the east coast.

When fishing from a club or within their territory, make 24 thread and a 16 oz. tip your heaviest rig as it is the top limit allowed by most organizations. At Montauk, Nova Scotia, Lower California or the Mexican coast, No. 39 should be plenty large enough and the angler should have no regrets about using it, but when in a new country with a tremendous depth of water unfortunately infested by sharks and hard-striking line-cutting fish, such as Bimini, Perlas Islands, the Galapagos and Tahiti, then in my opinion if the angler so wishes, 54 thread is a necessity that must be employed without criticism from anybody.

TUNA. These fish come north on the east side of the Gulf Stream from May 15th to June 15th every year in great numbers. In my opinion 3,000 feet of 54 thread line on a 16-0 Edward Vom Hofe reel and 25 to 29 oz. Vom Hofe hickory tip is the only and correct tackle to use. If a fisherman prefers a bamboo rod of that size, then I would suggest the No. 6 Hardy special made from palakona wood with the steel center weighing around 29 ozs. The new Vom Hofe triple enamel, made of extra fine bamboo, is also first class. Many men are using 72 thread line in these waters with the giant Knowles reel, attached to a 40 oz. hickory tip, made in Miami last winter and with which I have had some experience, but which, while a fine machine, makes fishing just a trifle too mechanical for me and the line is far too heavy in case you hook a blue marlin of average size. Light or heavy tackle men will laugh, no doubt, at the above statement comparing 72 to 54, but I have had 27 jumps in 18 minutes with a small 180 pound blue marlin on 54 and while 24 thread would have been just right for him, one of these tuna would have cleaned that in one to two minutes and a 12-0 filled with 39 usually goes almost equally as quick. Bimini in late spring is no goldfish pond or any other time for that matter and while unbelievable as it sounds, a 10-0 and 12-0 reel filled with 24 to 39 thread line is far too small for these tuna and, as already stated owing to its importance, using 54 eliminates the long double line which other fish in the school, not to mention wahoo and sharks, are attracted to strike at. Use the heavy airplane-wire leader with the loop in the end for a swivel and a snap on the end of your line to tie it to, then cover this with tire tape and with luck you may again have reduced your chances of a cut line. A 14-0 Pflueger Sobey hook or Vom Hofe Grinnell, with a large blue runner or mackerel and sometimes a very large cut bait, is what they like best and the same size hook with a very large Japanese feather is often a tempting morsel to these magnificent bulls of the sea. When one hits your bait you certainly must strike him many times, as hard as you can, for they have the hardest mouth of any fish. Personally I believe a great many never know they are hooked for one or two minutes, as I have seen them swim parallel with the boat, with a light line. But when they get started, each one heads right for the north and you settle down for a long hard fight and murmur many prayers to keep the sharks away which, as I have said before, have so far remained unanswered. However, I firmly believe that these fish will be taken unscarred in Bimini waters if the extra-heavy tackle is used and the spring of 1935 will only be the beginning. A few of the Allison or long-fin tuna have been caught on this side of the Stream but I, myself, have never had the good fortune to see one.

FISHING AT BIMINI

BLUE MARLIN. Some fishing guides of my acquaintance and a good many more anglers still refuse to believe there is a difference between the blue and black marlin. I am inclined to believe that this observation comes from parties who have never caught one of either kind. While I readily admit I have never been fortunate enough to land a black marlin, my opinion is that he is a much wider, thicker fish, has a smaller bill and his head and shoulders are much blunter and there is a wide difference in the shape of the lower jaw. Also, from what I have been able to ascertain, the color of this Bimini marlin is also much lighter. It may be that their colors change in different temperatures of water in different localities but the shape certainly speaks for itself. These blue marlin also show a very dull silver stripe on their entire blue body and this stripe does not change much in color after the fish is taken out of the water. You will never mistake one if you see it following your bait as he usually makes a very, very fast rush and hits instantly, not hanging back like his small cousin, the white marlin, and sailfish. I have seen over 16 of these fish come up to the outrigger baits and have never known but one not to strike. The largest variation the blue marlin has is the difference in his weight relative to length. For instance I have taken a 180 pound fish measuring 8 feet 6 inches long, as compared with one whose weight was only 191 pounds and measuring 10 feet 6 inches long. This I believe was a male fish and that I imagine constitutes the difference in size and proportion. At any rate the long and lanky ones seem to fight harder and put up a much better scrap. The largest blue marlin taken by Mrs. Moore and Mr. Wasey in March, 1933, weighed 505 pounds when 18 hours out of water and was 12 feet 8 inches in length. My guess is that very little is known of any of the marlin family, their types, sex and classification, but if we live long enough and a few more large ones are taken, we may be able to find out more; at least I will always be hoping to. To illustrate my point, a lady acquaintance of mine recently wrote to me from Bimini about the *royal* blue marlin she had raised and which had promptly cleaned her tackle. While that is a new one on me, calling them royal blues, I must admit it is a very appropriate name for a couple I hooked and lost and I have two or three friends who saw them who will ardently agree with me.

The tackle for these marlin, in my opinion, is 2,000 feet of No. 24 line on the Edward Vom Hofe 10-0, up to May 1st and then 1,600 feet of No. 36 or No. 39 thread on the Edward Vom Hofe 12-0 using a 16 to 20 oz. rod. In the winter time, with the small chance of hooking one over 300 pounds, No. 24 is ideal; in fact we use that on each outrigger with No. 18 on the 6-o Edwards, trolled short in the middle, thus preventing the larger fish from getting inside and grabbing the lighter line. Laugh, if you will at the No. 18 thread being too light, but remember that every five minutes wasted in these shark-infested waters just brings one that much nearer to a good size chunk of your precious blue marlin and believe me they look pretty poorly on the dock or over a fire-place with a large piece torn out of them. My motto is larger line, less time and more whole fish. The light and very pliable airplane wire, as supplied by Abercrombie & Fitch, is ideal for leaders to use on these fish but once again, not after May 1st. For bait, as long as it is fresh, I believe they have no preference. Captain Tom Gifford, who has caught over four times as many of these fish for his parties as any other fishing captain, always preaches big bait for big fish and he is dead right. I have hooked blue marlin on Gifford's exquisitely prepared cut bait of bonito and tuna, his special dolphin for blue marlin, baby barracuda which he shoots with a .22 rifle walking along the shore, and up to five and six pound mackerel and bonefish; the last named, I believe having no superior. A small eagle ray is also to be recommended. Most blue marlin in Bimini waters range in weight from 150 to 200 pounds but many over six and seven hundred, judged most conservatively, have been lost and I absolutely believe two different tales of fish of at least 1,000 pounds being hooked. The fish boated that were whole and unscarred by sharks range from the already described 505 pounder of Mrs. Moore and Mr. Wasey which took six hours and one-half to land, sixteen miles from where it was hooked, down to 110 pounds, also taken by the owner of Cat Cay. In between these are three of over 300 and about the same number over 200. I think I am correct when I state there have been about 30 of these fish caught in the last two seasons and most of them in the three or four hot spots off south Bimini, Pickett's Rock, the lonely pine on Gun Cay and one of the largest down off the Victory Keys. My humble advice to a man who has been to Bimini on one preceding trip is to stick to his large baits, forget about white marlin and smaller fish, concentrate on the blue devils and believe me his trip will be made if he hangs one. I have found that in fishing, as in everything else, you can't do two or three things at once.

WHITE MARLIN. Put all the different varieties of marlin up against this baby of the family, the white or common marlin, sometimes called skillygoelle

A FINE ATLANTIC COAST MARLIN. 353 POUNDS.

THREE WAHOO TAKEN IN ONE HOUR.

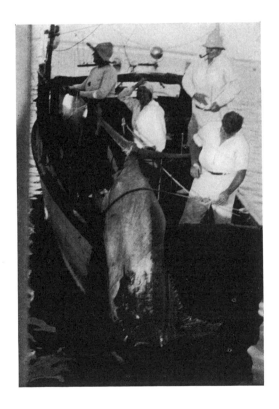

LANDING AT CAT CAY WITH A 502 POUND BLUE
MARLIN.

Photos by courtesy of S. Kip Farrington, Jr.
ALL THAT WAS LEFT WHEN THE SHARKS WERE
THROUGH.

as the commercial man of New England has so insultingly named him, and bet your money on this little fellow to out-jump them all on any line up to and including 24 thread and with the light airplane or piano wire leader. No hook larger than a 10-0 should be used. There seems to me, in Bimini waters and particularly in the late spring, to be more of these white marlin than there are sailfish off Palm Beach and that is certainly comparing them with some fishing that is far famed for its excellency, any month of the year. I have personally had four of these fish astern of Captain Gifford's "Lady Grace" at one time and that morning raised 12 in two hours' fishing, five minutes from Mr. Wasey's dock at Cat Cay. I have to admit, however, out of the six hooked we only caught two, a very sour showing. Strange as it may sound, I have taken my blue marlin baits away from eight of these fish in one day. We had no time to stop nor spare baits to be ruined, so Tommy speeded up and took the baits away from them, much to their disgust. I will never forget the first white marlin I caught. He jumped by actual count 45 times in one hour and two minutes, on a 12 thread line and weighed 92 pounds. A little one of 50 pounds gave me 37 leaps in 12 minutes on 24 thread and I had one go in the air for the count of 35, using No. 9. On 3-6 tackle I imagine there is no limit to what they could do, but I have never had the time to waste in stopping to try. While I never use anything else for sailfish on the Florida side, it is a tough proposition here with the sharks, plus the fact that they are three times the fish a sailfish is and there is always the possibility of one of the big boys grabbing your bait on the 6 thread line.

Mrs. Grace Gifford, Captain Tommy's wife, hung one after many hard days of disappointment. However, she probably has no superior as a 3/6 fisherman in the East and has even managed to hang on to a broadbill for an hour and a half with her little outfit. Mr. Cooney Bispham, the great bonefisherman of Bimini, catches them out of a canoe on flat days and says the sport can not be equalled. I have had the experience from a row boat and it sure has a power boat licked to death. The record white marlin at Bimini was taken by George Blabon of Philadelphia. It weighed 145 pounds. I believe Captain John Cass holds the east coast record for this beautiful fish that also tipped the scales at 145 pounds. The largest and first white marlin I ever caught at Bimini weighed 110 pounds. His bill was broken off and when Gifford skinned him he found in his shoulder, over which the skin and tissues had completely healed up, a piece of bill about four inches long, belonging to either a white marlin or sailfish and still in pretty good shape. This to me proves that these fish ram their enemies, while slapping their food to kill it. Many of them have broken bills and others healed up broken ends. A number of times I have seen these marlin hit a bait when I am sure they were not the least bit hungry, but possessed with a great curiosity and a savageness, coupled with a desire to kill, that is uncontrollable. In this they are entirely different from 95 percent of the sailfish who approach so suspiciously and are much more particular with regard to their food. White marlin will hit any of the smaller cut baits and ballyhoo has no superior. Personally I always release all of them unless the hook has injured them so badly that they surely will become prey to the sharks. I might add that Mr. Ernest Hemingway's chapter on marlin in this book is one of the greatest works ever written about them and there is no man in the world who has had more experience or is better qualified to write about them.

WAHOO. By all odds, after the marlin and giant tuna, wahoo are the most sought-after species in these waters. Pound for pound they have no equal — their beautiful bodies outlined with the heavy silver stripe and their rows of ferocious small teeth and the funny little dorsal fins. They will take any bait, and how they love feathers! One weighing 30 pounds or more will run out from 600 to 900 feet of 18 or 24 thread line; on 9 thread line or smaller — we won't even discuss that! While they do not jump on occasions when hitting the bait, they usually give a fine surface fight at the beginning, breaking water and raising a first-class commotion, with another good run or two thrown in. Then down they go and it reminds you of the fight of a tuna at least twice their size. The largest taken at Bimini, as far as I have been able to ascertain, weighed around 82 pounds. There have been a good many in the 60's and practically none under 25 or 30. However, don't let any one tell you there are many there. You can go a good many days without seeing one, in fact, on my first trip to Cat Cay, the second time out, I caught three in one hour off South Cat, all weighing between 44 and 46 pounds each, and they were the last I saw that trip. They seem to draw sharks quicker than any of the other fish that you hook in these waters, and why, I am at a loss to explain, as they do not seem to bleed much worse than any of the mackerel family. Last June a friend of mine had a fish of, I should judge, around 60 pounds, up to the side of the boat and refused to let Gifford land it, much to his great disgust. He kept taking pictures of the fish in the water and remarking how swell it would look mounted in his library. He was still going on with his speech making when the next thing he knew a shark had left him only a head for the library. This, of course, is a common occurrence when a man is slow and I only mention it here to show how fast different situations arise in these waters. As a food fish I rank him among the first five.

SAILFISH. Sailfish in these waters are most abundant in December and January but there are always enough to go around. Captain Capo, of Cat Cay, had four hooked at once, one day and succeeded in landing three of them. Fish of 80 to 90 pounds are not strangers over there and I am sure the average size is much larger than on the Florida Coast.

DOLPHIN. Keep your 3-6 and 6-9 outfits ready when you get in a school of dolphin. For sheer beauty, speed and strength they are unmatched. A purple fish streaked with yellow comes dashing in as far as the eye can see and bang— he has your feather. *Sock* — another one is on! The man-of-war birds are diving overhead. You are in a school and these marvelous birds always follow them. There is a story told in Bimini that a man-of-war bird will get his altitude in the Bahamas and will then make Florida without a flap of his wings. We certainly owe all birds a vote of appreciation and thanks for the aid they give us in catching any kind of big game fish. I have seen whole schools of dolphin chase flying fish and ballyhoo for miles, and what a sight. They remind me of the giant jack rabbits found in the western part of the United States or the kangaroos of Australia. When hooked, 20 to 25 jumps is nothing and I once saw one go in the air 18 times on a 24 thread. For cut bait there is hardly any better meat to be had and for food they rate the top. Their roe is equal to that of the shad. When boated I believe they are the hardest fish to handle, dying slower, showing more strength and fight than any other game fish that swims. I never heard the weight of the largest dolphin caught at Bimini but I saw Captain Leo Droughton bring in one of 45 pounds, and have seen many around 40. The largest I ever took weighed 35 and believe me if you are not tired of hearing me repeat myself, there are not many under that figure in the late spring. In short, dolphin fishing at Bimini has no equal any place else in the world.

BONEFISH AND TARPON. The bonefishing at Bimini has no superior and it is being wonderfully described elsewhere in this book. Fish of over 10 and 11 pounds are not uncommon and the record is 13¾ pounds and they can be caught night or day either from a boat or wading, using conch for bait.

Tarpon are plentiful in the harbor mouth and weigh up to 100 pounds. They are taken trolling from row boats on cut baits and feathers. Now that the rum running is over, your party should be safe when evening fishing from being run down by rum runners, Florida bound, with a heavy load and no lights. In fact, the tarpon fishing should improve, due to the smaller number of boats going in and out of the entrance to the harbor.

KINGFISH, BONITO, LITTLE TUNA AND REEF FISHING. All of the varieties of bonito and the little southern tuna, the largest of which I ever saw weighed 15 pounds, are plentiful and provide action at all times. Kingfish do not run as large as they do at Key West but put on a great show, grabbing the outrigger baits and leaping 15 and 20 feet in the air with practically the same motion but rarely hooking themselves. However, there is nothing that is more spectacular. These fish do not school up over there as they do on the Florida side.

The houndfish are a terrible nuisance. If one gets in too near the reefs, many a good bait is ruined by these pests. They run to 12 and 15 pounds and are a laughable sight jumping along chasing a fine piece of cut bait, dangling so temptingly from its outrigger, but they rarely take hold.

Barracuda, amberjack, grouper, jewfish and African pompano are always plentiful but I personally do not believe the first two named run so large as those caught at Key West and south to Tortugas. However, they are big enough, and there are some jewfish over there nobody has been able to pull up, and some beautiful big African pompano have been caught. The giant manta and different varieties of rays are numerous, but no one bothers with them very much. I saw the only whale shark (*Rhineodon typus*) I ever had the good fortune to see, off Turtle Rocks. He was a good 35 feet in length and must have weighed 8 or 9 tons. A miniature submarine and I was just as glad when Gifford's great whaling harpoon did not take hold; we would have been out there all night and the next day. Captain Bill Hatch and other guides who should know, tell me the shark that raises the most disaster with your hooked fish and particularly the giant tuna, is one called the black tip and from Zane Grey's description of his Tahiti misfortunes, I believe it is the same one he writes of. Of course, there are all kinds, but I have only heard of two mako sharks being seen and none caught. It is too bad there are not more of them for they certainly belong in the first four of the world's great game fish.

TACKLE AND WEATHER CONDITIONS. I am sure when I say that the Edward

Vom Hofe reel has no superior and most particularly the Commander Ross 10-0 and 12-0 for a general purpose all-round reel, that most American anglers will agree with me. They are perfectly balanced, hand constructed by skilled machinists who do nothing else, and the 12-0 is the only large reel made with the throw-off feature. This, to me, is indispensable when slacking back line to large marlin or broadbill swordfish. It is a great deal faster and more accurate than winding and releasing the star drag. There is no changing of your tension from where you had previously set it at its correct amount before your fish shows himself. I have seen good fishermen, who were not the least bit excitable, screw the star handle up so tightly as to cause line breaks and hooks being thrown on the initial rush. While it is probably true that a reel equipped with this device takes most of its pounding when the brake is thrown on, the Edward Vom Hofe experts have eliminated this and the new 16-0's are also equipped with this important feature. I have never had any difficulty with any Edward Vom Hofc reels and I have given a few of them some pretty good workouts. I oil them with special reel oil once a month when not in use, and every other day when fishing. Every two years I return them to the Vom Hofe store and have them given a thorough overhauling. If I were buying only one reel, it would be a 12-0 large enough for marlin and broadbill anywhere and tuna in most depths of water the world over.

The 16-0 is a magnificent machine and it recovers line as if wound by an electric dynamo. I have never seen mine even get warm and I have had over 2500 feet stripped off it in one rush of a giant tuna.

For 54 thread line they are indispensable and they do not strike you as being half as heavy as they appear, when attached to your rod and harness.

If the difference in price is making you hesitate in deciding between a 9-0 and 10-0, purchase the larger one and forget it. The 9-0 is the poorest size ever constructed and is a perfect misfit for any size line. It will only carry 1200 or possibly 1300 feet of 24 against 1900 and upwards for the 10-0, which can also carry 1200 feet of No. 39 — if one thought that would be enough. Personally I fill my 6-0 with No. 18 and it carries a thousand feet, using it on my 12 oz. tip. My 4-0 with 1,000 feet of No. 12 on my 8 oz. tip and my 3-0 with 1,100 feet of No. 9 to use on my regulation 6-9 rod and the 3-6 carries a 2-0 filled with 900 feet of No. 6. This reel is a trifle too small and a 3-0 would be much better on account of its larger line-carrying capacity. Give me smaller line and more of it on a reel every time. For bonefish I prefer the Edward Vom Hofe No. 800, known as the Matacumbe and use No. 6 thread line, but most of the well-known bonefishermen who are after big fish use No. 9 thread.

I also have had experience with the Coxe; a good reel much used and admired by California anglers. However, for Atlantic Ocean work, I prefer a reel made in New York due to its accessibility for any repairs that might have to be made and the fact that you can go into the Vom Hofe factory and store on Fulton Street, New York, and see your reel made for you. I have also had experience with the Pflueger Atlapac and Hardy's Zane Grey reels.

For bamboo rods up to 12 oz., I use the Edward Vom Hofe models and there are none better. All of my large hickory rods, which are the finest made anywhere, also have been purchased from them. I have never yet broken a single Vom Hofe rod. They have a first-class reel seat built of the best material and there is no danger of any part of the butt letting go. The rods set beautifully, which I prefer mine to do, and even the largest and heaviest tips have a fine feel and balance to them. All of my grips are made of the very finest felt which is very comfortable to the left hand after many hours of fighting a fish. This feature was developed by Hardy Brothers of London, whose heavy palakona bamboo tips I also use. The reel is secured to the butt with a magnificent reel seat which is screwed up with a wrench that comes with the rod and it is impossible to move it, once it is tightened. The male ferrule has a slot device which locks itself automatically in the female ferrule, making it impossible to move the tip or turn it around at any time. While I believe I am in the minority, I prefer agate guides, for if a rod does break, your line may not break and your fish would be saved with the line against the agate, whereas the line rubbing against the edge of the metal guide would instantly be worn through, even though you would automatically be disqualified in a club competition. If a rod is kept in shape at all, the agates will never fall out and are rarely broken, particularly when equipped with the Hardy protectors. For the tip I am not particular, but I have had fine success with the Hardy double wheel tip; care must be exercised, however, in seeing that the line does not catch or wrap around it, which can happen quite easily when fishing from outriggers. Of course, with novices, the agate tip is extremely dangerous, if they persist in reeling the swivel up against it and a crack results without being noticed.

For line, there are only two kinds; the original Ashaway Cuttyhunk made

Rods, left to right: Vom Hofe Weakfish Special for catching bait; Vom Hofe regulation 3/6; Vom Hofe bonefish; Vom Hofe 6/9; Vom Hofe 8 oz. tip; Vom Hofe 12 oz. tip; Hardy 29 oz.; Hardy 24 oz.; Hardy 16 oz. Catalina Special; Hardy 14 oz. Catalina Special; A. & F. 18 oz. hickory; Vom Hofe 16 oz. hickory; Vom Hofe 29 oz. hickory for big tuna. *Reels, left to right*: Vom Hofe 10/0, 16/0, 12/0, 6/0, 3/0, Bonefish Special, 2/0, 4/0. Rod belts, harness, 14/0 Pflueger Sobey Swordfish hooks with aeroplane wire leader.

Photos by F. M. Demarest.

THE FOUR GREAT EDWARD VOM HOFE REELS.
Left to right: 16/0 (8½ inches in diameter), 14/0, 12/0, 10/0.

at Ashaway, Rhode Island, and the Edward Vom Hofe special, manufactured and produced by them. The color should be no other than natural white. No dyed lines for me. Captain Gifford and Howard Lance have made exhaustive tests on this subject from under water and both tell me that the white line is far less conspicuous than the green, at least to the human eye.

As for hooks, and in this I believe that all anglers and captains will agree, there is only one kind — the Pflueger Sobey for any size fish and the Vom Hofe Grinnell is also satisfactory for swordfish. For the heavy work, the strong and non-rustable airplane-wire cable, which at the same time has not the sharp cutting tendencies that raised such havoc at Catalina some years ago, is supplied by Abercrombie & Fitch. This firm also makes the light airplane wire which is the only thing for marlin fishing. William Baxter, head of the fishing tackle department of A. & F. as a designer of harnesses, has no superior. In fact, I believe most well-known anglers have been measured by him. He even made one for Mrs. Farrington, which is lined with sheep's wool to prevent it from cutting her shoulders. Cheap cotton gloves should be good enough for most men if they are forced to put them on. For women I recommend regulation polo gloves which protect their hands and are remarkably cool, having open backs.

Weather conditions at Bimini vary so much and the fishing is so uniformly good that it is hard to make or write a statement regarding it. In fact, more than once I have said that the more I fish over there, the less I know about weather. I think, however, it is generally agreed that the best fishing times are early morning and late afternoon. While it has not been tried very often, many of the captains believe that a moonlight night can not be beaten. A smooth, flat and very hot day is by far the poorest. You must have a wind of some sort and the consensus of opinion is that for marlin, any kind of a northeast wind is the best; then southwest which is also perfect for the giant tuna, followed by west and northwest. East and southeasterly winds usually bring grass out in the Stream from the shoal water, although this condition is never very annoying off these islands. It takes a real storm to keep a boat in at Bimini or Cat Cay, as these islands also afford a magnificent lee. I have been able to get out many a day when 65 miles distant in Florida, not a boat left its dock. Don't let anyone ever tell you that fish won't bite in the rain. I have seen some fine tuna hooked and was fast to my second largest marlin in a tropical downpour with a visibility of not over 50 feet.

BIG GAME FISHING

BOATS AND EQUIPMENT. The perfect boat to catch these fish from, to my mind, is a twin-motored, twin-screw craft of 30 feet in length and 7 to 9 feet in width. It must have double rudders for fast handling and steer from the fishing cockpit so the man handling the boat may constantly be right beside the angler. Controls on top are also a decided asset in locating fins and watching the wake. In fact, one pair of eyes should never be off the bait and two are much the better. Many fine fish are lost through this carelessness. After a few days, monotonous and trying on the eyes as it is, you will become more accustomed to it and many times repaid in the end. Fish, ice and bait boxes should be conveniently located in the fishing cockpit and a well, if desired, directly behind the fishing chairs. Bait wells, if not kept clean and care exercised in putting bleeding fish into them, turn out once more to be a first-class attraction for sharks. Many species of fish will live a long while in them, but all of the mackerel family die instantly.

If two swivel fishing chairs are installed, have a bracket screwed between them for the angler who is fighting the fish. He can then have his chair moved over and continue the battle with ample room on both sides, in a much more advantageous position. All chairs must be equipped with rod sockets that turn in any direction and have removable backs which can instantly be taken out so as not to interfere with the pumping.

I know many will disagree with me in choosing a boat as small as 30 feet. I don't mean to be critical of any boat up to 38 nor possibly of one or two I know over 40 feet, but the smaller size is easier to handle in fighting big fish. Particularly at Bimini where there is but a short run off shore there is no need for a boat of larger size.

By all odds the greatest contribution to big game fishing in recent years are the outriggers, and when I say outriggers I do not refer to 10 or 15 foot bamboo poles such as one sees on many charter boats, but shafts of aluminum with wood and bamboo ends which reach out from 40 to 60 feet from the boat, reinforced with heavy wire spreaders and supporting guy lines running their entire length. The rig, if made right, will cost from $700 to $1,000. They are fastened to each side of the boat with heavy steel bracings and are raised and lowered upon hinges connected to an intricate maze of ropes and pulleys.

Your line runs from your rod tip to a clothespin tied on the outrigger's end, and then drops back in the water any length you desire. When the fish strikes your bait, the line falls out of the pin and into the water and when it comes up tight you let him have it. You determine beforehand how much slack line you want to give your fish and this flies in the wind until the strike takes place.

This outfit was designed and first used on the Atlantic Coast by Captain Tom Gifford in 1933 and since then all of the leading guides and some of the private boats have adopted them. Gifford was not satisfied with a kite — which is in itself a splendid way to fish, — due to the difficulty of running the boat in different directions, and at the same time combating the wind while trying to keep the kite in the air, plus the annoying situation which arose on calm days when it was sometimes practically impossible to fly the kite.

Some fishermen have made the ridiculous claim that outriggers are not sporting and simplify fishing, making the hooking of bill fish automatic. This to my mind is nothing but "sour grapes," and I have recently noticed that some of the hardest knockers have now put them on their charter boats. My answer to them is as follows: Nobody ever made the claim that the kite was unsporting and made the hooking of fish any easier and there is very little if any difference. Admitted, you don't have to give line with the outriggers but you will be surprised how many times you have to reel in fast to get your fish back, having missed him on the initial strike. This results from hitting him too late or too soon, for it is, in itself, an art to catch the right moment. Gifford's idea was to get a skipping bait and keep it out of the wake, making it much more exciting and attractive, and enabling a party to fish four lines at once with no interference. He also wanted to eliminate the use of wooden teasers, and by using outriggers your baits are your teasers — and where could you find a better or more practical one? With the wooden style of Tarp-oreno or teaser, once a billed fish hits them he is not going to be very, if at all, interested in the bait as you reel it up to him. My comparison is that a human being would not hit his head against the top of an automobile door or any hard object and go back and do it again. Once is enough and believe me none of these fish are fools. I think I am giving away a professional secret in telling this, but if it helps some fisherman to hang a record marlin I will gladly take the consequences. If a teaser must be used, it should be some kind of a dead fish sewed up so as not to be torn to pieces in the wake, and it can be conveniently towed from one half way up the outrigger. All I can tell you is, go to Bimini, try a fishing boat without outriggers for two weeks, then switch to one equipped with them and I will let you tell me the difference.

They have done remarkable work wherever they have been used, and last but not least have been a big aid in presenting a bait to broadbill swordfish at Montauk. Every kind of fish is just so much more interested in the aggravating, skipping and irritating bait which is made doubly so on account of being out of the wake. I firmly believe if Zane Grey or Captain Laurie D. Mitchell and other famous anglers had used these in New Zealand, Tahiti and California, their catch of record fish would have been doubled. I might also add, let one of the outrigger "knockers" catch a blue marlin and he will go ashore mighty glad to have a bed sheet, the blue marlin flag of Bimini, flying from it, and he will not think that hooking his magnificent prize was any less fun or was made any easier for him in so doing from this interesting device.

PERSONAL EQUIPMENT. For personal equipment, I advocate the original Block Island swordfish cap with the long visor as the ideal hat for fishing. It is cooler and affords fine protection from the sun, protects your face and is a great help in locating fins. Every angler should have two pairs of dark glasses with him as it is very easy to break or lose a pair. If a dark glass is desired, I prefer the Crook lens, and a lighter one is the Aninfra, which was brought out by E. B. Meyrowitz. These glasses have been endorsed by the U. S. Air Service and cannot be improved upon. I would never make a fishing trip without a pair of field glasses and believe the Zeiss Silvarem 6x30 is the ideal glass to use on a small boat with plenty of motion. The Binoctem or 7/50 regulation yachting glass is a trifle too large and hard to hold in looking for fins and other small objects over water, but, of course, is a much more powerful all-round glass. For a camera, give me the Leica or Zeiss Contax, but remember if you want shots of jumping fish, a telephoto lens must be attached with a special lens finder. For movie work the Bell and Howell will probably prove to do the best work and if you can get a 35 millimeter, so much the better. Again a telephoto lens is needed. E. B. Meyrowitz, at 43rd Street and Fifth Avenue, New York, have a special department devoted to anglers on the above mentioned articles and will give any one interested all of the correct opinions regarding accessories that go with the art of picture taking.

I would bring one oil coat, or a duck shooting pullover with hood attached for the head, and a sweat shirt comes in handy sometimes. Personally I always fish stripped, with only a pair of trunks and sneakers on my feet. Rubber soled shoes, of course, to wear on the boat, a good supply of cocoanut oil, and Un-

A GROUP OF FAMOUS BOAT CAPTAINS.

Left to right: S. K. Farrington, Jr., in white coat; Capt. Bobby Cass, Capt. Howard Lance, Capt. Doug. Osborne, Capt. Bill Fagen, Capt. Kenneth Foster weighing fish, Capt. Tom Gifford, Capt. John Cass with peaked cap, Capt. Archie Cass in rear.

guentine should be taken along to guard against sunburn, and I find Absorbine, Jr., the best rub down and will not bother a bad sunburn to any great extent. A man can be massaged in the middle of a battle and continue the fight feeling much refreshed. A large silk handkerchief to tie around the chin is also a big help in killing the reflection of the sun on the water, where it usually gives one the worst burn.

I would advise anyone going to Bimini, and particularly in the spring, to do a little gym work beforehand. Pulling both chest weights with one hand, and a rowing machine I find are the best exercises to build one up for hours of heavy pumping on a big fish. It is also a good idea to soak one's hands in brine, night and morning, for two or three weeks before starting out. In the spring we always go 12 hours a day in the Gulf Stream and then come in for bonefishing after supper. So being in good condition is a decided asset. I have sat in a swivel chair without a back on the "Lady Grace" for 8 or 9 hours a day without moving and never taking my eyes from the baits.

GUIDES AND FISHING HEADQUARTERS. At the present there are probably 12 fishing guides who know the waters of Bimini as they should be known and who have fished here more than any others the past few years. A great deal of credit is due Mr. L. R. Wasey for bringing Tom Gifford and his fishing boat, "Lady Grace," from Miami to do such great work in developing the fishing to what it is today. Gifford not only caught fish, but trained Captain Elmo Capo, now the head guide at Cat Cay, to be one of the leading Captains in the East, and also developed a Bahamian boy, Eric Stewart by name, who is blessed with the best pair of fishing eyes I have ever known.

The name Tommy Gifford speaks for itself and is known all over the United States. Gifford is a small man of amazing strength and not a nerve in his body. He never uses a gaff, thus eliminating bleeding fish when landing any size marlin, always grabbing them by the bill and hanging on until his mate gets the rope around their tails. No matter how green they are he sticks with them, and if they jump he goes in the air and comes down with their bill still in his vise-like grip. If a fish is bleeding or there are sharks around, he wastes no time in backing down on them and grabbing the leader. This I believe explains why none of the twenty blue marlin he has caught have ever had a tooth mark on them. In short, he is a fishing fool, marlin mad, and when he has a day off always takes his wife and goes fishing by himself. His boat, the "Lady Grace," has twin screws, high-speed motors, double rudders, steers from three different places and will turn on a dime. For fighting big fish there is no power boat afloat that has anything on her. Gifford held a commission in the Navy during the war, and is a fine navigator.

Captain Howard Lance, of West Palm Beach, is one of the outstanding fishing captains of the United States and his boat the "Cheerio" is a dream, twin motored, and 35 feet in length. She has a dandy pair of outriggers, elegant fish chairs, steers from on top of the cabin, is very easy to handle and a splendid sea boat. Lance, who incidentally was high man at Montauk this summer for all kinds of fish, was in command of a submarine chaser in the United States Navy during the World War and has enjoyed great success at Bimini. He has a marvelous personality and I have never heard a word spoken against him.

Captain Bill Hatch, whose headquarters are Pier 5, Miami, is the dean of fishing captains and his mate Jimmy has been with him over 20 years. Hatch was the first captain to take a broadbill swordfish on rod and reel on the east coast and was very near, if not the first, to catch a sailfish in a like manner. He has a very able boat, "Patsy," and is one of the most popular men in the fishing world today.

Captain Elmo Capo of Cat Cay fishes out of Bimini after May 1st when Mr. Wasey leaves for the North, and uses his employer's new fishing boat "Cookie" which is the latest and most modern addition to the sport fishing fleet.

Captain Bill Fagen, also sailing from Pier 5, Miami, has put in many days of fishing at Bimini, with plenty of luck for his parties. Fagen's boat, the "Florida Cracker II," is one of the best equipped and fastest in the fishing fleet, twin-motored and is well known for her grand accommodations.

The four Cass Brothers, also from Miami, all have their own boats and can usually be found at Bimini. They are all very hard fishermen and know their way around the Bahamas as well as they know Biscayne Bay.

Captains Leo Droughton and Rudy Steinhauser have fine boats, make their headquarters at Bimini and will give any party a great trip.

Other well known guides who have fished Bimini are Captains Bill Spooner, Owen Duffy, Charlie Thompson, Walter Stark and Douglas Osborne of Miami, and Herman Gray and Kenneth Foster of Palm Beach. All of these men are geniuses at cutting and making baits, which of course, is just about the most important thing in fishing. Such little matters as taking backbones out of whole fish and wiring them so they will be cut off instead of knocked up the leaders, are no jobs for the uninitiated, and handling the boat in proper fashion when the big one is finally on, needs a man with plenty of experience. In fact, I venture the statement that your guide and his boat are 75 percent of a successful fishing trip, your tackle 20 percent and yourself the remaining 5 percent.

Of course, it stands to reason, you simply can't catch big fish on poor tackle and that goes for the best fisherman in the world, unlike the crack shot who will do fine work with a very mediocre gun.

The Dower House at Bimini offers splendid accommodations for anglers of both sexes while fishing on that side. It is situated on the Kings Highway and was built by Mrs. Helen Duncombe, wife of the ex-British Commissioner at the Island; rooms with shower baths, hot and cold running fresh water, are available at very fair prices, and the food is delicious with all kinds of magnificently cooked fish on the menu, headed by the crawfish and famous conch broth, both made from the national food fish of Bimini.

Some time in the near future Mr. Wasey will probably build what will be the finest fishing Club in the world on Cat Cay and I understand the well known guide and salmon fisherman of New Brunswick, Jack Russell, is opening a camp at Bimini in the near future.

When you are at Bimini and things may not be working right or the picture does not look quite as rosy as I have painted it, just keep the following in mind and don't forget it. On three successive days of fishing with Captain Tom Gifford, less than five minutes from Mrs. Duncombe's breakfast table directly off the mouth of Bimini harbor, I have been fast to giant tuna that would go well over 600 pounds, great marlin of equal size and last, but far from the least, worked the great gladiator of them all, *Xiphias gladius*, the broadbill swordfish. I put a bait across this fellow eleven times before he finally went down and I suppose headed for the North and the Georges Banks. True, he was a straggler. There have only been two or three seen to my knowledge but he was there just the same and he brought the total up to 26 that I have presented a bait to and I should know him by now. Just let me ask you one final question. In how many bodies of water could you see three of the four great game fish of the world on three successive days? Only one other place to my knowledge, New Zealand; and my comeback to that is — travel over 7,000 miles if you care to, but leave me at Bimini on the way.

BROADBILL SWORDFISH

Charles Lehmann handling the rod aboard his boat "Alibi."

CHAPTER VI.

SWORDFISH

BY

CHARLES L. LEHMANN

N having been asked to write a chapter on my old friend the broadbill swordfish, which would give a few highlights to the fisherman who is contemplating taking a broadbill on rod and reel, it occurred to me that perhaps the best way to do this would be to answer the questions that are most frequently asked me about this fishing.

The first question that we have to consider is, "Where shall I go to catch one?"

The answer is, if you are on the West Coast, you are where the sport originated, and I advise you to apply to the famous Tuna and Swordfish Clubs. They will give you all the information, and supply you with everything that you could possibly need. If, however, you happen to be on the East Coast of the United States, I believe I can be of real assistance to you. My advice would be to start by going out with a guide who specialized in swordfishing with rod and reel — using his boat and his tackle. By no means invest in a large assortment of rods, reels, hooks, etc., until you have been out and have some idea of what you are up against. A 10/0 reel will not be of much use if you decide to go back to weakfishing.

The best of these men are to be found at Montauk, Long Island, although

I believe that there are boats available all along the coast from Long Island to Nova Scotia, but I have had no experience with any but the Montauk crew. These men fish the year round, going south in winter, and arriving in Montauk at about the time the swordfish do. They have, in nearly every instance, very good boats, as well as all the equipment that is necessary. Besides this, they are out every day, and are in touch with the local commercial men who know more about the movements of the swordfish than anyone else. I have found these guides all very keen, and willing to do everything in their power to get you a fish.

So much for the man who has no boat and has never done the fishing.

The next man to come along wants to know what's the best boat for sword-fishing with rod and reel.

Now, to answer this takes a lot of thought, because there are so many things that enter into this game. In the first place, the ideal boat for finding fish is most certainly not the best boat to fight him from, or to manoeuver about him when presenting the bait. Also, a small open boat in which you could fight him to the best advantage might be most uncomfortable when one of the not infrequent squalls suddenly appears between you and dry land.

Therefore, we must decide between the great big commercial fisherman, with seven to eight men in the mast (this type I think we will all admit is the best equipment to find a fish but out of the question when it comes to fighting him on a rod) and a small open boat with one fishing chair and no rigging to get in the way when the fish changes his course without taking you into his confidence.

We finally settle on a good seaboat from thirty to forty feet over-all with a large cockpit that is self-bailing, and lowsided enough to enable the man with the gaff to get at the fish as easily as possible. There should be one or two regular fishing chairs that can be turned in all directions, also a well-designed foot rest will be of great help during a four or five hour fight. In my opinion, a most necessary part of the ship's design is the location of the steering gear and controls, as I firmly believe that the ability of the skipper to see the fish or line at all times is a very large part of the battle. My idea on this point is to have the controls not only in the pilot-house but also on top of the cabin, where the man manoeuvering the boat has a clear view all around the horizon, and does not have to wait for the man fighting the fish to tell him what the fish is doing. This may not seem so important, but all I can say is, that if you have once fought a fish from a boat so equipped, you will never be satisfied to try to handle one from inside a pilot-house if you can help it.

I shall show a drawing of my "Alibi," which I think shows about all you need in the way of a boat for this work.

There are, of course, so many things to take into consideration when choosing a boat, that have nothing whatsoever to do with swordfishing, that the best thing I can do is to point out the requirements that seem to me most important, and let the fisherman decide whether the boat he has in mind, or may even own, can be used or not.

In the first place, at Montauk Point, the fish are found from five to twenty-five miles offshore. Therefore, I suggest that the boat be powered with two motors. I know that one two-hundred horsepower motor will drive a given boat faster than two one-hundred horsepower engines, but it is well worth taking into consideration that two motors give you two complete sets of parts which are more or less interchangeable. Remember you are outside the steamer lane, and while there is a big fleet of commercial boats that may pick you up, you have to be able to take care of yourself far more than you do in inland waters. Also, two motors permit you to cut out one, which gives you a trolling speed that might be hard to obtain with one big machine.

It is my opinion that two rudders, one located directly in back of each propeller, are far better than one, placed amidships, when it is necessary to follow a circling fish or when running with one engine, as you do when on the fishing grounds.

All these things may be only matters of opinion, but I can truthfully say that I have often come in with one motor, and at other times have had to use parts of both motors to keep one running. I have lost one of my rudders, and have had my steering cable break, but I still had a tiller packed away under the floor boards which came in very handy as I was crossing the bar at Fire Island Inlet when the cable parted. Oversized strainers on the gas lines may save you a few minutes of discomfort, as the tide-rips that you fish in most of the time seem to kick up a sea that will roll all the dirt and water out of your tanks, and do it just when you are trying to keep your eyes on a fin.

There can't be too much said in favor of ample fire-fighting apparatus, as well as something to hold fast to if you have to abandon ship. Most of the boats don't carry a tender, or if they do, it is not as good as a raft in rough weather.

Plenty of fresh water, and canned goods that don't have to be cooked, about cover the sensible things to have aboard. A sea anchor will be a blessing if you have to make any repairs, as it will keep you headed to the seas, and keep all the tools from rolling into the bilge. So much for the boat.

Now, having a boat equipped about as I have suggested, let's consider our gear.

One rod with 12 oz. tip, plain metal guides	$30.00
1200 yards in two lines of 600 yards each	28.80
One 9/0 star drag reel	100.00
18 yards of 150 lb. test, stainless steel leader wire	3.24
OR,	
3 made-up leaders and hooks at $3.00	9.00
6 toggle or Apex swivels	.90
2 gaff hooks, at least 4⅜ in. hook	8.00
1 leather harness	8.00
1 oil can	.40
1 flat-jawed cutting pliers	1.50
2 flat files	.60
6 12/0 Pflueger Sobey hooks	1.50
6 10/0 Pflueger Sobey hooks	1.50
1 or more 6 power field glasses (large field)	85.00 each
1 ice-box, as described in text	
2 bait knives	.50 each
1 medium-sized whetstone	1.50

My reason for suggesting tackle of this size is the result of six years' fishing off Montauk Point, starting early in the spring and ending in late September, with a total score of three broadbill and one marlin. Not very good fishing, you will say, but it is not the fish we caught that we must consider, but the ones that got away, some of them because the tackle was too heavy, and some because it was too light. I frankly admit that I discarded the 12/0 reel with 39 thread line, because I thought that we were pulling the hook out of the fish's jaws. I refused to use anything lighter than a 9/0 reel and 24 thread line, because I did not think that the lighter stuff would stand four or five hours of constant friction under the great strain on the tip and guides. My reason for insisting on

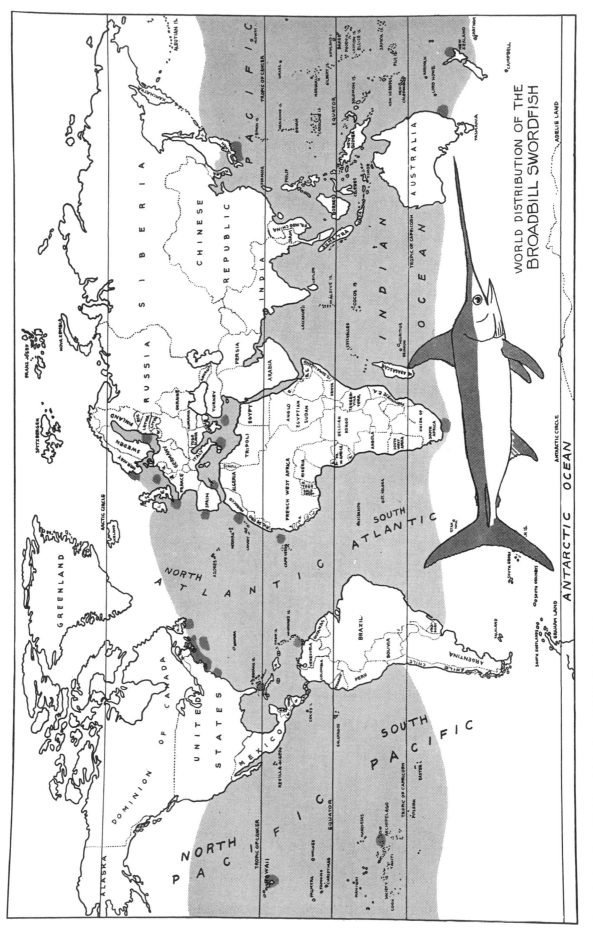

WORLD DISTRIBUTION OF THE
BROADBILL SWORDFISH

Drawn by Lynn Bogue Hunt from information supplied by Charles L. Lehmann.

all metal guides is that no man knows what a swordfish is going to do when he is hooked, and the number of times I have seen a rod slammed down on the deck by a fish that has seen the boat for the first time makes me positive that the chances of cracking an agate guide and having it cut the line are so great that it outweighs all the wear and tear that you save by having your rod equipped with them. I also shall never forget the feeling in the pit of my stomach when, after four hours in which a friend of mine had been fighting his second swordfish in one day (he had landed the first one), I saw the agate lining to the tip come out and slide slowly down the line. Although the fish was in his last struggles on the surface, in plain sight, we watched one strand of the line after the other fray out, and finally the last one parted, allowing our fish (which would have made an all-time record of two broadbill in one day) to sink slowly to the bottom.

So much for the rod.

The next and most important, as well as the most expensive, item to consider is the reel. The object of these notes is to suggest what equipment is necessary to land the average broadbill swordfish. Therefore we must leave it to the fisherman to make up his mind how much more equipment than I shall mention he wishes to buy, or how much more he wishes to pay for it, as it can be easily understood that there is practically no limit to price, where big game fishing tackle is concerned.

I think we can safely say that we will use a 9/0 reel, capable of holding six hundred yards of 24-thread line. It must have what is known as a star drag, as well as the free-spool attachment. It should also have a well-designed method of attaching the reel to the rod, as a fight lasting four or five hours will loosen a reel, unless it is almost one piece with the rod.

Six hundred yards of line, in my opinion, are rather more than is absolutely necessary, but the first fifty yards of a line get so much use that it is a good precaution to have enough line to permit you to cut off a frayed end, without having to splice or tie on more line.

I have never had a reel go bad on a swordfish, but I have never tried to land one on less than a 9/0, and so cannot say how small an outfit would do the trick. The reel must be able to stand at least 200 yards being taken without a let-up, with as much as fourteen to twenty pounds drag. It must have adequate methods of lubrication, and be made to stand salt water and plenty of it. The spool must be strong enough to withstand the swelling of the line when it gets wet, or jammed from too much drag. If the sides of the spool spread, they will jam against the side of the reel and part the line.

The line does not require much description. There are not many to choose from, and a linen line of 24 threads that will test about three pounds to the thread when wet will do the work. I must emphasize the fact that there is no economy in buying a cheap line. You save so little, and you risk so much, that only the best is good enough. Careful inspection of your reel to see that there is nothing that can rub or chafe the line, as well as a close examination of all guides and tip to see that they have not been bent or cracked so that they present the slightest rough or sharp edge, will save you a great deal more money than a cheap line. Many fish owe their freedom to the fisherman's failure to check his guides for cracks or rough places.

There is a good leather harness that puts the strain on a large area of the back, and hooks to the reel with snap hooks, that seems to be the most satisfactory rig I have found.

The swivel leader and hook can be bought all made up, which is the easiest way, although perfectly satisfactory rigs can be made up on the boat without much trouble. I think that a 12/0 hook and a 15 foot leader made of stainless steel of about 85 pounds test is about what you need.

A universal reel-seat, or just a plain leather one, firmly attached to the chair, is essential, as most of the pull of the fish, multiplied by the length of the rod, comes on this.

The fishing chair should be able to turn in all directions, and some of the best of them are capable of being locked in any position desired by the fisherman, which is a help.

A well-sharpened knife should be in a sheath within easy reach of the fisherman, so that, in the event of a backlash, he or someone else can cut the line and save the rest of the rig that might otherwise be pulled overboard.

The next on the list is the gaff. I have been using a standard 4⅜ inch hook on a long enough handle to reach at least three or four feet under water. This small hook will hold a fish when he is ready to quit, and it is my opinion that the gaff should not be used until the fish is practically dead.

The rest of the list speaks more or less for itself, with the exception of the ice box which, while not essential, helps a lot when bait is hard to get and has to be kept several days. I found that squid, when kept off the ice, but still at a temperature of freezing or a little less, retained their color and crispness, so that after three days, they were almost as good as fresh ones. The mackerel, which is a fish that gets soft very quickly, also lasts far better when kept dry but very cold. So I built an ice box which I will describe.

It consists of an insulated box 18 x 18 x 24 inches, through which is run an

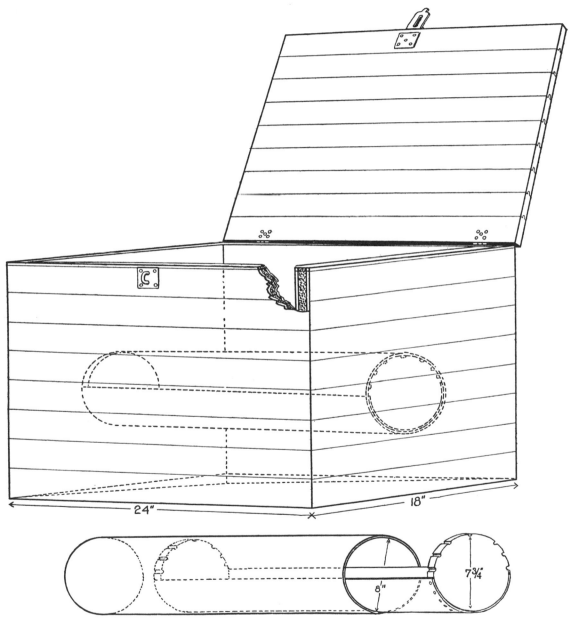

The Lehmann Bait Box.

ordinary 8 inch galvanized iron stove pipe, which is fastened to the back, but allowed to come through the front. Two circular pieces of wood are then cut out, which are small enough to slide inside the pipe. A sheet of galvanized iron is then tacked halfway around these round plugs, making a tray which will slide inside the pipe, the outside plug closing the pipe and the inside one touching the back of the box. Cracked ice and salt are then packed in the box around the pipe like an ice cream freezer, and the bait is put in the tray inside the pipe. This is a very simple thing to make, and I find it works beautifully.

Now, having acquired a boat and equipped it as I have suggested, let us assume that we are at Montauk Point, ready to take our first trip. Lady Luck is with us, and we have been able to get five or six beautiful fresh squid and a couple of mackerel from eight to twelve inches long. The weather is light air out of the southwest, and it is the early part of July. What more could a man want! So cast off and head for the Lighthouse, from which we take our point of departure, and mark our time carefully. At eleven miles an hour, we should run south by west for one hour and a half, unless we see something first. We now shut off one motor, and all hands really start to hunt for a fin.

On the way out, we must make up a few baits, because it takes about a half hour to prepare one, and we must have a second rig to put out if the swordfish knocks the first bait off the hook, as he is quite likely to do.

I shall do my best to describe the making up of a bait, and what it is expected to do after it is made up, but I am afraid it is going to be hard to follow unless you can watch it being done. We will start with the squid bait first, not that I think it is so much better than the mackerel, but it is so much tougher that it is more likely to stay on the hook after it has been struck.

The first thing to do is to thoroughly wash all the ink out of the squid, as this gets all over everything, and prevents you from seeing what you are doing. Next we lay the squid out on the bait board, and pass a piece of solid wire, which has been attached to the swivel, through the body of the squid in such a way that the leader will come out at the tail end of the squid, and the hook will be entirely covered by the cape-like body. In order to keep the tail of the squid from slipping down the leader and making a ball at the hook, a small ball of string is wrapped about the leader, at a point that will be just inside the tail, and when the split in the tail, made by drawing the swivel through the body of the squid and out the tail, is sewed up, the whole drag of the bait comes on the ball of

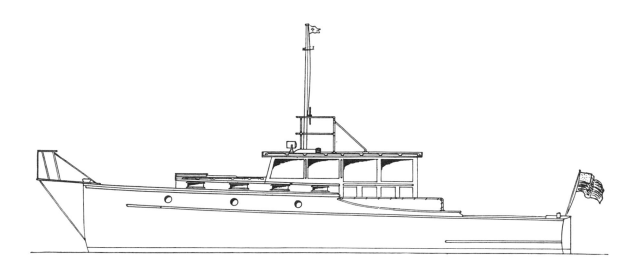

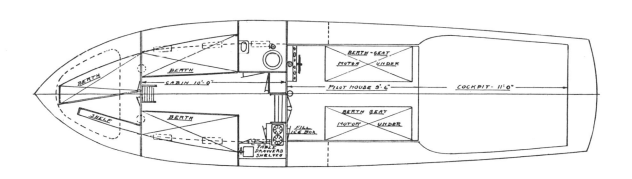

PLANS OF THE "ALIBI," 41 FOOT SWORDFISHERMAN.

Designed by Ralph H. Wiley.

Whole mackerel attached by nose to hook. Dotted lines show spine. Black marks show where spine is severed to make bait swim naturally.

Top view of whole mackerel, showing incision for removal of section of spine, also the hook as it protrudes from the back.

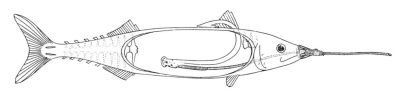

Side view of same bait as above, with side cut away to show position of hook, short chain and leader and section of spine removed. Bait towed by the nose attached to the leader by non-slipping knot.

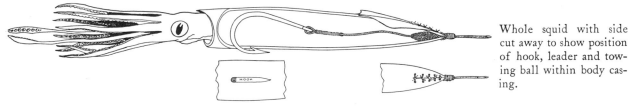

Whole squid with side cut away to show position of hook, leader and towing ball within body casing.

Bottom view of squid bait, showing protruding hook.

Top view of squid, showing incision for introduction of towing ball.

WHOLE MACKEREL AND SQUID BAITS AS RIGGED BY CHARLES L. LEHMANN.

string on the leader, which makes the bait troll perfectly true in the water. Great care should be taken to wrap the end of the squid that is up the leader in such a way that there will be a smooth joint, with no danger of slipping down into a ball.

Next we make up one of the mackerel baits. This requires a different method entirely. Instead of attaching the wire leader directly to the hook, we use a short piece of chain between the hook and the leader. The chain is flexible and permits us to lay the leader along the back of the hook, as shown in the drawing. This is necessary, because, after striking, and apparently killing his prey, the swordfish is supposed to return and swallow the fish headfirst, which he could not do if the point of the hook protruded from the fish pointing toward the head, as in the case of the squid bait. In order to do this, we split the fish down the back, starting directly back of the head and cutting enough to imbed the hook as shown in the drawing. Next, we remove enough of the backbone to make room for the hook and chain. Removing the backbone not only makes room for the hook and chain, but it makes the fish limber and much more lifelike. Having placed the hook in the fish with the point pointing aft and the leader folded back toward the head, we pull the swivel through the head of the fish and out the mouth. The mouth is then sewed up and the thread is attached to the leader in such a way that the pull all comes on the head of the fish and not on the hook. The fish is then carefully sewed up and the bait is ready to use.

Another method of using the mackerel is to attach it by the head, as shown in the diagram. This method works well, but requires some practice before the bait will troll right side up. The advantages are that the bait is easily and quickly made up. The backbone should be severed by passing a narrow knife through the fish at about two inch intervals, which makes the bait limber and lifelike. It also leaves the hook entirely uncovered, which I think increases the chances of getting fast to a fish.

There now remains only one thing more to do before we are ready to attach whichever bait we decide to use to the line, and that is to wet the line. This is most important, as it not only adds greatly to the strength, but it also permits you to put the line back on the reel after it has swelled, and removes all slack places, caused by drying out.

The procedure is very simple, and consists simply of permitting the line to run overboard until it is nearly all out and then stopping the boat until you have reeled it in again, taking particular care to distribute the line evenly on the spool and with a reasonable amount of tension.

We are now all set, out at sea with all hands keeping a sharp lookout, and possibly a swordfish over the crest of the next wave.

At this point, it behooves us to give a little thought to the problems that confront us. In the first place, you may ask why do commercial fishermen never fish for swordfish with a line, and why are so very few fish taken in this way? Of course, the answer to the first question is that it is so much easier and surer, and saves so much time, to take them on a harpoon, that it would not pay to use anything else. The answer to the second is that the swordfish seldom is feeding when we see him on the surface, but, to our sorrow, has probably just gorged himself, and is sleeping off the effects; hence his lack of interest in the prime morsel with which we are trying to tempt him. Put yourself in his place, and you will have a better idea of what we are up against. Suppose you had just finished a large Sunday dinner, and were stretched out on a porch chair in the sun, when the butler suddenly passed you a large plate of sandwiches. I am afraid he might get the plate broken over his head, but if not, at any rate he would meet what is known as sales resistance. There are several methods used to overcome this sales resistance which we encounter, none of which is altogether successful, I must confess. The procedure is about as follows, with certain variations which I shall endeavor to describe:

When the fish is sighted, the bait is put over and trolled far enough astern to permit the captain to get the bait in front of the fish without the fish crossing the boat's wake. Crossing the wake is apt to put him down. This can be done by crossing in front of the fish after you have come up behind him and passed him. The swordfish hunts by eye, not by smell, so that the bait must be near enough for him to see it. If he is hungry, he will attack the bait, at once slashing at it with his sword, at which time the drag is thrown off the reel and the bait is allowed to sink down, giving the fish the impression that he has killed it. Allowing the line to run off until he has come back and picked up the bait requires a lot of nerve, but if the bait moves after the strike, it may make the fish suspicious and cause him to sound. When he has picked up the bait you will notice the line begin to move slowly out at an increasing rate. This is the time to throw on the drag and strike him, as hard as you can.

A hungry fish, I am sorry to say, is the exception and not the rule, so we must consider how to interest the rest of them. This is where the fascination of swordfishing with rod and reel comes in. It is the same feeling of satisfaction that must be felt by a trout fisherman when he has gotten a rise on a fly tied by himself, when the other fishermen have been unable to get a strike on any kind.

The first swordfishing I ever did was with Tommy Gifford, who, I consider, is one of the best. No one could want to catch a fish as much as Tommy and not be good at it. He made up the most beautiful baits I have ever seen, but with all his knowledge and skill, there were plenty of fish that passed him by. If they were in the mood, they struck, and he handled the boat to perfection, but if not, he had to look for another.

The first swordfish I ever saw, we caught after fighting for four hours and thirty minutes. He weighed 430 pounds. The fish struck, after we had given him up and let the bait sink — not what he was supposed to do at all. The method used was to present the bait slowly, giving the fish plenty of time to look it over, and I believe this to be the most successful way when the fish is hungry, as there is a much better chance of his swallowing the bait.

The next man I fished with was Bill Fagen. Nobody could accuse Bill of not being keen, and no one could find fault with his baits. They worked beautifully, and as Bill's method was to present the bait at a good speed, with the idea of attracting the attention of a dormant fish and getting him to follow up and strike, the ability to make a bait troll was most important.

This method, I think, will produce more strikes, but the fish will be hooked in the jaw which is fibrous and has little strength, and so allows the hook to pull out. So we still have to admit it's anybody's guess. Bill and I managed to land one that weighed 393 pounds. He fought for four hours and thirty-one minutes, and struck in the conventional way, striking the bait, which was moving at a good speed, and picking it up at once.

Both Gifford and Fagen know as much as there is to know about swordfishing, but nevertheless whole seasons go by without their getting one, so we must come to the conclusion that we don't know it all by a long way.

The last man I fished with was Owen Duffy. He was mate with both Gifford and Fagen before he became captain, and a better fisherman it would be hard to find. He has several fish to his credit, one of which I caught with him, using an outrigger 45 feet long, built like a wireless mast, which skipped the bait over the surface of the water. It so happened that just as the fish was about to strike, the boat rolled, causing the bait to leave the water. The fish, thinking the bait was jumping, jumped with it, and made a beautiful strike. Perhaps the outrigger will be the solution of this fishing, but I am inclined to think not.

The only difference between fishing with an outrigger and the usual way is that the line, after being let out to the desired length, is attached to the end of the outrigger by means of a piece of thread, which breaks when the bait is struck, after which the procedure is the same. The advantages are that it is easier to place the bait in front of a circling fish, and the fish is less apt to get in the boat's wake. The disadvantages are that the fisherman is unable to regulate the length of line after it has once been attached to the outrigger. As it is frequently necessary to reel in or pay out line, according to the speed and direction the fish is moving, this is a great inconvenience.

Now, having gone over in our minds the different methods used and difficulties to be encountered, we check over our gear, and wonder of wonders, find that it is all on board. We now take the swivel end of one of the leaders, of which the baited end is in our little freezer, and attach it to the double line on the swordfish rig. Suddenly we hear from the lookout that hail which all hands have been waiting for.

"Swordfish! Swordfish!"

In a minute all is excitement, even among the old-timers, because this fish may be the one that has slept off the effects of his last meal and is ready to take an interest in the next one. The motors are shut down to very slow, and the best bait is reverently lowered over the stern and slowly allowed to slack back to about two hundred feet; then the drag is set for about twelve pounds and thrown on, causing the bait to come to the surface. By this time the boat has been manoeuvered into a position in back and to one side of that sickle-like fin and tail that is languidly slicing its way through the seas. Now we approach the fin and finally pass at a speed not much greater than that of the fish, and when the bait is approximately abreast of the fin we edge over so as to get the bait closer and closer to that great saucer-like eye, which will appraise it with interest or not, as the case may be. Is he moving any faster? I think he is, but not coming any closer. Now the rhythm of that tail begins ever so little to increase in speed. Now he is keeping pace with the bait, but still ten or twelve feet to one side. Will he see it? And if so, what will he do? Get ready to throw off that drag, and look out for a backlash when he hits the bait.

Atlantic record broadbill swordfish weighing 505 pounds. Caught off Montauk by A. Rex Flinn of Pittsburgh, Pa. Guide, "Bill" Hatch.

Broadbill swordfish caught by Charles L. Lehmann off Montauk Point. Length 14 ft. 6 in. Girth 60 in. Weight 430 pounds.

Wham! What happened?

"The rod was almost jerked out of my hand," yells the man with the rod.

But by this time one of the cool heads on board has thrown off the drag, and the captain has thrown out the clutches, while all hands watch the line to see whether the fish will pick up the bait, or whether he just took a good bat at it for the hell of it, as I sometimes think they do.

Suddenly the sag is out of the line, and the spool begins to revolve with little jerks, then more steadily, and now with a rush that may end in a back lash, if the fisherman loses his head.

"Strike him!" yells the captain, and throws in both clutches at once, yanking open the throttles. There is a tremendous roar from the exhausts as the boat leaps ahead. The drag is on and the young man has struck with all his might, holding on for dear life, while, with horrified eyes he watches the line go tearing out over the stern, as though he had tossed his hook into the back door of a subway train. Smaller and smaller grows the size of the whirling spool. The temptation is to tighten down on the brake, and just as he is about to do this, one of the old-timers leans over and slacks it off a notch or two, because, as the spool of line gets smaller, the tension of the drag increases.

Now the boat has been stopped, and the line is only moving out in short jerks, showing that the first run is over, but still no slack must get in that line, whatever happens. However, we have time to get our breath and get on the leather harness, so that it will not take off too much meat during the next four hours' fight.

We now back up slowly and regain about half the line, but lose most of it again in a long series of jerks that make your arms and shoulders ache. So it goes, back and forth, now gaining, now losing, until somebody yells:

"He's coming up!"

The line is almost level with the water, and away out, much further than you thought, you suddenly see a great splash, and a long sword describes an arch, back and forth, and then disappears, not to be seen again for an hour. Now he is so close that the double line is at the end of the rod, but just as you have come to the conclusion that there is not so much to this fight after all, the fish sees the boat and away he goes. All that hard work for nothing. The thought now occurs to you that you don't want a swordfish as badly as you did, and you can't imagine what ever made you think that you did want one. But whether you have caught the fish, or he has caught you, you can't give up now, so you work away until he finally is back where he was, and this time you get a turn or two of double line on your reel and you tighten down on the drag, knowing that you have twice the breaking strain you had. Foot by foot you get him up to the boat, until he is almost near enough to use the gaff. The fight is nearly over, but not quite. When the gaff is used, unless he is almost dead, a lot may happen. One loop of that wire leader about a man's wrist might mean the loss of a hand, so make haste slowly. Have a sling ready to put on his tail as soon as you can, because until that is fast, he's not your fish. That being done, all hands on the block and fall, and in he comes.

The end of a perfect day!

Having read over these notes, and realized that I have tried to condense into these few pages all the experience and knowledge which is the result of watching the best men do everything in their power to make these contrary fish take a bait, I am reminded of the man who said that he was going to learn to play the violin if it took him all day.

There is this to be said, however, which should be an incentive to all who take up this sport — that the correct method has not yet been hit upon, I am convinced, and it is still anyone's game.

GIANT TUNA

Francis Low handling the rod aboard his boat "Mullet."

CHAPTER VII.

TUNA

BY

FRANCIS H. LOW

THE tuna (*Thunnus thynnus*) has played a major part in the fishing world since the days when the mighty Caesars ruled the world. His flesh sold on the market streets of Rome along with nightingale tongues and delicacies from the Orient. There were no feather lures in those days or anglers who gazed stupefied at 12/0 reels stripped clean by one rush of these bronze torpedoes. The tuna was merely a food fish and treated accordingly. He was netted in enormous quantities and shipped to market much the same way as he is now, only in galleys instead of in high-powered fishing smacks equipped with modern inventions such as radios, refrigeration, etc.

The slaughter of these magnificent fish has gone on down through the ages and it seems impossible that they have been able to withstand the drain on the supply. The answer to this is due to the enormous number and the fact that tuna never stay long in one place. They have to keep moving because of their enormous appetite, and as they always travel in schools, they soon clean out the bait in any locality and have to move on in search of more.

There are three varieties of tuna; — the bluefin, the Allison and the yellowfin. The bluefin tuna are by far the most numerous, and are the species to which this chapter is devoted. The Allison and the yellowfin tuna are most common on the West Coast, although one specimen of the yellowfin variety was chased ashore at Fort Lauderdale last spring by a large shark. This particular fish weighed 132 pounds. There have been several schools reported off Bimini but very few taken.

The bluefin tuna, besides being the most numerous, are by far the largest of the tuna family. They have been reported up to 2000 pounds but the largest I know of weighed 1260 pounds dressed, and was harpooned by Captain Herman P. Gray, famous fishing guide. On the Atlantic side, they range from Bimini to Nova Scotia. The small tuna are taken in Florida and Bahama waters all winter, but the large fish suddenly put in an appearance off Bimini about the middle of May and work north to Nova Scotia, where they arrive in the middle of the summer. Where do they spend the winter? *"Quién sabe!"* Possibly in the Caribbean. So far, no one has been able to successfully land a big tuna whole off Bimini, due to the great number of sharks which infest those waters. On the other hand, the anglers, who have fished the Nova Scotia waters, have been extremely successful in landing quite a few of the big ones. The world's record of 956 pounds was taken last summer by Mr. Thomas Howell of Chicago. The reason for the large catches of big fish here is due to great concentration in a relatively small area. One has only to be present during the run of herring and he can be almost assured of hooking at least one. However, as we are only concerned here with tuna of local waters, we will confine ourselves to New Jersey and Long Island.

Up to recent years, the tuna or "horse mackerel," as it is often called, was never regarded as anything but a menace. There were no deep water sport fishermen, and the tuna raised Cain with the commercial fishermen, especially the bluefishermen. The dories would chum up a school of blues when suddenly a great tuna would appear, smash all the lines and scatter the bluefish. The air would become filled with Portuguese and Jersey "cuss" words, but to no avail. The only thing to do would be to move. Occasionally, a fish would be harpooned out of spite, but there was no thought of taking one on a rod and reel, principally because there was no rod or reel powerful enough to stop these monsters, or a boat fast enough to keep up with their long runs.

About 1913, a few hardy anglers began to venture off the Jersey Coast in the old fashioned crooked skiffs powered with a make-and-break gas engine. Equipped with handlines, "knuckle-duster" reels and "hickory clubs" they caught bluefish and a few small tuna on lead and cedar squids. As the products of the machine age became more and more developed, tackle and boats became more modernized and consequently larger fish were taken. However, no real large tuna were captured, nothing over 100 pounds. Big fish were hooked but not for long, as the tackle would not hold. Lines that tested only a pound or so to the thread could not stand the strain. Many stories came in about tuna as big as dories, with eyes like dinner plates, that would grab the cedar squids and strip the reels in ten seconds flat. Most anglers avoided these monsters as much as possible, but one of the greatest anglers that ever lived, who now rests among the immortals, decided to have a try at them. That man was William G. Scheer, who with his son, Otto, were the pioneer tuna fishermen off the Jersey Coast. Mr. Scheer saw that the lines of his day were not strong enough so he had special wire lines made to stand the strain. His method of procedure was as follows: He first made friends with the commercial fishermen and then arranged that they should telegraph him when big tuna were reported. Upon receiving a wire as to the whereabouts of the big tuna, he would set sail in his yacht "Venture" and join the smacks. When a tuna was raised by one of the chumming dories, the fisherman would raise a boot on an oar and Mr. Scheer would lower a small boat and go over to where the dory was anchored. A cash prize was given for each fish raised and an additional one for each one hooked. Mr. Scheer hooked several fish in this manner and fought one for nine hours, the steel line eventually breaking. He was never able though to land a large tuna. Zane Grey then came East with his brother and followed much the same procedure. He met with all kinds of hard luck, and never succeeded in landing any, but in a letter last fall he told me of seeing fish taken in Jersey pound nets that went well over 1,000 pounds. There is one record of a large one being taken off Jersey in 1915 by Mr. Jacob Wirtheim on rod and reel, which weighed 285 pounds.

My first introduction to big tuna was in the fall of 1931. We were trolling for bluefish in a Portuguese chum line, on Commodore Newbold Herrick's "Gannet," when suddenly I had a terrific strike. The 18 thread hummed off the 6/0 reel at a great speed and we were barely able to turn the boat and follow the fish before the reel had been stripped clean. We fought this fish for forty minutes and then the light piano wire leader parted. I was heartbroken, but this soon gave way to the satisfaction of knowing that big tuna were to be found a scant twenty miles from the Woolworth Building. Father, Captain Fred Wicht and myself immediately planned a campaign against these "critters." Our first piece of information came from the diary of a bygone angler who told of having fought a tuna for three hours near Ambrose Lightship, only to have his line parted by the swells from the wake of the "Lusitania" as she passed outward bound, on her last voyage. Captain Fred then got some valuable information from the Canarsie lobstermen and bottom fishermen. They reported seeing many huge tuna in the early fall.

In 1932, Captain Wicht and I equipped my 22 foot Jersey skiff "Mullet," with a swivel chair, and a few other weird gadgets. Armed with a 9/0 Vom Hofe reel, 24 thread line, a heavy split bamboo rod and a barrel of bunkers, we made several expeditions around Ambrose but caught nothing but a few ling and dogfish.

The summer of 1933, we spent fishing for swordfish off Montauk, with little success. We hooked and lost three, one of which I had on for 2 hours and 35 minutes, after which he proceeded to foul the line on the bottom of the "Akela." I dove overboard to try to clear the line and nearly succeeded in cutting all my fingers off. Freddie finally cleared the line with a boathook but the fish had recovered enough strength to make a final dash for China, where to the best of my knowledge he is enjoying a very pleasant old age. We returned to Cedarhurst about the first of September, extremely disgusted with fishing in general. No sooner had we arrived, however, than our hopes were rekindled by the news that Francis Geer had hooked and lost several big tuna off Manasquan, and that the bluefishermen off Jersey had seen several. We immediately put the "Mullet" in condition and on September 11th, headed bright and early for the ridge northwest of Ambrose Lightship. This year we had strengthened our equipment by the addition of a 12/0 Vom Hofe reel and 600 yards of 39 thread Ashaway line. Instead of a bamboo rod, I had a huge hickory club, as big around as a baseball bat, and as limber as a lead pipe. This I was very shortly to learn was not the type of rod to use on a big tuna.

We anchored about a half mile northwest of the Lightship and started chumming with ground-up bunkers. Freddie put a whole mackerel on my 13/0 swordfish hook and I let it drift back to the chum line some fifty feet. About eleven o'clock, I had a terrific strike and the line smoked off the reel. Captain Fred and young Harold Herrick got the motor going and the anchor up. The fish made a run of some four hundred yards and then turned and made for the

FRANCIS H. LOW WITH HIS U. S. RECORD TUNA OF 705 POUNDS.

boat. We got out of the way and managed to get a tight line again. This fish would surface and circle the boat a hundred yards away. As it was slick calm, we could see him plainly but had no idea of his great size. After surfacing a while, he would then sound and head for sea, towing the "Mullet" after him. This performance kept up for five hours, at which point I thought my back would break, as all the play of the fish was taken up there instead of by the rod. Incidentally, I don't believe the rod bent two inches during the whole performance. I was exhausted and felt ready to cash in, when suddenly the tuna made a long run and then lay motionless on the bottom. We put the boat in a position directly over the fish, which lay in some seventy feet of water, and after a "wee bracer," I proceeded to pump him up. Although this method is perhaps the best way to break a line, had I used the conventional method of slowly circling at a distance and procuring a better leverage, I would have lost him surely as he was only hooked in the side.

I have never had such a thrill as I did when that great forked tail shot out of water a scant two feet from my nose. Captain Fred grabbed the leader and in my excitement I proceeded to break two perfectly good swordfish gaffs, jabbing them into an already stone-dead tuna. We put ropes around his tail and towed him over to a nearby commercial fisherman, where, with the aid of a steam winch, our prize was lowered into the "Mullet." Upon reaching shore the fish was placed in a truck and taken to the nearest tested scales where it was found to weigh 705 pounds — a United States record.

This tuna taught us many things. First, and most important, that fish of this size could be caught close to New York. Second, that a small, fast boat which can be easily handled is essential. Third, a man with unerring judgment and a quick thinking mind to handle it is equally important. The main secret of big game fishing lies in the boatman. I don't care how good a fisherman a man is, he is absolutely lost without a good guide that can be depended on to do the right thing at the right time. We would have lost the 705 pound tuna a dozen times if it had not been for Captain Fred's split-second thinking. The fourth thing is don't use tackle so heavy that it tires you more than the fish. After much experimenting, we found that a fairly limber hickory tip from 18 to 22 ounces was the most practical. The rod must be strong enough to stand the strain of towing a small boat, and to lift the weight of a dead tuna from the bottom; as I have found that most big tuna fight to the finish and then plunge to the bottom in a death flurry from which they have to be raised by "pumping." I prefer hickory to bamboo as it will take more severe punishment, even though both ends almost meet after a long fight. As far as reels go, I think a 12/0 is the most practical. A 9/0 is a little small and the 16/0 is too awkward. In fishing Long Island and Jersey waters, one does not need a mile of line. A 12/0 will hold 600 yards of 39 thread line which I think is long and strong enough to hold a fish up to seven or eight hundred pounds. The only time that I feel that this is too light is in raising a dead fish from the bottom. For this reason, I had a line made last summer that consisted of 50 yards of 72 thread line backed by 500 of 39 thread. This, however, failed, as the first big tuna I hooked broke the line at the splice.

As a tuna's head comprises approximately a third of his body and contains a huge mouth, a large hook is necessary. A 13/0 Sobey Pflueger is none too big. It is important though to have this hook filed to a needle point, and the cutting surface as sharp as a razor, as a tuna has a mouth of iron and it takes a hard strike to "sink it." To the hook we attach a heavy 16 foot stainless steel cable.

The summer of 1934 found us "rarin' to go" after the big ones and as soon as the first reports of fish came in, we made several expeditions to the Ambrose grounds, from which we returned empty handed. Francis Geer got four one day about two miles south of the Lightship, ranging from 96 to 231 pounds. Except for that one day, the fish seemed to be offshore. As a result we determined to play around the bluefish smacks, which were anchored some 35 miles southeast of Debs Inlet. When in doubt as to the whereabouts of big tuna, the safe bet is to fish among the smacks. They chum so heavily that they are bound to attract a great number of fish. We kept on the good side of the skippers by keeping them well supplied with cigarettes, papers and magazines, in return for which they were only too glad to give us all the information they could.

The morning of September 16th found us rolling and pitching in the midst of the smacks. It was blowing hard from the southeast and spitting rain. The heavy ground swells made it almost impossible to hold anchor and we were glad to be on board the "Akela" rather than the little "Mullet." We ran up alongside the "William A. Morse" and upon hailing her, learned that the big tuna had been raised the day before. We then decided to have a try at it and accordingly anchored a hundred yards to leeward. After having made the anchor line fast to a swordfish keg, we put over two big rigs and a couple of bluefish lines and started chumming. We caught a nice mess of blues but for a long time nothing exceptional happened. While Dad was having a siesta in the forward cabin, and Captain Fred was having lunch on the bridge, suddenly the line began to scream off the 12/0 so fast that the reel became hot. Instantly all was confusion. Everybody tried to do seven things at once. In vain I tried to turn the fish by clamping down on the drag but I might just as well have tried to turn the "Bremen." Suddenly the line went slack and I reeled in the remains only to find that the splice between the 72 thread and the 39 thread lines had pulled out. Feeling very much like the man who locked the stable door after the horse had been stolen, I tied another hook and leader on the end of the 39 thread line and cast it over again. Within five minutes, I had another strike but this time we were all set. The anchor buoy was cut loose, the motors started and the battle was on. This fish started off on a slow ponderous run right through the thirty odd smacks anchored around us. We almost died of fright a dozen times, fearing that the tuna would foul on some anchor cable, but for once the gods were with us. We cleared the fleet and headed out to sea, stern first. As the tuna went to windward against the heavy seas, we shipped a great deal of water which added to my discomfort, as I was drenched. After several long runs, this fish circled the boat several times and then made a long rush to the bottom. As the fish had only been on about an hour, we could not believe it was dead. I pumped it up very carefully, expecting a rush any minute, and you can imagine our surprise when it came to the surface, belly up and stone dead. In an hour and ten minutes, we had a rope around his tail and had him hoisted up on the davits. From then, it was only a few minutes until he was safely stowed in the cockpit and we were back trying to find the anchor buoy. It is hard to understand why this tuna which weighed 550 pounds was so easily killed, especially when he was only lightly hooked. The only answer I can give is that this fish was very fat, due to living around the smacks for some time. He had apparently been gorging himself and was all out of condition.

The following week we hooked into a tuna that behaved in a far different manner. He never made any long rushes but just plugged near the boat. I would get in 50 yards of line and then he would take 50. He would then circle the boat on the surface, his tail showing, and pushing a huge wave in front of him. It was impossible to tire him, but the same did not hold for me. After three hours and a half, I thought my back would break and stars began to gyrate in front of me. When eight bells struck (the performance started at noon), I was ready to let the tuna take me home as a trophy. However, having been administered a slight tonic of a well-known brand, I was again prepared to do or die; preferably die. Suddenly there was a loud report as the big hickory rod snapped into a dozen splinters and I was pitched into the scuppers. As far as we were concerned, it was all over, as the fish was disqualified. Much to our surprise the line had not parted and the fish was still on. Captain Fred put on a pair of gloves and handlined the half-dead tuna to the surface. We gaffed him and slung him into the cockpit where he was soon dispatched with the aid of two clubs. This fish weighed only 320 pounds, but had apparently been raised on a combination of steel squid and sucker fishermen. He was hooked deeper than the first fish and was bleeding when brought to the surface. I hope I do not mix up with many more of this type.

Before I close the first part of this chapter, I will try to answer a few of the thousand and one questions asked me with regard to fishing for big tuna. The first is, "How can it be developed into a poor man's sport?" The answer to this is rather simple. Fish long enough and you will soon be as poor as you wish. Five or six men cannot charter a boat and go big tuna fishing. It is a one-man job. If you fish four or five lines you are sure to get in a mess and lose an opportunity, let alone taking a chance on someone's being pulled overboard. In fishing for these fish you must have patience and forget about everything else. The strike is just as apt to come when you are pulling up a porgy from the bottom as at any other time, and then you are out of luck. In three years, we hooked only four big tuna and landed three, which is a good percentage, but when you think of the time and effort put in, it is not a lot of fish. Another point which I wish to mention is that I would not advise anyone who is not in good physical condition to tackle these big fish, as the results might be disastrous. The next question that comes up is, "When is the best time to fish?" That is almost impossible to answer. Tuna will strike at almost anything when they are feeding, but when they are full, they will not touch a thing. I have seen them swim by even the choicest live ling, and yet when they were taking, gulp down a rotten bunker. Nor does the weather seem to affect the big tuna, except that we have had best luck on cloudy days, probably because the heavy leader cannot be so easily seen. A light southwest or northwest wind is usually the best for most offshore fishing, but both big tuna we took last summer were taken in hard, rainy southeasters. Some wind helps as it ruffles up the water and the fish do not get scared. It is almost impossible to chum in a hard blow, as the boat is sure to swing out of the chum line and it is hard to handle a fish.

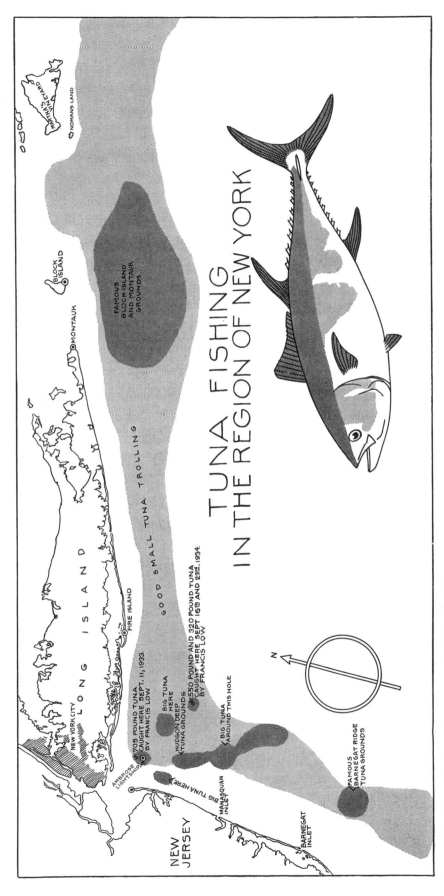

TUNA FISHING
IN THE REGION OF NEW YORK

MARTHAS VINEYARD

NOMANS LAND

BLOCK ISLAND

MONTAUK

FAMOUS BLOCK ISLAND AND MONTAUK GROUNDS

NEW YORK CITY

LONG ISLAND

FIRE ISLAND

GOOD SMALL TUNA TROLLING

705 POUND TUNA CAUGHT HERE SEPT. 11, 1933. BY FRANCIS LOW

BIG TUNA HERE

HUDSON DEEP TUNA GROUNDS

550 POUND AND 320 POUND TUNA CAUGHT HERE SEPT 16th AND 23rd, 1934. BY FRANCIS LOW

AMBROSE LIGHTSHIP

BIG TUNA AROUND THIS HOLE

MANASQUAN INLET

BIG TUNA HERE

NEW JERSEY

BARNEGAT INLET

FAMOUS BARNEGAT RIDGE TUNA GROUNDS

N

Drawn by Lynn Bogue Hunt from information supplied by Francis H. Low.

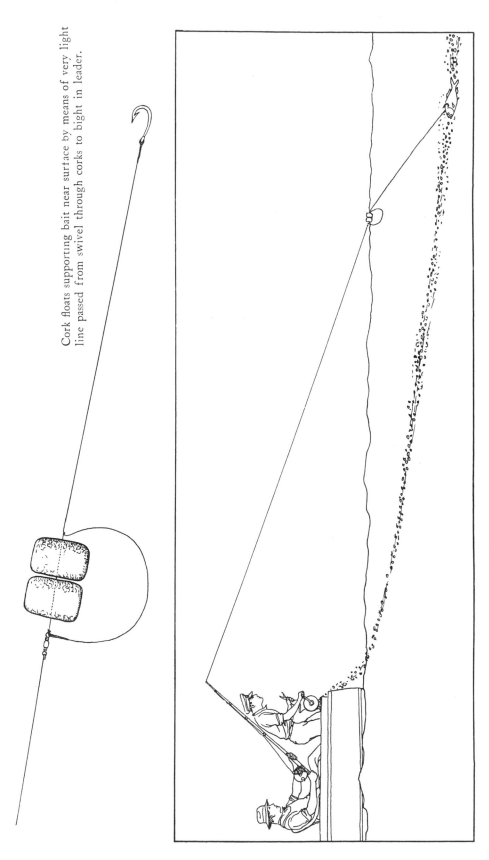

Cork floats supporting bait near surface by means of very light line passed from swivel through corks to bight in leader.

Drawn by Lynn Bogue Hunt from information supplied by Francis H. Low.

CHUMMING, BAITING AND FISHING FOR GIANT TUNA.

To summarize the sport of big tuna fishing, I will try to give a brief description of the procedure. First, find out where the tuna have been last seen. The chances are that they will remain in one locality for a few days. As it is impossible to raise a heavy anchor and get underway before the big tuna has run off all the line, it is best to tie the end of your anchor rope to a buoy so that it may be slipped "at an instant's notice." In chumming, at least 200 pounds of bunkers should be used. Although this sounds like a lot of bait, it will only last about six hours because chum streaks should be continuous and fairly heavy. I have found that tying a few light corks at the swivel will float the heavy leader and the bait in such a manner that at about 100 feet, it will lie in the middle of the chum slick.

The method of attaching the corks is as follows: A light line that will break, such as sail twine, is run through the corks, one end being fastened to the swivel and the other to the leader in such a way that a loop is formed in the leader. When a fish strikes, the twine will break, allowing the corks to float away and giving the fish free play.

At all times, watch your chum line so that you can see any swirl that will indicate the presence of big tuna. In baiting the hook, I suggest hooking the bait so that it will lie in a natural position in the water. Although the rod may be laid down in the boat with a light drag, keep an eye on it at all times and be ready for the strike. The minute a tuna strikes, set a good tight drag. At the same time, have somebody cast the buoy loose, start the motors and prepare to follow the fish. In fighting a big tuna, never get so close that you cannot anticipate his next move. Many fish have been broken off because the anglers became over-enthusiastic and tried to bring them in too soon. The result was that the fish made a sudden dive and either broke the rod or the line, or else fouled itself in the propeller. Do not attempt to bring your fish to gaff until he is either dead or thoroughly exhausted.

In chumming for big tuna, I have found that in nine cases out of ten, bluefish were raised first. After catching seven or eight, suddenly they would leave and that was the time to look out for the big tuna.

As a last little hint, I suggest lowering a line to the bottom, armed with a few small hooks in the hopes of catching a ling or porgy, because on a calm day especially, a live ling or porgy will prove deadly where all other baits will fail.

We now turn to the small tuna which, as far as the catching is concerned, might almost be regarded as a different fish. I have taken small tuna chumming only once. That was last summer when Dad, Herm Gray and myself caught thirteen from the "Akela" off Manasquan. These fish ran from 47 to 55 pounds and offered grand sport on light tackle. The old-fashioned way of taking small tuna was to troll a heavy single-hook cedar squid some forty feet behind the boat. A good many fish were lost by this rig, as the heavy squid very often tore out. In the summer of 1926, offshore trolling was revolutionized by the introduction of the famous Japanese feather lure which my father, Ethelbert Ide Low, imported from California. These lures proved deadly for any fish that would take a trolling bait. This made trolling for tuna doubly exciting, for not only were more tuna taken, but one never knew what was going to strike next. It might be a big blue, a bonito, dolphin, and sometimes a marlin.

Tuna are very curious fish and love a lot of fuss in the water. For this reason, boats that throw a big propeller wash seem to get more fish than those that slip through the water with no wake. There are lots of ways to attract tuna. Boats that have no wash, sometimes tow a whole automobile tire right under the stern. Others chromium plate their propellers. Another effective attraction is the brilliant-colored wooden or metal teaser. However, I am inclined to agree with a good many boatmen who claim that the best place for a teaser is in a store window. The reason for this is that if you do not watch it like a hawk, it will foul every line overboard in no time. As a substitute for a teaser, we put over as many lines as we can. Six or seven feathers give a good imitation of a school of squid. We usually stagger them by having some under the stern about twenty feet back and then running the rest back to about seventy-five feet. When it is found out at what distance the fish are taking best, the other lines can be easily adjusted. The same holds for trolling speeds. We have found that eight miles an hour was about right but there are times when the fish seem to take better at a slower speed. While eight miles is all right for tuna, it is a little fast for marlin and other fish, although I once hooked a bonito while doing sixteen. The result was startling.

It seems hard to think of one or two men handling six rods at once but I have seen it done many times. We have rod holders on either side of the coaming and then put two more in the chair sockets. These are made doubly secure by a snap hook which fastens to the reel. I have even committed the horrible offense of sticking a rod in the flagstaff socket. So far I have only broken one tip, and I never did like that one anyway. Newbold Herrick has designed an ingenious rod holder that proved very effective. He built a large brass candelabrum that screwed into a deck plate. This rig alone takes care of three rods. Another trick that boatmen use is to throw the boat into a tight circle when a fish is hooked. By always keeping one tuna on the hook, the school is kept right under the stern, attracted by the struggles of their companion. I saw Bill Fagen do this last summer and catch thirty tuna while a dozen boats circling around him failed to get a strike. I would not advise doing this with very many lines overboard as they are sure to foul.

Charlie Lehmann has devised another ingenious method of catching small tuna. He takes four or five one-gallon jugs and ties about twenty feet of line to the handle of each one and then sets them up on the after deck. When the tuna strikes, it pulls the jugs overboard and then the dancing jug is chased all over the ocean. When four or five fish strike at the same time, it is quite a job to keep track of all of them. Although this is not sporting from a rod and reel fisherman's point of view, it affords a lot of amusement.

As I mentioned before, one is very likely to raise a marlin while trolling for tuna. While marlin have been taken on feather jigs, I recommend while trolling that a cut bait be kept ready on ice for any emergency. When a marlin is raised behind feathered jigs, put over the cut bait and reel in the feathers, because you will have a much better chance of getting him. Dolphin and bonito will strike a feather readily.

Before closing this chapter on Long Island and Jersey trolling, it is only fair to say a word about the bluefish. As I have already mentioned, a good many are taken while chumming for big tuna. However, the commonest method is by trolling. Bluefish do not readily strike a fast-moving bait although occasionally big fish are taken in this manner. In trolling for bluefish, a slightly smaller hook and lighter leader are used. Instead of trolling eight miles an hour, four is about the right speed. The feather should be trolled about 150 feet or more behind the boat. Sometimes 300 feet is none too far, depending upon whether or not the fish are feeding on the surface or just below.

In closing, I will say that boats for small tuna and bluefish can be chartered from Montauk Point, Bayshore, Babylon, Lindenhurst, Freeport, Far Rockaway and Sheepshead Bay on the Long Island side, and from Shark River, Manasquan and Beach Haven on the Jersey side. The price for a day's outing runs from $25 to $35 a day, and split among four or five anglers, a good day's sport can be had for about $5.00. On some boats this includes tackle; on others all the necessary equipment can be hired for $2.00 or $3.00 extra.

[153]

Photos by courtesy of Otto J. Scheer.

Solid line indicates passage of the boat. Broken line shows where the bait was trolled past the rock where the fish was lying.

Showing broad beam and comfortable cockpit arrangement.

Ideal boat of shallow draft and great stability used for trolling inshore.

Five striped bass totaling 143 pounds.

CHAPTER VIII.

STRIPED BASS

BY

OTTO J. SCHEER

HE striped bass, *Roccus lineatus*, a native shore fish of the Atlantic Coast of the United States from northern Florida to southern Maine, is most highly esteemed as both a game and a food fish. This beautiful striped salt water fish, being anadromous, ascends the fresh water rivers of the Coast for breeding the same as our salmon and shad, the spawning season being generally about the same time as the shad or directly following.

This fish is known to have been taken by casting from the shore as well as from boats and in nets, miles above tide water and swiftly running rapids. They will ascend very swift rapids and are often injured in doing so, which accounts for the frequent scars found on these fish. After spawning they return to the salt water in a sluggish, weakened, poor condition, as proven by the fish taken at this season of the year. On their ascent the gills and bodies are usually found to contain large quantities of lice from which they are freed by fresh water.

It is generally believed that the striped bass does not spawn until it reaches a fair size and the roe in the large bass are decidedly larger than in other fish their comparative size.

These fish many years ago were caught both by sportsmen and market fishermen far up the Hudson, Connecticut, Thames, Potomac, Susquehanna, Delaware and other coastal rivers in the spawning season. The State of Maryland has admirably placed a closed season on striped bass above tide waters from December 1st to June 1st and also has restricted taking them over 15 pounds.

Following the spawning season they return to the salt water and, unlike the anadromous salmon and shad, stay close to the ocean shores or in the bays and sounds, and so furnish endless sport to the surf caster on the ocean shores and to others trolling in the bays, sounds and the mouths of our rivers.

Mention must be made of a most admirable act of the United States Bureau of Fisheries in the transplanting of this superb Atlantic shore fish to the Pacific Ocean where a few hundred fish have so thrived and multiplied that at this time they are believed to be as abundant on the Pacific Coast as on the Atlantic.

This fish in Massachusetts, Rhode Island, Connecticut, New York and New Jersey is generally referred to as the "striped bass," whereas in Delaware, Maryland, Virginia and Southern States it is usually called "rock fish" or "rock."

Although considered a migratory fish, the striped bass should not be classed so in the same sense as the salmon and shad, or the tuna and mackerel, or bluefish and weakfish, as the migrations of the bass are really local and not oceanic. In very severe winters they have been found frozen in outlets into Long Island Sound and in some of the fresh water rivers of New Jersey.

The foods of this delectable game fish vary greatly with the seasons, conditions and locations. It is well known that they feed on eels, sardines and small fish, not even disdaining the baby blowfish, fiddler crabs, blue crabs, shrimp, worms, squid and sea insects.

During the summer and fall months preceding and following storms they are a most temperamental fish, refusing to take all sorts of baits and lures and often move from grounds where they are usually most abundant. The temperament and diet combined with the craftiness of this fish and his natural habitat make him a true test for the sportsman.

From the earliest colonial days striped bass were taken for sport and food by surf casters from the ocean shores. The methods, lures and baits of this type of fishing have changed with the times, and thousands yearly enjoy this sport. Others were caught in the quiet waters of the bays, sounds and lower reaches of the rivers from small trolling rowed boats, using the various natural foods as bait. The more adventurous sportsmen on the ocean shores occasionally launched small boats through the surf and fished just beyond the breakers with rowed or sailed boats. This, however, except in large runs of fish, proved a hard task for the guide and often resulted in a wetting for the sportsman.

With the advent of dependable power for small boats, trolling changed. Now there are small boats available with heavy bottoms, high sides and protected propellers, very maneuverable and powered with quiet motors, making it possible to fish among the rocks and just beyond the break of the surf, and sometimes edging inshore between the swells, permitting the trolling of baits very close inshore where the striped bass live. The power enables one to fish and hunt them over miles of coast in a few hours which would take days to do with a rowed boat. The same methods have been used in the quiet waters of Long Island Sound, Chesapeake and other bays with the same result, enabling the sportsman to try various grounds and find his fish without causing physical hardship to the guides.

In the Chesapeake the drone spoon has proven a great success, while on the Long Island Shore, especially at Montauk, the Japanese feather lure, combined with worms, with the hook rigged well up into the feather, has proven a tremendous success.

In using the feather bait it is essential that it is trolled at sufficient speed that the feathers wiggle, in order to give it a live, fish-like appearance. Too slow a speed with the feather produces no results. When a fish strikes the feather or a drone spoon at this speed, the sportsman needs no further notice and it is seldom that the striking fish is not hooked. Over rocky ground it is advisable to use a long, fine steel leader and a line of sufficient strength to turn the fish on his first rush, as the striped bass will bore down and run behind a rock and so cut the line. Over muddy or sandy bottom a lighter line is more desirable.

A noteworthy trait of the striped bass, which has been observed many times on quiet days with very clear water, is, that when the trolling boat comes near them, they will run inshore the majority of times, although they have a better chance to evade the boat by going offshore; while other fish will run offshore. If a bass is lying beside a big rock, and the boat nears him on the same side, he will not rush off like other fish, but will skulk around the other side of the rock and lie there until the boat passes. These fish are so wary that an unnecessary noise in a boat is considered a great offense and muffled oars and expert boatmen are insisted upon.

Striped bass like eddies of running water, both salt and fresh, and on their way up and down the fresh water rivers in the spring they are usually found in eddies created by deep holes in rivers or behind large boulders where they lie in wait for their food and rush out to take it on its way downstream. In channels of bays they are found on edges of stunt banks where parts of the bank have fallen in, behind which they wait for passing food, or at intersections of small dreans where they lie in wait for food coming down into the channels.

In Long Island Sound and Rhode Island they are found at points and in channels or deep holes along the shore where tides create eddies and where they lie in wait for passing foods.

On the Rhode Island shore they have been chummed from stands on shore in slow-moving tides with ground menhaden with exceptional results and on the Potomac and in bays have been chummed with shrimp or crushed blue crabs. They may stay a day to a week or more in natural feeding places and then for reasons unknown seem to completely disappear.

Having fished many years and taken the many ocean and bay game fish of the United States Atlantic Seaboard, I believe one of the most intriguing, thrilling and all-absorbing fishing to be the trolling with power among the rocks in the surf for the gamey striped bass. This necessitates a guide who knows his surf and can judge when best to take a making sea on the beam or a rock on the bottom. The sportsman and guide to have success must be 100 percent team-mates and in approaching likely grounds should use very long lines, often 300 feet; the guide should keep the boat well offshore of the ground and describe an arc around the "spot;" the fisherman holds his rod up and inshore and reels in sufficiently to compensate for the speed loss and in doing so drags the bait across the arc over the ground without having the boat pass over it. This will not drive the fish out and often many fish can be taken before the trolling boat drives them. When a fish is hooked, the guides work the boat gradually offshore to deeper water to keep the fish free from the rocks and the boat clear of surf.

The fascination of expecting the strike at the moment the bait passes the spot fished is most gratifying to both sportsman and guide, particularly if a thirty pounder is taken.

On quiet days with clear water, large schools of fish are often observed and identified and a careful study of bottom conditions can be noted for future conquest. This adds hunting to fishing. Last, but not least, it is no place to dream or nap and constant cautious judgment and action is imperative, as the penalty may prove a good wetting or a boat ashore.

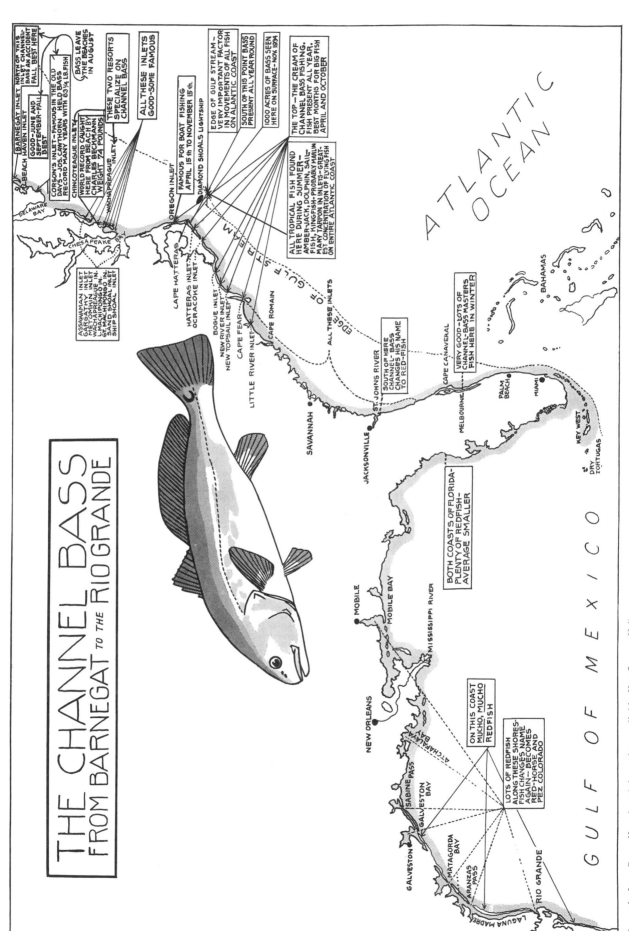

THE CHANNEL BASS FROM BARNEGAT TO THE RIO GRANDE

BARNEGAT INLET NORTH OF THIS INLET CHANNEL BASS AN ACCIDENT FALL BEST HERE

BEACH HAVEN INLET GOOD—JUNE AND SEPTEMBER-FALL BEST

CORSON'S INLET—FAMOUS IN THE OLD DAYS—JOS.CAWTHORN HELD BASS RECORD MANY YEARS WITH 63¼ LB. FISH

BASS LEAVE THE BEACHES IN AUGUST

CHINCOTEAGUE INLET WORLD RECORD CAUGHT HERE FROM BEACH BY A. BECKMANN WEIGHT 74 POUNDS

WACHAPREAGUE INLET

THESE TWO RESORTS SPECIALIZE ON CHANNEL BASS

ALL THESE INLETS GOOD—SOME FAMOUS

OREGON INLET FAMOUS FOR BOAT FISHING APRIL 15th TO NOVEMBER 15th.

DIAMOND SHOALS LIGHTSHIP

EDGE OF GULF STREAM—VERY IMPORTANT FACTOR IN MOVEMENTS OF ALL FISH ON ATLANTIC COAST

SOUTH OF THIS POINT BASS PRESENT ALL YEAR ROUND

1000 ACRES OF BASS SEEN HERE ON SURFACE—NOV 1994

THE TOP—THE CREAM OF CHANNEL BASS FISHING. FISH PRESENT ALL YEAR. BEST MONTHS FOR BIG FISH APRIL AND OCTOBER

ALL TROPICAL FISH FOUND HERE DURING SUMMER—AMBER-JACK, DOLPHIN, SAIL-FISH, KINGFISH—PROBABLY MARLIN MANY TARPON IN INLETS—GREATEST CONCENTRATION OF FLYING FISH ON ENTIRE ATLANTIC COAST

ASSAWAMAN INLET GARGATHY INLET METOMKIN INLET WACHAPREAGUE IN. L.MACHIPONGO IN. GT.MACHIPONGO IN. SAND SHOAL INLET SHIP SHOAL INLET

HATTERAS INLET OCRACOKE INLET

BOGUE INLET NEW RIVER INLET NEW TOPSAIL INLET

CAPE FEAR LITTLE RIVER INLET

CAPE ROMAIN

ALL THESE INLETS

EDGE OF GULF ST.

DELAWARE BAY

CHESAPEAKE BAY

CAPE HATTERAS

SAVANNAH

JACKSONVILLE

St JOHNS RIVER

SOUTH OF HERE CHANNEL-BASS CHANGES HIS NAME TO RED-FISH

CAPE CANAVERAL

MELBOURNE

VERY GOOD—LOTS OF CHANNEL-BASS MASTERS FISH HERE IN WINTER

PALM BEACH

MIAMI

KEY WEST

DRY TORTUGAS

BAHAMAS

ATLANTIC OCEAN

BOTH COASTS OF FLORIDA—PLENTY OF REDFISH—AVERAGE SMALLER

MOBILE

MOBILE BAY

MISSISSIPPI RIVER

NEW ORLEANS

ATCHAFALAYA BAY

SABINE PASS

GALVESTON BAY

GALVESTON

MATAGORDA BAY

ARANSAS PASS

RIO GRANDE

LAGUNA MADRE

ON THIS COAST MUCHO, MUCHO REDFISH

LOTS OF REDFISH ALONG THESE SHORES—FISH CHANGES NAME AGAIN—BECOMES RED-HORSE AND PEZ COLORADO

GULF OF MEXICO

Drawn by Lynn Bogue Hunt from information supplied by Van Campen Heilner.

CHAPTER IX.

THE CHANNEL BASS

BY

VAN CAMPEN HEILNER

MOST of us, I suppose, have a first love, and without doubt this writer's is the channel bass. Perhaps because this fish was associated with my early youth or perhaps because he was the first large fish I ever caught (a 41 pounder by the way), the place he occupies in my heart is a very near and dear one.

Memories of autumn days with the snipe trading down the beaches and the first flock of wild geese etched high against the sunset above the golden marshes, seagrass on the dunes bending against the hiss of the first northwester, spring days with the miles of rolling breakers creaming in across the bar and the nesting terns and laughing gulls setting up their ceaseless clamor in behind the thoroughfare — these all mean but one thing to me, that lovable old coppery warrior of the tides, *Sciaenops ocellatus*, the channel bass.

From Barnegat Light to the Gulf of Mexico I have pursued him down the years with a relentlessness that has amounted to a mania. Other fish have I caught which proved gamier; other fish have I caught which were more spectacular, more deserving perhaps of their place in the sun (or sea); but none gives me a greater thrill or a greater desire to repeat sensations which each year seem as new and exciting as they seemed when first I experienced them.

He goes by many names. From Jersey to Florida he is the channel bass or red drum. But the name red drum should be discouraged because it only confuses him with his cousin, the black drum, an oafish fellow with a beard, a hump on his back, stripes like a convict and the fighting abilities of a sack of potatoes. From Florida south he is the redfish and as you wend your way around the Gulf coast and approach Texas and Spanish America he becomes the red horse or the *pez colorado*. But he's still the channel bass to me, no matter under what name he masquerades.

The sportiest way to take him is by surf fishing. Surf fishing is to salt water angling what trout fishing is to fresh water. It is a one-man game from start to finish. You are the one and only factor. It is the same as still-hunting is to deer driving. Here you are and there he is. If he runs out all your line you can't pick up the oars or start the engine and follow him. No cushion or comfortable seat or chair supports your fundament, no thwarts against which to brace your feet, no companion to assist you or guide you. You must find your quarry yourself, you must rig and bait your hook yourself, you must become proficient in the art of casting so you may reach him, and you must bring him through a line of foaming breakers and surging tides until at last, whipped to a standstill, he lies gasping on the wet sands at your very feet. Then you must let him go because he deserves it.

Some bright morning in early summer you pack your duffle and rods and hie yourself to your favorite inlet. You have been mulling over that tackle all winter. Your rod is two-piece split bamboo, — maybe one piece — and the tip is from 6′6″ to over 7′. It has a "spring butt" or a straight one, 24″ or longer. Maybe you've rewrapped it during the winter and given it three or four coats of varnish. You've certainly oiled and cleaned your 2/0 reel and filled it with new 12 thread line. You've sharpened your hooks which may run from 5/0 to 9/0, put on new leaders, cleaned your fish knife and sharpened it to a razor edge, re-riveted your rod belt, molded some new sinkers of your pet shape and weight, cleaned out your bait box.

This season you have a couple of new gadgets. You've put a throat on the inside pocket of your beach bag with a drawstring, so the blowing sand can't get inside. You've made a disgorger out of a copper tube with a handle 18″ long so you can get that hook out of the tummy of the bass without cutting your hands to pieces. And you have a finger gaff which is a big strong 10/0 hook drilled into a small barrel-shaped piece of wood so you can grasp it with your fingers. It only weighs a few ounces and you can hang it in one of the buckle holes in your belt where it's easy to reach and weighs nothing.

At the fish-house you've picked up a dozen fresh bunkers. They are nice and fat and fairly ooze oil. If you're beach camping or on your boat you have them already iced down, or you've made arrangements for some one to supply you with fresh ones every day.

At last you arrive at the inlet. You've judged it about right. The tide is some two hours down, the wind is onshore and while there isn't a heavy sea running, there's plenty of "fight" to the surf. You first make a survey to determine the most likely place. The formation has changed since you were here in the fall. Where is that beautiful pocket that lay just north of the point? It's gone and the beach there is as flat as a flounder. You walk on and pretty soon you find what you are looking for. A good cast from the beach lies a long bar over which the sea is breaking with diminishing intensity. It will be nearly dry at low water. Between it and the beach runs a long narrow slue, maybe half a mile long. Another hour or less and you'll be able to wade it. Thousands of broken clam shells strew the beach in all directions. You can see lots of small bait in the undertow. You drop your beach bag near the high-water mark, take out your sand spike and stand your rod up in it. You heave a big sigh. "This is the place!" you say; "If they're anywhere, they ought to be here!"

While you're waiting for the tide you cut some bait. You find a board and lay your mossbunker on it. First you scale him. Then you cut off his head and split him down the side, keeping the knife just this side of the backbone. Then the other side. Now you have two nice scaleless, boneless slabs of bunker. If he was a big one, cut these diagonally in half and you have four baits. Cut just enough to fill your bait box, as fresh cut bait is much better. Later when the bunkers are a couple of days old, if you can't get any more you will have to wrap them on the hook with thread or they'll fall to pieces.

Now you're all set. If the water and weather are warm you'll discard boots and wade in. If it were late in the fall you'd probably be wearing boot-foot waders. Waders are better than boots, because sometimes the slues are deep. It's almost waist deep in the slue and you climb out on the outer bar which is nearly dry. A short cast to wet your line, bait up, swing back and heave her out.

For a long time nothing happens. Then your heart skips a beat. Something moved in with your bait. You wait. There it is again! This time the line runs slowly out. You set the hook but instead of the expected rush, something flies to the surface and flaps the water furiously about. A skate! You reel in disgustedly and spend five minutes stabbing and sawing the grotesque nuisance into several pieces before you can recover your hook.

Cast again. What a peach of a cast! Your form was perfect! If some of your friends could have seen that one! Maybe you had better enter the tournament this summer. You are so busy congratulating yourself that before you know it your line is whizzing out in long steady surges that you know can mean but one thing. You clamp down your thumb and the fight is on!

Out he goes, then the tide catches him and he goes with it. You have him almost in and out he goes again. But each rush is shorter. In fifteen minutes you see him on the surface twenty feet away. He's swimming slowly but still headed out to sea. The tide has changed now and the waves are getting larger. The bar is starting to cover. You bring him slowly to your feet and a receding wave leaves him flopping in a few inches of water. Luckily he's hooked in the mouth. You work the hook loose and with the next wave kick him back. About thirty-five pounds you guess. A good fighter.

It's getting pretty deep on the bar now and it's time you were leaving. You wade back across the slue and take up your station on the main beach. There's lots of movement in the surf now. 'Way to your left you see the gulls working over something that is breaking all over the surface. Blues! You're sorely tempted but you're after bigger game. Then you have a strong slashing strike and in a minute or two beach a beautiful weakfish, five pounder at least. Well, you'll take anything that comes. But you won't move from this spot, because — ah! that unmistakable pull! You'd know it anywhere, anytime. He drops it, he's picked it up again. Let him have it, let him have it, let him have it . . . NOW!

Thus the mechanics of surf fishing for channel bass. But to me the fish are but incidental. The miles and miles of lonely beaches stretching from Montauk to the Florida Straits. The dunes, shading from white to golden brown. The sedge grass blowing in the wind. The little "teeters" scurrying up the beach just ahead of the waves and right-about-facing just as quickly, to stab their long little bills in the moist sand behind the retreating surge. The confused clamor of hundreds of terns "working" over a school of blues. The wild fury of a "northeaster" pounding down on a deserted coast, with the whole beach under water

ON THE OUTER BAR.

"HERE'S HOPING!"

FRESH FROM THE BRINEY.

"C" STANDS FOR CHANNEL BASS.

WHAT COULD BE SWEETER?

Photographs copyright 1935, by Van Campen Heilner.
A LULL IN PROCEEDINGS.

and the flash of the distant lighthouse showing faint and blurred through the driving rain. Autumn, with the first crisp tang of a northwester, blue skies and blue surf and the first blackducks coming in at sunset to the marshes behind the inlet.

These are what I think of when I think of channel bass. And for myself I can think of nothing better.

SONG OF THE OLD TIMERS

Famous wherever surfmen gather.
Tune: "Watermelon Hanging On The Vine."

Oh, the weakfish am good
And the kingfish am great
The striped bass am very, very fine;
But give me, oh give me,
Oh, how I wish you would!
A channel bass a-hangin' on my line!

SLIDE RULE FOR CHANNEL BASS FISHERMEN

SCIENTIFIC NAME: *Sciaenops ocellatus*, channel bass, red drum, redfin, redfish, red horse, *pez colorado*.

DISTRIBUTION — Atlantic Coast from New Jersey to Texas.

FAVORITE GROUNDS — In the vicinity of all inlets from Barnegat to the Rio Grande. Bass are found next to the beach in slue and channels between the bars. In boat fishing, fish as close to the break on the bar as you can.

TACKLE — Great difference of opinion. No two anglers will agree and each one is right. The author uses the standard surf tackle, tip 6′6″ to 7′ in length, 12 thread line, 4 oz. pyramid or cone sinker (5 or 6 ozs. if strong current or heavy surf) and 7/0 Harrison White Label Sproat hook with 2′ wire gimp leader. A 2/0 reel, thumb stall, rod belt, sand spike, belt gaff, bait box, knife, disgorger and towel complete your equipment. But every surfman you meet will have a new gadget or wrinkle to show you.

BAIT — Cut open nearly any channel bass and you will find crabs in his stomach. Undoubtedly the best bait for all bottom-feeding fish of any species wherever found. But the old standbys are "bunkers" (menhaden) and mullet in the fall. Scale and split. Squid, fresh, frozen or salted, will do if the others are not obtainable. In trolling in Southern waters I have had redfish take 'most any moving lure.

BOATS — The writer prefers surf fishing above all other methods. It is the one way from start to finish where you are the sole arbiter. If you insist on boat fishing, get a boat and guide at any of the places where they specialize in this sport, go out the inlet and fish as close to the "break" on the bars as you can. Fish right in the "break" or in any little slue going through it. You should have a strong stomach, however, as it's sometimes quite rough.

HOOKING, PLAYING, LANDING — Channel bass will bite in any of three different ways. They will "fool" with the bait, picking it up and dropping it several times, they will grab it and run, they will pick it up and run in with you. In either case, wait until the fish starts off and you feel the weight of him — then set the hook. At all times give the fish his head, allow no slack line and don't, under any circumstances, "horse" him. When you get him in the undertow and he seems all in, watch your chance and as a wave comes lift him just ahead of it. This will shoot him up on the beach where you can gaff him or get your fingers in his gills.

WEATHER — TIDES — The last two hours of the ebb and the first three hours of the flood. Sometimes on the falling tide the point of the inlet is excellent. Find a "rip" if there is one and fish there. At dead low water, if you can wade to the outer bar, do so, and cast out beyond it. Back up as the tide comes in and fish in the slue and pockets as they commence to fill. The writer's experience has been that an onshore wind is best. It blows the warm surface water onto the beach. With the wind offshore, the warm surface water is blown out and the cold water wells up from underneath. Onshore wind, water warm; offshore wind water cold will always hold.

WHERE TO GO — North and south sides of inlets from Barnegat to the Rio Grande. Barnegat is best in the autumn which after all seems to be the best time, certainly the weather is most pleasant then. Chincoteague and Wachapreague, Va., specialize in channel bass fishing. Also Oregon Inlet (town of Manteo) and Ocracoke, N. C. Good fishing around the jetty at Mayport near Jacksonville, Fla., and Melbourne on the Indian River good also. All the North and South Carolina inlets excellent. Mid-June to mid-July and mid-September to mid-October best north of the Carolinas. April and October best for big fish from Oregon Inlet south. Barnegat is the northern limit. You will be more sure of fish from Beach Haven south. August appears to be a bad month everywhere and during this time the fish either drop off the beaches or go up in the big sounds and bays to eat oysters. Never heard of good bass fishing in August anywhere.

RECORD FISH — For many years the world's record was held by Joseph Cawthorn, the famous comedian, with a fish of 63¼ lbs., taken at Corson's Inlet, N. J., on July 17th, 1910, which was a famous hang-out of all the old timers. Then the record shifted to New Inlet, N. J., where Charles H. Smith chalked up a 65-pounder caught on Sept. 24, 1919. In 1935 the record stood at 74 lbs. with a fish taken by Charles D. Beckmann at Chincoteague, Va., on June 27, 1929. This fish was caught from the beach. The average channel bass will run on one side or the other of 30 lbs. Forty pounds is a gold button fish and if you catch a 50-pounder bring on the refreshments. You'll need them. "Puppy drum" of 8 to 15 lbs. literally swarm on the beaches of the Carolinas at all times of the year. The largest channel bass ever taken by any method was a fish of 75 lbs. reported by Jordan & Evermann, so there's still hope.

Courtesy of George C. Thomas, III.

Photo by Reyes.

THE TUNA CLUB, CATALINA.

CHAPTER X.

CATALINA ISLAND AND
SOUTHERN CALIFORNIA FISHING

BY
GEORGE C. THOMAS, III

THE main big game fishing grounds of America's Pacific are composed of the waters adjacent to and immediately surrounding the Channel Islands of Southern California. These islands are eleven in number and lie in an almost northwest southeast position, ranging over some three hundred miles of semi-tropic coastline. They may be divided into three groups: the Santa Barbara Islands, which are the furthest north, being below Point Concepcion, and extending southward to Ventura; the Catalina group, which are in the vicinity of Los Angeles; and the Coronado Islands, directly south of San Diego. Most offer extreme beauty of coastline, with an abundance of anchorages which intrigue the yachtsman. The two former groups are in American territorial waters, but the latter are owned by Mexico, and permission to visit them within the three-mile limit must be obtained from the Mexican government. The Santa Barbara Islands are composed of San Miguel, Santa Rosa, Santa Cruz and Anacapa, of which Santa Cruz is the largest, being twenty-one miles in length, with an extreme width of about six and one-half miles. With the exception of Anacapa, they are privately owned or leased, and permission to land is difficult to secure. Anacapa is under the control of the United States Government Lighthouse Service. Santa Cruz is the most widely fished, Santa Barbara craft making it their rendezvous, and at times swordfish and tuna are plentiful there. The more northern islands are quite desolate with much rough water, and anglers seldom visit them.

The Catalina group, with which we are most concerned, since they afford the best general fishing, are made up of Santa Barbara Island, a tiny offshore islet which occasionally offers fine fishing, but where anchorage is undependable and which is now absolutely uninhabited; Santa Catalina Island, by far the most important, and which we will discuss at length later; and San Clemente, her sister island. San Nicolas Island, the most desolate of all under this heading, far offshore, with rough seas predominating, offers little or nothing to the average angler.

The Coronados, comprising three islands, all of which go under this name, being designated and differentiated by the prefixes Northern, Middle and Southern, are small, none being over two miles in greatest dimension. They are fished chiefly by San Diego anglers, although others visit them from neighboring waters. They frequently provide excellent fishing, especially for smaller game.

All of these islands were discovered by the Spaniard, Cortez, and later were renamed by his countryman, Viscanio, in 1652. Volcanic in character and rocky in the extreme, they are supposed at one time to have been connected to the mainland, but it is of interest to note that their vegetation and animal life differ greatly, both from each other and that of the mainland. Most of them harbor goats or sheep, now gone wild. The former were placed there in early days by the Spaniards, who wished to provide against food shortage in various expeditions to these waters. Catalina is overrun with goats, having some forty thousand in the many herds on various parts of the island. Many of the other islands, particularly Santa Cruz and San Clemente are given up to the sheep raising industry, and Santa Cruz in addition has a number of wild pigs, also placed there by the Spaniards. The boars are quite dangerous, and provide good shooting to those who are fortunate enough to obtain permission to hunt them. Originally, at least in so far as their history has been disclosed, they were inhabited by Indians, who made fishing their livelihood. Relics continually are found of much interest to scientists. Much could be written of their historical background, and many fascinating accounts of them are on record.

Santa Catalina Island is the cradle of modern big game fishing. Other lands and other waters may boast stranger or mightier fighters, larger or more abundant fish and greater variety. Florida and New Zealand, Britain and Mexico, Cuba and Nova Scotia each have their claims, and all have their merits, but there is only one Catalina. Here sea angling is a tradition. It was here that bluefin tuna first were killed on rod and reel, then marlin, then broadbill. Avalon, Catalina's harbor and village, became the first base for modern big game fishermen.

Avalon is unique. Situated near the eastern end of the Island and facing the mainland, twenty-two nautical miles due south from San Pedro, the seaport of Los Angeles, it is easily accessible by frequently timed steamers and airplanes. Avalon is an enchanting combination of the old and the new — a mixture of its own tranquility and its tourist hustle. Originally a fishing town where anglers and fishermen from all parts of the world congregated, intent upon the sport to be furnished by the yellowtail and tuna, and later marlin and broadbill, it has now become a holiday land, beckoning vacationists from all walks of life. Though for the angler the changes have not wrought improvement, and most certainly it has become commercialized, it has a fascination all of its own, and those who know it love it.

While it may be assumed from the frequent mention of Catalina that the best general fishing is to be found only at this Island, this is not the case. During several seasons the members of the Tuna Club have sponsored an anglers' camp at San Clemente due to the abundance of yellowtail, marlin or tuna found there. At other times those more fortunate fishermen with ample leisure have haunted the Coronados. Often the wondrous coves of Santa Cruz have sheltered part of Avalon's fleet. And even Santa Barbara Island has harbored our boats after some days of unusual luck in that vicinity.

By the same token that Catalina has been called the cradle, so is the Tuna Club the parent of big game fishing as a sport, and no history of Pacific Coast sea angling would be complete without its mention. It is there that are preserved the legends of the past, of Mexican Joe, Harry Elms and other famous boatmen of early years. It is there that the great catches of other days may be viewed in the Club albums, and it is there also that the largest and most unusual specimens are found, adorning the walls and cabinets.

Founded in 1897 by the late Charles Frederick Holder, the Tuna Club has watched over the growth of sea angling. It has prescribed to its wants and doctored its hurts. It has helped more than any other single factor in putting this great sport on the high plane which it now enjoys. Standardization of tackle and development of sportsmanlike rules for the angler are the contributions of this distinguished club. Its traditions and rules are accepted by all on this coast. For this reason the reader's attention is called to the photograph on the opposite page of the official Tuna Club Record Board which hangs in the club, and also to the copy of the tackle specifications and rules appearing in the text. Since the larger game fishes of the Pacific Coast constitute the subject of this chapter, it would seem wise to limit its scope to those species which appear on this board, with only casual mention of other, smaller game varieties.

One of Catalina's chief appeals lies in its weather. Both on land and at sea, especially during the summer months of the fishing season, it is ideal. The island has a natural lee from the prevailing westerly winds, with no severe storms to hamper offshore trolling. Occasional rough days, of course, are to be expected, but they prove the exception rather than the rule, and even during the worst of them there is the island lee where game will be found. It is a comfort to know that the morning will be calm, with a westerly breeze which commences in the late forenoon, increases during the rest of the day to die with sundown. High fogs are not unusual, but low, thick ones are rare, appearing about six or seven times during the entire year, and never do they interfere with fishing. The temperature of the water, too, is fairly high, ranging throughout the year between fifty-eight and seventy-four degrees. More perfect conditions would be hard to find.

Aside from the Tuna Club, where rooms are available to members and guests, there are many hotels and lodgings which cater to anglers, and which may be had for any price which the visitor cares to pay.

Although many of the anglers fish from their own boats, there are available a number of excellent guides with fully equipped fishing launches. Each guide, or boatman, as they are known at the Island, furnishes bait, standard Tuna Club tackle and other equipment at a reasonable price (from fifteen to twenty-five dollars per day, according to the size and speed of the boats). These boats are seaworthy, comfortable fishing machines, with twin swivel chairs mounted in the stern, fitted with brass universal-jointed butt sockets. The sole purpose of their captains is to provide sport, and since most of these men have grown up at the Island, they are thoroughly familiar with the fishing grounds and the conditions which will be encountered. The newcomer would do well to engage one of these boatmen.

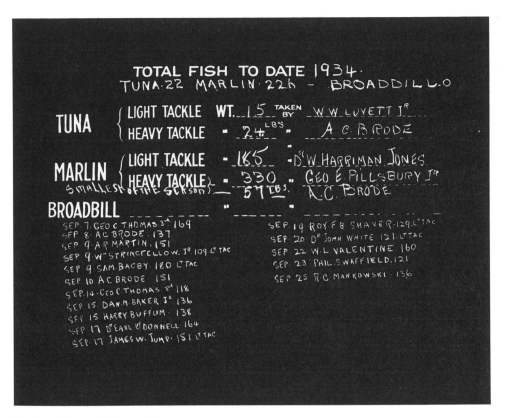

Courtesy of George C. Thomas, III.

TUNA CLUB DAILY CATCH BOARD.

This photograph was taken during a lull in the fishing. In 1934 there were no large tuna taken.

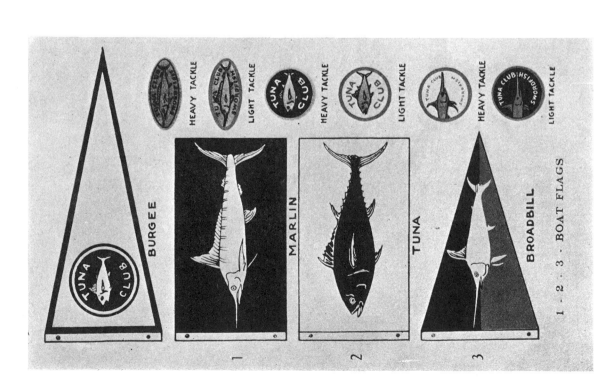

One of the picturesque touches of Catalina fishing is the habit of flying the Tuna Club flags which signalize the catch of each boat as the fish come aboard. This custom is not confined to members of the Tuna Club, but has been adopted by all who fish from this base. Tuna, marlin and broadbill, as well as giant sea-bass, each have a separate and distinct flag which is run up on the mast when a capture is made. The flag for tuna is a blue fish on a white field; for marlin the colors are reversed; the broadbill flag is somewhat similar to that of the marlin except that the lower half of the field is red. Thus it is easy for those ashore, as well as the other boats, to know when a fish has been landed. These flags are shrouded in tradition, and many rites are observed in their use. The custom was established at the Island in 1898.

On the question of tackle and rules, one could do no better than quote the Tuna Club rules verbatim:

"The following tackle specifications and rules are the result of over thirty-five years experience. Strict adherence to both the spirit and letter of these rules is vitally necessary in order that the Tuna Club may maintain the high standards set by its founders and retain the enviable reputation it now enjoys. In fairness to all, involuntary infractions of these rules can be no more condoned than can willful violations. Members should be sure that they understand the rules and that their tackle complies with the specifications. The underlying spirit to angling should be that it is a sport in which the skill of the angler is pitted against the instinct and strength of the fish and that the latter is entitled to an even chance for his life.

"Heavy Tackle — Rod to be of wood, with usual mountings, and shall consist of butt and tip and shall not be shorter than six feet nine inches over all. Tip shall be not less than five feet in length and shall not weigh more than sixteen ounces. Line shall not exceed standard twenty-four thread linen line and shall have a maximum breaking strain when dry of not to exceed sixty-six pounds.

"Light Tackle — Rod to be of wood, with usual mountings, and shall consist of butt and tip and shall not be shorter than six feet over all. Butt shall not exceed fourteen inches in length. Tip shall be not less than five feet in length, and shall not weigh more than six ounces. Line shall not exceed standard nine-thread linen line and shall have a maximum breaking strain, when dry, of not to exceed twenty-six pounds.

"Three-Six — Rod to be of wood, with usual mountings, and shall consist of butt and tip (butt may be of metal), and shall be not shorter than six feet over all. Butt to be twelve inches in length. Weight of entire rod shall not exceed six ounces. Line shall not exceed standard six-thread linen line and shall have a maximum breaking strain, when dry, of not to exceed sixteen pounds.

"The word tackle shall be defined as consisting of rod, reel, line, leader, hooks, and harness.

"Leaders shall not exceed fifteen feet in length. Double line, not to exceed fifteen feet in length, may be attached to leader.

"By length of rod over all is meant with tip fully seated in butt. By length of tip is meant from the shoulder of ferrule to outer end of tip.

"Every angler must bring his fish to gaff unaided and by the use of regulation tackle only.

"The following acts or omissions will disqualify a catch: a broken rod; handlining a fish; any person other than the angler touching any part of the tackle, excepting kite line and leader, while the angler is fighting a fish; handlining the double line or use of a boatman's handline snapped on or in any way attached to the double line or leader; failure to have rod weighed and measured and line tested before competing; failure to comply with tackle specifications; shooting a fish; throwing gaff at fish before leader is within reach of boatman; use of harpoon, lance or lily iron; anyone other than the angler and one gaffer assisting in gaffing or killing a fish; use of more than two hooks attached to leader at any one time or use of cluster hooks.

"All fish entered for competition for Club buttons or prizes must be officially weighed in and recorded. Tackle must be exhibited when fish is weighed in. Any protest relative to weight of fish or manner of weighing must be made before fish is removed from scales.

"Any protest relative to tackle or manner of killing fish must be filed, in writing, at the office of the Tuna Club within twenty-four hours after fish is weighed in.

"Every member competing for Club prizes or buttons must have his line tested and rod weighed, measured, and stamped by the Club and a record thereof will be kept. The Club expressly reserves the right to require an additional line test and to call for an examination of tackle whenever such action may be deemed advisable.

"Competition for Club prizes or buttons is limited to waters between a line drawn due west of Point Concepcion and a line drawn due south from the international boundary line (United States and Mexico) until you clear the Coronado Islands; thence due west.

"The award of buttons will be governed by the tackle upon which the fish was caught."

These rules and tackle specifications have become standardized to a certain extent all over the world, but at the Island they are practically law, and anyone fishing there must compete under them, because all of the boatmen recognize them, and their tackle is so constructed. What is fair for one, is fair for all, and it seems rather too bad that tackle is not more restricted at other fishing grounds. Twenty-four thread line is adequate for all except extremely large fish.

There is an art to fighting a large fish on standard tackle. It is not, as so many people seem to think, merely a matter of strength and stamina. It is not the superman, in the best of condition, with a peculiar liking for punishment, who makes the records. Perhaps modern accounts emphasize long fights; perhaps modern anglers glorify themselves by telling of hardships which they endured in landing a giant marlin or broadbill; but in the main, strength is not the governing factor. Angling is a matter of skill, where rhythm, grace and perfection of form count far more than brute strength. Much of the tackle and equipment used in parts of the world is indeed cumbersome, and in its use, finesse is impossible. How often do we see photographs of straining men with huge winches for reels, and miniature telegraph poles for rods, fighting a fish for hours, when it could be landed on lighter tackle in far less time. Such equipment tells more on the angler than the quarry; it is foolish and altogether needless. It makes a harness necessary, which spoils technique. Twenty-four thread line is ample for virtually all needs; few are the anglers who can break it except through misuse. If one considers that the record weight lift from a standing position without harness on a six-foot rod, no matter how heavy, is less than thirty pounds, and that twenty-four thread breaks at about sixty pounds dead weight, the fallacy of heavier equipment is evident. With very large, fast fish, where friction might break a line, thirty-nine thread is perhaps admissible. Large tuna in deep water, giant marlin and broadbill can call for this heavy line under some conditions.

Overly large reels are an abomination — they are unwieldy and heavy, as well as unnecessary. If more than three hundred yards of line are taken out on a tuna's first run, the fish generally is lost. If a swordfish sounds to a greater depth than one hundred and fifty fathoms, especially if he dies there, he cannot be brought to the surface without breaking the rules, regardless of tackle, unless his weight is well under five hundred pounds. These are the underlying reasons behind the tackle specifications of the Tuna Club.

Knowledge of the fish's actions, too, are most important. The angler must be able to tell from the feel of the rod exactly what the fish is doing. He should know when to exert power, and when to relax. There is little gain in working a fish hard when it is taking line, for the small amount of pressure which is exerted by the rod, will not stop him. When he turns toward the boat, however, the rodsman instantly must be aware of the action; it is his turn to gain line. A great fish will not be led until he wants to be, or until he is so weakened that he cannot resist, and much strength can be saved by knowledge of this fact. The line tires the fish more than the rod in the early part of the fight, and line soon gained is soon lost. Another fallacy in fighting large fish is that the line always must be kept tight. When a marlin is jumping toward the angler at speed, this is impossible. Of course, the angler must reel fast, but he cannot keep up with the fish. The line will belly behind the fish, and thus keep the pull from behind him, too, unless the fish is very close to the boat, and the line itself comes out of the water for its total length. With the line pulling from behind, as generally is the case, a fish is much less likely to be lost, since the hook will not readily be pulled from his open mouth. It must be realized that no matter how much strain is exerted upon a moving fish, the line will never go directly to him. Rather, it will bow or belly out behind, forming a cushion against shocks and jerks. This is as it should be, since this belly in the line forms a friction through the water against the fish, and greatly helps in the process of wearing him out. It must be understood, however, that the fish must be fought too; simply following him around with the boat, waiting for him to tire, is a poor system. Knowledge of tackle and its handling can be gained only through practice, but the angler should study and strive for form in fishing. Pumping, especially, is an art. It is not simply lifting and lowering the rod to reel in slack; it is the angler's way of feeling the fish. It must be rhythmical, and the rod tip should be lowered down the tight line in a smooth, even sweep. Both the upward and downward movements must be timed to the fish's actions, the swell, and the position of the boat. So much for rod technique; suffice to say that it is all important in the handling of large fish.

FISHING AT CATALINA

Of all the big game fishes which I have landed, I prefer the bluefin tuna (*Thunnus thynnus*) taken in deep water, as is invariably the case off California. There is a mystery in hunting them, and a charm in their capture which is lacking in other varieties. The beauty of using the kite, a necessity in these waters, is perhaps the chief charm; the terrific first run is another. The fish themselves, their schooling habits, the uncertainty, and the care necessary to produce the strike combine to make them my favorites.

In the 1890's tuna made Catalina their all-year habitat. Avalon Bay was full of them, and one needed but a skiff and a bait to hook on. The fish stayed down deep, and would bite readily in the mornings or evenings. They did not school in the true sense of the word — they merely stayed at the Island in great numbers. Today it is different; for some inexplicable reason, in the summer of 1904 they changed their habits, coming to the surface in great schools and beginning an exodus. At that time it became almost impossible to catch them on rod and reel. Although fish still were plentiful, they would not bite on a bait with a hook in it. They fed, of course, both on flying-fish and small bait, but few of the varied and ingenious methods which were devised to hook them succeeded. The fish became boat-shy and would sound at the approach of a fishing launch. Then Captain George C. Farnsworth, then as now the outstanding expert, hit upon a truly brilliant idea. As a boy in Northern California, he had been tremendously interested in kite flying. He remembered his kites, and realized that he could employ one to keep a tuna bait to one side of the boat; it also would give the dead flying-fish a lifelike action, making it skip and skitter over the water as if chased by tuna. He tried it out, and found it an instant success. For a time this invention was jealously guarded, but the secret when perfected was disclosed. Today kite fishing is the only method by which large bluefin tuna may be caught on the Pacific Coast. To see Farnsworth and Tad Gray alternately work a school of tuna with the kite is one of the most thrilling sights an angler ever witnessed.

Truly, this is a remarkable and beautiful type of angling. The handling of the kite and the working of the bait over the school, putting it into the correct spot for the strike, is most exacting, and requires perfect timing on the part of the boatman. When two can accomplish this feat in the same school without interfering with each other, the very acme of this sport is attained.

The general procedure, after locating a school of tuna, is to head directly down wind for several hundred yards, in order that the kite may be launched when the boat is turned back into the breeze. Then, with the kite directly behind the boat, at an altitude of several hundred feet, the hook is baited and fishing line let out a short distance. The kite line is tied to the main fishing line, just above the leader, with a piece of lighter-breaking thread between, so that after the strike, the kite will be free, and will fall into the water, to be retrieved when the fish has been landed. As the tuna are approached and passed, the boat is turned across the wind, and since the kite will stay to leeward, the bait is carried off the beam and over the fish. The best place to put it is just behind the leaders of the school, for it is there that the largest fish will be found. When properly handled, it is small wonder that tuna go wild over this amazing replica of a crippled flying-fish, and that anglers are enchanted by this novel and interesting method of fishing.

When schooling, tuna travel either on the surface of the water or at a depth, according to weather conditions and their fancy. If they are on top, their presence readily may be detected by their telltale ripple or wake, by the flashes of the sun on their backs, and occasionally by the view of their dorsal fins and tails. When deep, they are much harder to see, but the experienced eye learns to look for a slight disturbance on the water and other indications so delicate that it requires a sense rather than perception to recognize them.

At Catalina, flying-fish are the universal bait for tuna. These sixteen-inch fish weigh about a pound and one-half, and being tough, do not readily go to pieces when trolled at speed or by long use. The method of baiting is shown in the accompanying photograph. The most popular hook is a size 8/o to 10/o Sobey.

Although large bluefin tuna have been caught on light tackle, the record being James W. Jump's 117¾ pounder (the Tuna Club record of 145½ pounds, also taken by Mr. Jump, was a yellowfin), this tackle is not adequate for fish approaching one hundred pounds in weight. When first hooked, bluefin tuna make a tremendous run which reaches an estimated speed of over fifty miles an hour, and often take off many hundred feet of line in a few seconds. Except in rare instances, where good luck, rather than skill, plays the predominating part, nine-thread line will break from friction as the fish drags the bow through the water. This also is the reason why that heavy tackle record of two hundred and fifty-one pounds, made by Colonel C. P. Morehouse in 1898, has never been broken. (Incidentally, this fish also was a yellowfin.) The tremendous strain as

 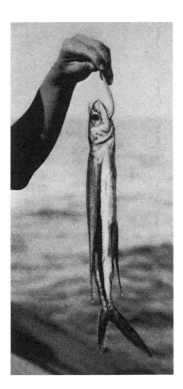 

One method of baiting for marlin. The looped thread sewn through flying fish's mouth makes rebaiting easy and allows freedom of bait when marlin strikes.

Another marlin bait. Note how flying fish is hooked through the head.

Flying fish as trolled by kite.

Sewing the mouth of flying fish closed to prevent spinning when trolled.

Photos by courtesy of George C. Thomas, III.
Hook baited with flying fish for tuna or to strike marlin with set drag.

giant tuna make their first rush breaks the line. This is not true in parts of the world where the water is shallower, but at Catalina literally hundreds of tuna over two hundred pounds have been hooked, and only two of this size have been landed on standard tackle. W. C. Boschen, one of the best deep sea anglers who ever lived, lost over five hundred big tuna in one season, simply because the line he used would not stand the fish's first run, and Tuna Club rules forbade the use of larger. Farnsworth, who was his boatman at the time, tells me that they would lose as many as a dozen hooks a day, and they never succeeded in stopping a single fish. I have seen schools of tuna at Catalina where individuals would weigh over five hundred pounds apiece, and have hooked some well over the two hundred pound mark with always the same result. Several fishermen in whom I have complete confidence have asserted that they have seen tuna in these waters over 800 pounds in weight. I have tried loose drags and tight ones, as well as all sorts of maneuvers with the boat, and I have never landed a tuna over one hundred sixty-three pounds. This undoubtedly explains why the record at the Island never has been broken during some forty years of angling, and possibly never will unless larger and heavier line is used. The rods and reels are adequate, but the line is too small. Perhaps, when the big tuna return to California waters, the Tuna Club will legalize a heavier tackle for them.

Bluefin tuna are a mystery. Where they come from and where they go is unknown. Early in the spring, schools appear off Guadalupe Island, some two hundred and fifty miles south of Catalina. These schools work up along the coastline of California as far as Point Concepcion (there are records of them as far north as San Francisco), where they swing southward offshore, and traveling down the coast in the fall at great speed, disappear seaward whence they came.

Let us suppose that tuna are schooling off the east end of Catalina and that we are starting on a day's fishing. Our boatman is waiting off the Tuna Club Float, and as we hurry to keep our appointment we pass other anglers; some walking briskly toward the fishing pier, others converging with us in the direction of the Club. Greetings are exchanged, and prophesies made on the day's prospects, and we stride down the boardwalk, skirting Avalon's picturesque, rambling tile-fronted buildings. No matter how often we may have seen the crystal clear waters of its crescent shaped bay, nestled in the steep slopes of the mountains, and dotted with yachts and fishing craft of all sizes, we can never fail to marvel at nature's wondrous handiwork. As we reach the Club, Mr. West, its capable assistant secretary, joins us to offer cheery words of encouragement and sees us down the gangway and safely aboard our boat. The motor roars; we are off.

As we run at high speed along the shoreline toward Seal Rocks, an easterly breeze daintily skims the top of the water, and the sun vainly tries to break through the mists of the upper air. Seals bark and gulls scream. Occasionally a bald-headed eagle wheels high above. The east end is passed, and our boat sways, rather than rolls, to the oily swell from the southwest as the lee is lost. The sky takes on a bluer hue. Soon the Island astern disappears in the haze as an offing is gained, and although the spell of the perfect morning still haunts us, thoughts turn toward the fish and the day's work ahead. As we sit on the forward bridge our eyes search for signs of tuna. Flying-fish skitter away on their smooth, graceful flight as they are scared up by the boat. Patches of kelp and schools of surfacing sardines are passed. Here and there a small shark swims lazily in apparently endless circles, his dorsal and flopping tail showing dark against the leaden water. Mackerel splash and swirl as they feed on small fry, and gulls hover momentarily to swoop on the cripples they miss. Shearwaters skim over the waves. The sea teems with life.

Seven miles southeast of the Island, the captain points seaward. A dark streak shows on the horizon. Is it a wind patch or current? No, it is fish; it is tuna! Cautiously the boat approaches them. Shimmering ripples make "tuna water," and we orient the school as it travels to windward. Conditions are perfect, and the spell of anticipation enthralls us.

Hurriedly rod is threaded and hooks baited, and the boat turns down wind. The captain carefully, and with exasperating slowness, adjusts his kite to the slight breeze, rigging it so that it will pull. Back into the wind turns the boat; up goes the kite. Quickly the line is fastened, and out goes the bait. All is in readiness.

"Make that bait jump; make it alive," calls the captain, as with great precision he judges his distance and approaches the fish. The angler lifts on the rod, making the bait skitter and splash over the water.

"Not too hard, or you'll foul it," comes the command.

The angler sets himself for the strike, and the bait enters the school. Then everything seems to happen at once. Splashes and ricocheting forms shoot behind the bait, three or four tuna miss, and then the great bronzed back of a bluefin appears, cuts the water in a seething arc, and hits the bait squarely between his open jaws.

"Strike," calls the angler. Quickly he reels to set the hook. "He's on!"

Away goes the fish, tearing off line, and the kite, freed from its breaking thread, flutters aimlessly to leeward. The reel sings a shrill scream and the rod nods rhythmically. Toward the end of the run the angler eases the drag, since the strain increases as the amount of line on the reel diminishes, and we watch him pump and reel, and pump and reel, again and again. How beautifully he handles his tackle, wasting not an inch of line, ever forcing the quarry nearer. How skillfully the boat follows his every action, backing and turning, sometimes speeding up to save line. It is perfect teamwork between boatman and angler. No words are spoken; no commands are necessary; each knows his part, and we revel in its precision.

The tuna makes several runs, but each one is shorter than the last, until finally we can look down into the blue-green depths and see his shimmering outline. The captain leaves the wheel, reaches for the gaff and steps into the cockpit. Carefully he grasps the leader; out goes the gaff, and with a deft movement born from long years of practice, it enters forward of the gill cover and back of the eye; the quarry is ours. We help slide the fish over the coaming and onto the stern deck, where he is made fast. The tuna flag is raised in triumph.

In addition to bluefin, the Channel Islands at times offer another species of tuna; the yellowfin (*Neothunnus macropterus*). This fish is almost identical in appearance with the former, save for the slightly longer fins and yellow cast to the coloring. They school and travel the same way, but a kite is not necessary to hook them. Since they are not so boat-shy, they may readily be taken on live bait cast from the fishing boat, and this is their undoing, because commercial boats make great hauls by chumming. These, together with the Allison, are the tuna generally taken in Mexican waters on the Pacific Coast. On occasions when yellowfins come northward along the coast as far as the Channel Islands, they provide excellent sport on rod and reel.

So much recently has been written on marlin that these greatest of all jumpers have become well known throughout the world. Truly, they are spectacular fighters, and it is small wonder that they are recognized by most authorities as the gamest fish that swims.

Marlin arrive in California waters during the middle of the summer. The vanguard of their migration from Mexico generally is seen in the Channel during July. They stay until October and later, the earliest capture having been made in 1926 when a marlin was landed July 13th, but the best fishing is in the latter part of August and throughout September. It is a peculiar fact that during the early days of Catalina fishing, marlin were not present; not until 1903 were they noted and hooked. Undoubtedly there would have been strikes on the tuna baits had the fish been there, and most certainly some of them would have been seen by the many anglers. The first boatmen at the Island who noted marlin came in with weird tales of zebra fish, the stripes suggesting the name. They were considered dangerous at that time by guides and anglers. Then after many had been hooked and a few landed, fishermen realized that they were a great new game fish. To date, some twenty-five hundred marlin have been landed at the Island.

The average weight of marlin at Catalina is about one hundred and sixty pounds. The largest ever killed off the California Coast weighed six hundred and ninety-two pounds, but fish of this size are rare in the extreme, and a three hundred pounder is considered large. Many seasons' records have been under this weight. The smallest marlin recorded tipped the scales at but fifty-seven pounds, but this is equally rare, and seldom are they taken under the hundred pound mark.

It is perhaps more difficult to lay down set rules for hunting marlin than any other fish. At different times of the year, during different seasons and under different weather conditions their actions are most dissimilar. During the height of a good season when marlin are plentiful, few problems present themselves, for the fish are readily found, being oriented through the action of the birds, by their peculiar tail fins, by their jumps and splashes, and by the frequent catches of other boats. At other times marlin rarely show themselves, and blind trolling is as productive as any other method. Some anglers insist upon the use of teasers (baits trolled close to the boat without hooks) as a means of attracting them under these conditions, but personally I do not favor this, since too often marlin will take one of these teasers without being seen. Had the teaser not been there the fish would have struck at the bait itself. It is remarkable how a fish of this size can steal a bait without being seen by the angler. Often I have had my eyes glued to the bait, and without seeing so much as a ripple have had a strike. When fish are scarce, the best method of locating them is to watch painstakingly for a jump or a splash, a sickle tail, or the action of only a brace of gulls as a single fish rounds up a small school of bait.

Since marlin drive small fish into a solid ball when they feed, slashing through and later returning to pick up the cripples, the birds which hover above them also restrict their activity to a small area. They wheel dizzily round and round, instead of dashing in all directions as they would where large schools of tuna, mackerel or bonito are feeding. When marlin are on the surface of the water, they almost invariably swim down wind, riding the swells as they go, and their peculiar sickle-like tails are easily spotted if the water is not too rough. By far the greatest number of fish are found this way, especially in the afternoon, when the wind has come up, and it is a simple procedure to troll the bait in front of them. The percentage of strikes, however, from surfacing fish is fairly small; sometimes they will hit and sometimes they will not. If marlin follow a bait, but will not take it, occasionally they may be enticed by speeding up the boat and by holding the bait high to make it skitter and splash. Since these fish have little fear, one may run quite close to them to get the bait nearer. I have had them strike while I was letting the line out and the bait was not further than five feet from the stern, right in the wake of the propeller. When the marlin are feeding and have rounded up mackerel, sardines, anchovies, sauri or other small fry, they nearly always will take a hook, and this is by far the most interesting type of marlin fishing. When ten or twelve marlin find a school of bait, they dash through it, slashing and killing as many as possible and use their bills as clubs, rather than rapiers. Once I saw a feeding marlin leap clear of the water with a mackerel impaled on his bill, but I believe this was an accident, rather than a deliberate attempt to spear the fish. The best way to fish when marlin are feeding is with a fairly short line, trolling slowly from three to five knots, right through the school. I shall never forget one of the most interesting experiences I ever had with marlin. We found eight or ten of them feeding close to shore off the east end of the Island. They had rounded up a small school of mackerel and were slashing through, knocking their quarry in all directions, and often splashing and jumping clear of the water. We were using flying-fish for bait, and although we got the hook into the middle of activities, the marlin were too much engrossed with the mackerel to take our flying-fish. It was most disconcerting to see so many fish and not be able to get a strike. As we slowed down, the mackerel saw the boat and made a dash to get under it for protection; they swam right along under us, but there was not room enough for all of them, and the marlin picked stragglers from under our very stern. I reeled the bait as close as I could and held it there, but the fish would not take it. What a sight it was! Marlin all around the boat, their stripes brilliant; so close that I could almost touch them. Then my boatman yelled:

"Quick! bring in your line!"

As I took the bait off the hook, he hurriedly rigged a snag gang to a light rod and dropped it over the side into the thickly packed mackerel. In a moment he had one impaled. I handed the big hook to him and on it he put the flashing, struggling mackerel, tossing it overboard. As it struck the water and before I could throw off the drag, a marlin grabbed it and cleaned the hook. Meanwhile, the skipper was snagging another mackerel. This time I released the drag before the bait went out and when the fish struck I was ready for him.

The usual bait for marlin is flying-fish, and the general procedure is to put a single hook through the head of the bait. Some anglers sew the mouth closed, and leave an inch or so of heavy line projecting, which is looped over the hook. Either method serves equally well and each has advantages. Of course, when the fish strikes, the line must be turned absolutely free, for marlin do not grab the bait in their mouths; rather they seize it between their upper and lower beaks. If the line is jerked even slightly when the fish strikes, the bait is pulled out of his mouth, he becomes suspicious and generally will not come back to it again. Quite a lot of line must be given; often a hundred feet or more is necessary, but there is no set rule. Each fish strikes and acts differently, and the novice must rely on the advice of his boatman as to when to set the hook.

There are several methods of rigging the bait, so that the fish may be struck without giving line. Some of these employ two hooks, not in gang which would violate the rules, but in tandem. Others consist in fastening the single hook far back in the bait so that it will catch in the corner of the marlin's mouth as he turns after striking. These methods as a rule are unsatisfactory, since the element of luck becomes too great, but there are times when marlin are not really hungry, hitting the bait solely out of the desire to kill. Then such methods are used to advantage, since there is a chance of hooking. Several ways of baiting are illustrated.

Heavy tackle generally is used for marlin since the chance of hooking a large fish always is present. However, there are many anglers who use light to the ex-

Heavy tackle equipment showing harness.

George C. Thomas, III, with light tackle rod and reel showing improved type of butt socket.

The three-six tackle.

Photos by courtesy of George C. Thomas, III.

Detachable swordfish gaff. The handle is removed and fish held on short rope to prevent injury to gaffer from heavy handle.

clusion of all else. Marlin are nice fish on nine-thread line since most of the fight
is on the surface. They seldom sound (some fish, especially large ones do, but this
depends to a great extent on how they are hooked), and are not too fast on their
runs. Their speed when hooked does not compare with that of tuna, and the danger of breaking the line through friction is not often encountered. A few of the
better anglers have even succeeded in landing them on three-six (my father was
the first on this coast), most notable of whom is R. C. Mankowski whose record
weighed one hundred and eighty-one pounds, but this is more in the nature of a
stunt, as the tackle is not adapted to general marlin fishing. Perhaps the nicest
tackle of all would be a light-tackle rod with fifteen-thread line, like that used
for sailfish in Florida, but this never has been adopted by the Tuna Club.

Since marlin fight on the surface, jumping and dashing in every direction,
boat handling counts a great deal in their capture. It is far better to follow the
fish, keeping behind it and turning as it turns, almost paralleling it on runs, than
it is to keep ahead as so many boats do. A popular method of boatmen is to run
away from the fish and let the angler pump it up to the boat. Many fish are lost
in this way, since the quarry often is facing the boat, thrashing on the surface
with his mouth open, which allows the hook to pull out easily. How much better
for the line to come back across his back to the boat behind. It also is much easier
on the angler. At gaff the marlin is usually quite docile, having played himself
out by his acrobatics. He should be gaffed under the front of the dorsal fin.

There is only one kind of marlin at Catalina. In fact, it is extremely doubtful
if there is any but the so-called striped variety (*Tetrapturus mitsukurii*) even in
Mexican waters. The numerous color variations all seem to be caused by color of
the water, weather, temperature, or the fact that when the fish are excited their
stripes become pronounced. I have landed marlin out of feeding schools which,
when they struck were very brilliantly striped at the beginning of the fight, but
when they were landed the bars were barely visible. I also have seen many fish
which apparently became aroused, whose colors flared brilliantly at the time of
landing. I believe that large, heavy-set fish with proportionally smaller dorsal
fins merely are old ones.

The best fishing grounds for marlin at Catalina are just off the east end of
the Island, out of the lee. Here fish seem to congregate and surface. Even if they
are not showing, the trolling angler will be rewarded with many blind strikes.
However, during the season, marlin are found throughout a widespread area.

To those who have never seen marlin at their best (which undoubtedly is in tropic or semi-tropic waters) it is almost impossible to describe their antics. Rushing, swerving, jumping, diving, splashing, thrashing and hurling themselves in every direction to shake the hook, their fight is the most spectacular of all fish. At times they dash for a hundred yards or so with only their tails in the water; at others they will start a fast run close to the surface, jumping with clocklike regularity every few feet, circling the boat. Then, tiring, they will bull-dog close to the boat, only to repeat the whole show all over again when you have relaxed in the confidence of apparent victory. There is just the slightest chance that one of them will come aboard in one of those mad dashes, which adds a bit of spice to the game.

It is a peculiar fact that marlin and tuna do not seem to run together in these waters. Each have apparent cycles; when one is abundant, the other usually is scarce. Perhaps this is the reason that marlin were unknown here during the best tuna years, and that during the great marlin run of 1929-1934 tuna of any size were absent. The year 1926 saw the end of the last great tuna migration, and the influx of the present excellent marlin fishing. Present conditions would indicate that marlin are now commencing a period when they will not be so plentiful on this coast. It is to be hoped that the tuna once more will return in great numbers. In fact, as I write, my boatman telephones that they are in the Channel at this season (February) for the first time in many years.

Broadbill (*Xiphias gladius*) swordfishing is on the wane in California; perhaps it may return. There are two reasons for this. The first is that commercial harpooners have wrought such depredations that the fish themselves are becoming scarce, being harpooned almost as they arrive, and the few which are seen have become so boat-shy through constant harassing by spearboats, that it is most difficult to work them. The other reason is that the fish seldom strike even if they have not been bothered, and that the chance of getting one is so small that it is hardly worth the effort. Several years ago, before harpooning started, and when there were lots of broadbill in the steamer lane off Point Fermin, it was not uncommon to see as many as a dozen or more of them a day. Throughout the season, which runs from June until October, one could generally find fish, although usually it meant a long run from Avalon. At that time it was estimated that, on the average, one out of every twenty-two fish worked would take a bait, and that one out of every three which struck would be hooked. Of those which were hooked, only one out of every five would be landed. So the chance of getting a fish even then was rare. It meant that one should expect to work a great number in order to land one, and if he was successful, he could consider himself lucky. The total catch at Catalina since the first one was taken on rod and reel by Boschen and Farnsworth in 1914 does not exceed two hundred.

I lost sixteen broadbill in fights ranging from five minutes to eight hours before I took my first one, and consumed five summers in fairly constant effort. In the past three seasons I have put a bait in front of perhaps one hundred and fifty, but have not had even one strike. Last summer none was landed at the Island.

Broadbill generally are solitary fish. Although they travel in migrations they do not often school, and it is unusual to see more than one at a time. I have noted as many as twelve in a square mile of water, but this was exceptional. They have been seen in Catalina waters throughout practically the whole year, but the summer months are the general period of their sojourn, since they travel leisurely up the coast from Mexico in the spring, returning in the fall. Their breeding grounds are unknown, but the only place I have seen small ones is in the Mediterranean. The curator of the aquarium at Naples found three for me, one of which, sword included, measures only fourteen inches.

They are best hunted on calm days, when it is easy to spot the telltale dorsal and tail fins. Under good conditions they may be seen for a distance of two miles, especially if the water is glassy, and this, too, is the best time to fight them, since a broadbill and a rough sea make a tough combination.

Practically any sort of small fish may be used as bait for broadbill. Flying-fish are used most commonly, since they are carried by all the fishing boats as tuna and marlin bait, and hence are at hand. However, mackerel, especially live ones, and small barracuda are used to better advantage, because broadbill often hit flying-fish so hard that the bait is ruined or the hook fouled. Perhaps this is because they fear the flying-fish is more likely to escape on account of its ability to leave the water. If a broadbill is hungry he will take practically anything that is offered. If he is not, nothing will tempt him. Occasionally these fish may be raised by the kite, after all else has failed, and in this connection, it is of interest to note that the first one ever landed was taken by Boschen and Farnsworth on a tuna kite, but then they are most difficult to hook, since the line cannot be turned loose with the kite pulling. The chance of hooking is slight. The ordinary method of offering the bait is by circling the surfacing fish and drawing the hook in front of him, but since broadbill do not always swim on a straight course and generally turn with the boat, keeping their side toward it, this is not always easy to do. Sometimes a great deal of maneuvering is required to get the bait in the right position. When the fish apparently sees the bait or is swimming toward it, the boat should be stopped, and the bait allowed to settle in the water. Frequently, the broadbill will go down to look it over, but the chances are that he will scorn it and come to the surface several minutes later. Broadbill, at least in Pacific waters, are the most exasperating fish that swim.

When hooked, these fish are slow. They seem to go about a deliberate method of wearing the angler down. Occasionally they jump. I had one fish clear the water sixteen times, but this is exceptional. More often, after the first few minutes of the fight, they sound to a depth of about two hundred feet or so, swimming almost due west. There they will stay, sometimes for hours, and it is seemingly impossible to raise them. They come to gaff when they want to, and not because they are forced. At the boat a large broadbill is truly a tough customer, and extreme care must be taken, especially with a green fish. They are best gaffed in the tail, because the sword is a dangerous weapon if thrashing above water, but great strength is required to hold a fish so gaffed and keep his tail out of the water. A detachable gaff, of course, is necessary.

One time I watched A. R. Martin, the present president of the Tuna Club, and one of the best anglers on the Coast, fight a three hundred pound broadbill for thirteen hours and twenty-three minutes. The fish was hooked at shortly after four o'clock in the afternoon, and landed at a quarter of six the next morning. Undoubtedly the night fight and the fact that we did not have adequate lights on the boat accounted to some extent for the length of time taken, but the chief cause was the fish itself. He was hooked in the pectoral fin, about half way out from his body, and the leverage and broadside pull which he had was almost too great for the angler to cope with.

The longest fight which I ever had with a broadbill was just under eight hours. This fish was large; we estimated his weight as close to seven hundred pounds; and just before the faulty leader broke, he was as fresh as when he started — in much better condition than the angler. The largest one which I have landed weighed five hundred and seventy-three pounds, and required over five hours to bring to gaff. He was hooked fairly in the corner of the mouth.

Personally, I do not enjoy this fishing. It is too uncertain, and the chances

Photos by courtesy of George C. Thomas, III.

George C. Thomas, Jr, with a morning's catch of light tackle marlin.

The author's 573 pound broadbill taken in 1927. This fish is still the world's record on regulation Tuna Club heavy tackle.

Small broadbill swordfish procured by the author in Naples, Italy. Note how dorsal fin extends back almost to tail. This fish is 22 inches long. Also note length of lower bill as compared to adult fish.

BROADBILL SWORDFISH ON THE SURFACE.

The author later hooked this fish and fought it for nearly eight hours before the leader broke.

LEAPING MARLIN.

MARLIN ARE UNDER THESE SARDINES.

A few moments after this picture was taken marlin broke loose among them. Boats in background trolling for marlin.

are too great against success. I believe that the average Catalina angler wants to land a broadbill simply for the sake of having done it, and after the first thrill has worn off, he is content to let them more or less alone. Of course, if he sees one, he will offer it a bait, but as far as fishing for them exclusively — that is another story.

The black seabass (*Stereolepis gigas*), often erroneously called a jewfish, is quite common at Catalina and in neighboring waters, and may be caught during practically any of the summer months. Although they range up to six hundred pounds in weight (the Tuna Club record is four hundred and ninety-three pounds), these giant bass are not particularly sought after by most anglers. They rate considerably under tuna, marlin and broadbill, but occasional days given up to fishing for them afford a pleasant change from the otherwise constant trolling. They live inshore, close to the kelp, and spend most of their time on the bottom. Still fishing at Catalina is the common method and with the boat at anchor in some pleasant cove one may while away a peacefully lazy day. Heavy tackle generally is used, but recently several anglers have taken to using nine-thread line, with surprising results. When the tuna and marlin are not biting, many boats may be seen at the jewfish grounds off the east end of the Island. The common bait for them is any kind of small fish.

A series of short, irresistible runs characterize the giant bass' fight, and he is easily gaffed in any part of his anatomy.

There are a great many varieties of smaller game to be found in California waters. Perhaps the best known offshore fish is the albacore (*Germo germo*). These miniature tuna, which reach a weight of fifty pounds or more, provide excellent sport on light tackle or three-six, and during the years in which they are plentiful, are greatly sought. They almost always are found in deep water far off shore, and running in schools, may be taken in great numbers. Their fight typically is that of tuna, with the long first run and the final circling before being brought to gaff. During recent years few albacore have been landed in the Channel waters; they seem to come and go with the large bluefin tuna, and have the same periodic absences. Last season marked the beginning of their return, and the coming summer undoubtedly will see them once more plentiful along the California Coast. Occasionally albacore visit the Channel Islands in the winter time, and it is then that the largest fish are caught. It should be noted that the albacore of the Pacific Coast are separate and entirely distinct from those of the

Atlantic, and I shall never forget an argument which I had with a Florida boatman about them which reached a rather hot stage. We saw a school of fish off Palm Beach which looked to me like some sort of small skipjack or bonito. I asked the boatman what they were, and he replied, "Albacore." The more I looked, the less I thought they were albacore, and I made no bones about saying so. We caught one and I found that the California albacore is altogether different from the so-called Florida variety.

Other small offshore game commonly found in these waters include mackerel, skipjack and bonito, all of which are taken by trolling or with live bait. The bonito run as large as sixteen pounds, and are most game, affording fine sport on three-six tackle.

Occasionally dolphin (*Coryphaena hippurus*) are found at the Islands, and when they come they are most welcome to light-tackle anglers. To many these fish are the most beautiful that swim, and the color changes which they show when landed are, to say the least, amazing. When they do run it is usually late in July and throughout August. It is probable that water temperature has a great deal to do with their visits, since they are more or less a tropical fish. In this connection it is of interest to note that their greatest run was in the summer of 1929, when the water at Catalina reached a maximum of seventy-eight degrees, the warmest on record. Since then, few have been caught. These fishes generally are found under floating patches of kelp, schooling in small groups of less than a dozen, and are caught most frequently on feather jigs trolled at good speed. Three-six tackle is perfect for them, and their jumping fight reminds one much of marlin.

Of the inshore fish, white seabass (*Cynoscion noblis*) and yellowtail (*Seriola dorsalis*) are the most sport, and it was this type of fishing which first attracted anglers to Catalina. Although recent years have not offered good inshore fishing, the cycle seems about to change. According to Farnsworth, periodic absences and returns are characteristic of practically all of California's marine life. He believes that the next few years will show a marked change, and that old-time conditions, with great schools of tuna, albacore, yellowtail and white seabass once more will return. It is to be hoped that he is right. Most certainly all present indications lend support to his theory, and the change already seems to be taking place.

If the albacore and yellowtail arrive, it will add great stimulus to sea angling in California, for it will mean a longer season and many more anglers. They are wonderful game, not too large for the novice, yet strong enough to intrigue the expert. On light tackle or three-six they cannot be surpassed.

White seabass are much like the yellowtail, but they are not so strong. Since they are night feeders in the main, they are not taken in such great numbers as yellowtail, but an afternoon's fishing, when they are plentiful, affords fine sport. Slowly trolled spoons generally are used. However, night fishing is much more interesting, and many of the anglers and boatmen form parties on the moonlight summer nights to hunt them. Perhaps this fishing brings us closer to the Island. It is then that one knows the beauty of the coves, the spell of inshore waters where he can look down into the depths and almost feel himself a part of the submarine gardens with their endless variety of strange tiny fishes. He can see sea cucumbers, anemones, abalones and other weird shapes. If he is lucky he may see a school of dozens of white seabass swimming majestically over the bottom. Perhaps he may troll a bit along the shore, landing rock bass or barracuda. (Not the savage fighter of Florida waters, but a smaller, thinner variety which reaches a maximum weight of sixteen pounds and which is excellent eating.) A group of boats generally leaves Avalon early in the afternoon, running up the coast of the Island to one of the numerous small bays. The afternoon is spent in preparing dinner, of which the chief course is fish, and the way in which these Avalon boatmen bake it in the rocks is something one remembers a long time. Just before sunset a gill net is set for flying-fish, which come inshore at dusk to feed. After dinner the net is pulled and a supply of fresh bait given to everyone. One cannot imagine a more beautiful setting, trolling slowly on these balmy summer evenings in glassy-smooth water, with the Island forming an almost black background, and the moon lighting the shimmering ocean. The silence is broken only by the sound of the boat's engines and the splashing of thousands of flying-fish.

White seabass are difficult to hook on this kind of bait. Plenty of line must be given before the hook is set, and many strikes will be lost. However, when the bass are running many of them will be taken.

One unusual fact in connection with fishing on the California Coast is that the angler knows and prepares beforehand for the variety he is going to catch. In so many noted fishing grounds any type of indigenous fish may strike. Here one fishes for what he likes best to the virtual exclusion of all else. Another perhaps pleasant feature is that one is not ordinarily surfeited with too good fishing. He learns to appreciate his catch; he works for it, but realizes that this very work will bring him a better understanding of his quarry, and a love for those days spent at sea which he might not otherwise have. To me this accounts for the universal acclaim of the fishing offered by the Channel Islands of Southern California.

THE PENINSULA OF LOWER CALIFORNIA

The waters between Point Concepcion, one hundred and fifty miles south of San Francisco, and Cedros Island, about four hundred and fifty miles below Catalina, offer approximately the same varieties of fish, under somewhat similar conditions. From Cedros (Cerros) Island south to and including the Gulf of California constitutes a new and very different fishing territory. It is these Mexican shores, covering some five hundred miles of latitude and with almost two thousand miles of coastline, exclusive of bays and islands, to which the remainder of this chapter will be devoted.

While practically all ocean fish are migratory, the ranges throughout which the various species travel differ greatly in extent. All of the mid-Pacific waters are visited upon occasion by the great game fishes whose habits and methods of capture have already been described in connection with fishing at the Channel Islands. In the Gulf and along the bleak coast of Lower California they are, with the exception of the bluefin tuna and the albacore, whose places are taken by the more tropical yellowfin and Allison tuna, even more abundant and grow to greater size. Here they furnish all the thrills attendant upon their capture elsewhere, with less effort expended in hunting them. In addition, the angler will find many new and untried varieties. Perhaps the very isolation of this coast is one of its chief charms — most certainly it is virgin territory, and the angler has it all to himself. So great in number are the species of fish here encountered that even an ichthyologist may find himself at a loss to classify all of the day's catch.

The angler who is equipped to fish these desolate shores will find sport beyond his most imaginative dreams. Here he will take fish of all sorts and descriptions, from the largest, fiercest marlin down to the wariest, daintiest lady-fish. There can be no question of the fact that fringing this narrow strip of land, both inside the Gulf and on the Pacific, is one of the world's greatest schooling and surfacing grounds, and the time is not far distant when its austere coast will be the Mecca for sea anglers of the North American Continent.

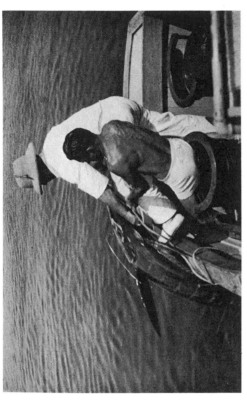

LANDING A BIG MARLIN.
Note the piano wire leader from corner of fish's mouth.

Photos by courtesy of George C. Thomas, III.

Marlin swimming on the surface. Note how dorsal fin is folded down. This fish struck a few moments after the photograph was taken.

A porpoise at Catalina. These mammals are plentiful on the coast.

P. West, assistant secretary of the Tuna Club, who is known to more sea anglers than perhaps any other man in the world.

FISHING AT CATALINA

At the present time all fishing expeditions to these waters must be self sustaining, since the poorly lighted, badly charted shoreline offers no bases where one may find boats and equipment. All supplies and all fishing launches must be carried aboard a mother ship. Even gasoline and oil are hard to procure, and then at a price only justified in an emergency.

In view of the fact that the average yacht is not capable of carrying a tender large and seaworthy enough to thoroughly explore the offshore fishing grounds surrounding each anchorage, and good anchorages are far apart, and that boats large enough to be self-sustaining are generally most unwieldy to fish from as well as too big for inshore work, comparatively little is really known of this coast. Certain ports, of course, are fished and have become well known, but there are many others which rarely are explored. The commercial live bait tuna boats have done most of the research, but since their activities are confined solely to tuna they have learned of little else. If one stops to consider that it has taken many years of constant effort to find the surfacing points and migration lanes of big game at our various fishing resorts, he will realize that the occasional well equipped boat which heads southward along Mexico has all too little time for anything but the briefest survey of this great country.

The selection of time of year one goes to Mexico is of the greatest importance, because during certain seasons there are severe storms as well as extreme heat. In the spring and early summer it is practicable for fairly small boats to go part way down the peninsula, but none except very able vessels should attempt extended cruises or exploring. The weather below Cedros Island often is dangerous during the summer months. The best time to visit the Gulf is from November to June, for then good fishing will be found, the climate is not too hot for comfort, and the weather may be relied upon.

Fishing tackle is an item upon which considerable care must be spent, and too much stress cannot be placed upon the fact that plenty of rods, lines, hooks and other essentials must be taken. In Mexican waters the angler never knows just what he will hook next, and the number of lines and hooks which will be lost is little short of appalling. Lines, especially, are most important, and each rod should have at least three spares. The various sizes of standard Tuna Club tackle of course will prove invaluable, and thirty-nine thread line for extremely large marlin and tuna is almost a necessity. In addition, I have found that a tip midway between the standard heavy and light tackle, used with a fifteen thread line, is ideal for trolling, especially in untried waters. It is not too small for the average large fish, and not too heavy for most of the smaller fighters. In trips to Mexico we found that spoons provided the best lures for general fishing, but we took the precaution of having heavier hooks fastened to them, as the havoc which large cabrilla (bass) play with the smaller, lighter ones is almost unbelievable. Many of our spoons were retrieved after a fight in such shape that we hardly recognized them as spoons at all. Of course for marlin and sailfish we used fresh bait — small fish of any variety which we happened to have at hand. Tuna bit well on feather and bone jigs.

I shall never forget my initiation into Mexican fishing. For many years before heading southward I had heard stories of the myriads of fish which were ravenous for the bait. Of course I was a bit skeptical, and considered most of the reports exaggerated — but I was soon to learn. We anchored at Santa Maria Bay early one afternoon, and immediately put the launch overboard for a bit of fishing. My father and I were using fifteen thread line as we did not know quite what to expect. We had no more than placed the spoons in the water when we simultaneously struck a pair of sierra or cero mackerel. As I was playing mine I felt a terrific commotion on the end of the line. Before I realized exactly what had happened I was fast to a large fish of some sort—he had taken my mackerel. My father sensed the situation, and tightened down his drag, endeavoring to bring his mackerel to the boat as quickly as possible in order to give me a clear field for my fight. Before he was able to do so another large fish grabbed it, and he, too, was hooked! Without any idea of what it was, although we knew that they were large, we fought for about ten minutes. My fish made a fast run toward the bottom, and upon being turned, came unhooked. Hurriedly I reeled so that I would not foul my father's line. Imagine my surprise when another fish grabbed the spoon, and again I was hooked on. We landed two cabrilla, one of which weighed eighty-three pounds.

This is typical of the fishing. One never knows just what he will hook next, and the unexpected is the rule. Of course, there will be times when fish are not biting, but those times are often welcome, since they add stimulus, and make one appreciate the great catches which follow.

Imagine a catch composed of ladyfish, roosterfish, dolphin, crevalle, cabrilla and a marlin, or again tuna, sierra mackerel, turel or torro (amberjack), white seabass, yellowtail, several large red snappers and a giant barracuda. Yet such is quite possible on two successive days, and even a third equally exciting catch may be made without repeating a single variety. You might as readily land a broadbill, a giant sea bass, a forty pound pompano, a wahoo, a skipjack and a two hundred pound sailfish.

Cape San Lucas, at the very tip of Lower California, is, so far as I have found, the greatest fishing spot in the world. Here migrations of divers fishes pass in endless array, and most of the great game varieties which we have mentioned, as well as others, may be taken within a mile of the anchorage. The bay itself is extremely beautiful and interesting. Semi-circular in shape, and bordered with a broad beach of the whitest sand, it runs out to a high rocky point on its westerly side. These rocks are most unusual, standing like sentinels to guard the southerly tip of the great peninsula. One forms a perfect arch, and is known as "The hole in the wall;" all offer protection from the prevailing west winds. High above, frigate birds wheel, while below on the water fish boil as they feed. Fortunate indeed is the angler who visits it. The town itself, located behind the beach and invisible from the bay, is a tiny settlement, its only business being its cannery. No provisions are available.

San José del Cabo, eighteen miles north of the Cape, on the Gulf side, is a larger village where some supplies may be procured, but landing here is difficult, being accomplished in dugout canoes through the surf.

In the Gulf, between the Cape and the town of La Paz, which is the only sizable port on the peninsula, are two other anchorages where great fishing may be had. The first is Los Frailes under Point Arena, about forty miles north; the second is Murales Bay, which is thirty miles further. Although neither of these places provides really dependable anchorage, they do give shelter of a sort. Ceralbo Island, off La Paz, has a good anchorage, (uncharted the last time I visited it), situated about one-third of the way from the east end. This island offers a fine lee, with excellent fishing, and interesting pearl fisheries.

In the Gulf above Ceralbo are a number of other islands which are well worth visiting, notably San José and Carmen, but the fishing which is to be found at them in the winter time does not generally compare with that at the Cape. North of Guaymas, the Gulf seaport on the mainland side, and some four hundred miles from Cape San Lucas, is Tiburon Island. Here white seabass run throughout practically the entire year. They reach one hundred and fifty pounds or over in weight and are excellent sport.

The experienced angler, upon leaving Los Angeles harbor for the Gulf, makes a quick trip of it to Cape San Lucas, well realizing that on the return journey he will buck headwinds and a somewhat disconcerting swell. Therefore he saves the several bays and islands on the west coast as resting places on the way home, rather than visiting them in the beginning. The first stop north of the Cape should be Santa Maria Bay, about one hundred and fifty miles up. Here inshore fishing is especially intriguing, and the beauty of the harbor, with its sheltering brown bluffs, and calm, clear water offer welcome refreshment after two days of pitching seas.

Magdalena Bay is only a short step on the homeward journey, but it should not be missed because of its unusual interest. It is here that the United States battle fleet often stops on its southern cruises, and the tiny village near the anchorage is aptly named Man of War Cove. Entered by a narrow opening, this bay opens up into a virtual inland sea many square miles in area. Here could be sheltered the battle fleets of the world. Truly this vast expanse of water is one of the greatest natural harbors in the western hemisphere. The sloughs and lagoons which border it teem with wild-fowl, and many varieties of fish may be taken.

Two hundred and forty miles further north is Turtle Bay, noted for its fine anchorage, its abalone fisheries and cannery, and its thousands of cormorants. Here one begins to enter the territory of the more northern fishes, and kelp makes its appearance for the first time. Here giant black seabass may be found in great numbers.

Passing through the Dewey Channel, one comes to Cedros Island, where an interesting stop may be made to fish for yellowtail.

By this time the angler will have realized that the reports of Mexican fishing were not exaggerated. He will have taken upwards of fifty different kinds of fishes, and he will feel that he has had more and greater sport than ever before in his life — then his thoughts will turn to getting home. Since the inshore passage would afford much rough water because of the adverse currents and winds, he will do well to go offshore, and if he has time he may wish to visit Guadalupe Island so famed for its herd of sea elephants. As his trip draws to a close his thoughts will turn back to these fish-laden waters and he will know that he has seen as good fishing as may be found anywhere in the world.

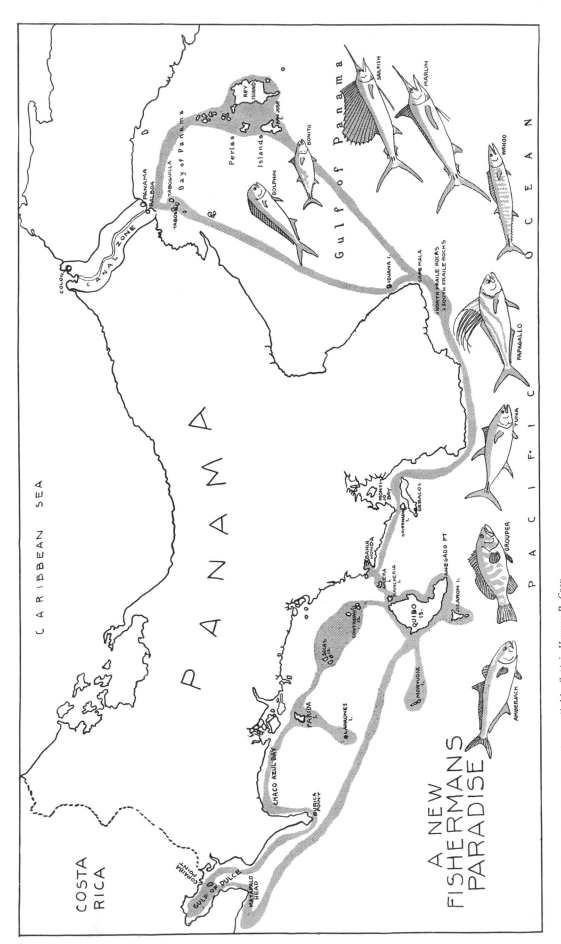

Drawn by Lynn Bogue Hunt from information supplied by Captain Herman P. Gray.

CHAPTER XI.

PANAMA WEST COAST FISHING

BY
CAPTAIN HERMAN P. GRAY

ETWEEN the equator and 30 degrees north, in almost any longitude, ocean fishing is sure to produce thrilling experiences that the angler will live over and over again in memory. Perhaps in fuller measure than elsewhere in the western hemisphere does this apply to that small bight of the Pacific bordering on Panama and other Central American countries. Certainly, in a fishing experience that covers waters from near the Arctic Circle to the Equator, I have not found the equal of this sport fisherman's paradise.

My attention was first directed to this strange country when, some years ago, in quest of new fishing grounds, I began making extensive inquiry among seafaring men, including many master mariners who had sailed the seven seas. While not as a whole particularly interested in fishing, these men are almost invariably keen observers of ocean life. Perhaps, to them, a tumbling porpoise or breaching sailfish or marlin becomes sort of a welcome relief in an endless expanse of blue; at any rate, such objects seldom escape their vigilant gaze.

Their reports all seemed to indicate that — whether due to some favorable quality in the topography of the ocean bed, an abundance of natural food, or perhaps some less understood factor — here were waters literally infested with big fish of many game varieties. Needless to say, I found little difficulty in persuading my sponsors that a personal investigation was in order. What sportsman wouldn't respond to the prospect of finding practically virgin fishing grounds, scarcely less accessible than the popular waters of Florida and California?

With a view to observing some of the waters off Nicaragua, Costa Rica and Panama on the way south, I took passage on a Pan-American air liner out of Miami. From Belize, British Honduras, a regular stopover, a few hours' flight across the mountains of Central America brought us a bird's-eye view of the blue Pacific lapping the shoreline of the beautiful little country Salvador. A brief stop for mail and we were off again over the water, following the coast as we headed for Managua, Nicaragua.

Due to a strong wind and the fact that we flew at great height to get the benefit of favorable air currents it was difficult to see anything but the larger forms of marine life, such as blackfish, porpoise, sharks and devilfish. Conditions were better next day when, after a night's rest at Managua, we took off for the final hop to Panama. Skimming along at from four to six hundred feet over the ocean, we had hardly cleared the beach when I saw several devilfish. The water was alive with sharks. From then on I could see fish of some kind anywhere I looked.

I wouldn't attempt to say what kind they all were, but there was no mistaking the broadbill swordfish, who stands out by himself in his beautiful deep purple. Marlin, too, were readily recognized by the purple stripes, distinctly visible as far as one can see the fish. There were great schools of smaller fish which I took to be tuna, clouds of gulls and boobies hovering and feeding over them. Fish of one kind or another were constantly in sight until we landed at Balboa. If I ever wanted to drop a hook over the side it was that day.

I called on Governor Burgess of the Canal Zone, who though more interested in golf than fishing, was good enough to introduce me to Mr. H. H. Hammer, whom I believe to be the best informed fisherman in the Zone. The largest sailfish ever taken until that time in those or any other waters had been landed by him in conjunction with his uncle, an elderly gentleman.

As I recall the story, they were in the habit of making week-end fishing trips to the Perlas Islands, a group lying twenty-five miles south of Balboa. Their angling wasn't confined to any particular species of fish, the baits used being mostly spoons of various makes and home-made feather baits that skipped along the surface. These latter consisted of a wooden, scooped-out head piece, to which chicken or parrot feathers were attached, concealing the hook. These feather jigs were very effective on dolphin, papagallo, tuna and yellowtail, but sailfish, marlin or swordfish were not easily hooked though they would often strike them.

On one of these trips, however, Mr. Hammer's uncle was trolling a feather bait when a huge sailfish took it. He managed to hook the fish securely, but it proved more than he could handle. Mr. Hammer landed it after a terrific fight, but he did not look for any more such fish that day. I believe he told me that it measured 10 feet 8 inches and weighed 187 pounds. He did not claim any record, however, as the catch was made by two persons.

So far as I could learn, cut or strip bait had not been used with any success in Panama waters prior to my first visit. I was told that they had tried it, but so many lines had been ruined by the bait turning over and over that they had given it up as a bad job and gone back to their feathers and spoons.

Another keen fisherman whom I later had the pleasure of meeting was Dr. Mitten, who had succeeded in landing a large silver marlin on this same type of home-made feather bait.

Well satisfied with the information I had gathered on my brief survey, I hurried back to Palm Beach to organize a real expedition to such promising waters.

There being no suitable fishing boats available south of Key West, we had two small, specially equipped power boats built and shipped down. Before leaving Panama, I had already chartered a boat of sufficient size to serve as headquarters for the expedition. Tackle and other equipment were soon assembled and in July (1931) we were en route by steamer to Colon. There we boarded our headquarters craft and after setting everything shipshape were soon nosing up to Gatun Locks.

Tarpon were rolling and splashing all around us, waiting for the big gates to open and let them in. They followed us through into Gatun Lake; whether they remained there or returned with the next outbound ship I cannot say. They seemed to be in every lock but, strange to say, there is no record of tarpon being caught on the Pacific side of the isthmus. Perhaps they are too well satisfied with their Atlantic home, where they occur from South Carolina to British Guiana.

Dropping the pilot a few miles out of Balboa, we headed for a little group of islands nine miles off the mainland in the Gulf of Panama. Here, in a beautiful land-locked harbor, surrounded by the islands of Taboga, Taboguilla and Little Taboga, we dropped anchor and went ashore for a look around. Back on board again that evening, we made preparations for some fishing next day.

Leaving the mother ship in one of the small boats soon after breakfast, we dropped two Japanese feather baits over the stern, and had hardly left the side of the big boat when a Spanish mackerel and a horse-eye jack were hooked. Both were immediately cut up for bait, but we did not put them out until we were well clear of the islands, not wishing to waste them on dolphin, tuna, mackerel, jacks and other lesser game fish.

We had just rounded the point of Taboguilla Island when we saw a fish breach, but couldn't make out the species as it was about half a mile away. Sword, sail and marlin are easily mistaken at that distance as they all breach in the same manner when not on a hook. Just why they breach is something that has never been explained to my satisfaction.

I jerked the throttle wide open, never taking my eyes off the spot, for distance on water is very deceiving and once you take your eyes off the spot where the splash was seen it is difficult to judge when you have reached the place, even if your course is true. The boys quickly changed their Jap feathers for the cut baits and, nearing the spot where I had seen the jump, I slowed down to about three or four miles per hour.

Hardly had the bait gotten thirty feet from the boat when a fin that looked like a small sailboat came clear of the water and with it the long rapier bill of the largest sailfish I had ever seen. The second bait was being put out while Number 1 line was being paid out to our big fish, which showed signs of being hungry from the start. Suddenly Number 2 bait was struck a terrific blow and line began whizzing off the reel at a great pace. With the drag thrown in and thumbs bearing down on the leather brake, my friend tried to halt the mad rush, the reel grinding and squealing as though it would fly into pieces.

Number 1 rod had meanwhile thrown on his brake and, the line coming tight, set back with such a strike that had he not set his hook in something solid, I believe he would have gone overboard. Almost at the same instant two of the largest and most beautiful sailfish I had ever hoped to see broke clear of the water. Believe me, that sight was worth the entire trip!

Then followed a grand exhibition of skyward leaps and fancy tail-walking, each fish seemingly trying to outdo the other in acrobatic stunts, or putting on an extra show for the newcomers to their uninvaded realm. Finally the fish on No. 2 line made a wild series of jumps straight toward the boat. I doubt that any angler could have taken in the slack, nor could it have been done with the boat, starting from a full stop. To attempt to run away from him with the boat was out of the question anyway, the other fish already having too much line out for us to give him more by such an operation. It didn't take No. 2 long to shake the hook and he was gone, to grow into a bigger and better sailfish.

Number 1 fish was still going, if anything stronger than ever, it seemed. My friend was beginning to realize that it wasn't one of our Atlantic sails he had on. I don't mean to belittle the Atlantic fish, as he is a fighter in his own right; the difference between this fish and his Eastern brother was one hundred pounds of fighting power.

After about one hour and thirty minutes of magnificent fight the splendid fish was finally brought alongside. It struck me as being just too much fish to take by the billing method and I decided to resort to the gaff rather than take any unnecessary chance of losing our prize at this late stage of the game. As the gaff went home, I was instantly convinced that I hadn't overestimated the strength of the fish, for it made one tremendous lunge and I came as near going for a ride in tow of a sailfish as I ever want to. Jerked clear of the deck, it was just by sheer luck that I caught the underside of the gunwale with my left hand while Mr. Sail was clear of the water. My right wrist being through the loop at the butt end of the gaff, I couldn't let go even if I had wanted to and only the fact that my companions threw their weight on my legs and held on prevented me from going overboard.

After a few exciting moments the big fish was in the boat. We didn't stop to try for any more, but headed straight for the big boat. The enthusiasm of the crew was high, as none of them had ever seen a sailfish close enough for examination. We quickly broke out yardstick and scales and found that this fine specimen registered 10 feet 2 inches, weighing a full 152 pounds.

There was great excitement in the little village of Taboga as the natives, mostly Panamanian, had never seen any of these fish caught in this vicinity before. After lunch, however, we were again ready for action and, fishing in nearby waters, caught a number of big sharks, mostly of the tiger species.

Next day we set sail for Cape Mala, about ninety miles west-northwest of Taboga and, arriving late in the afternoon, anchored behind a little island called Iguana. On this day's run we saw several sailfish breach; also any number of schools of tuna, two whales, porpoise of many sizes and flying-fish skimming at every angle.

My companions were towing Jap feathers on heavy hand lines, astern of the big boat, in front of the two fishing boats which we were compelled to tow, the davits on the mother ship not being strong enough to hoist them aboard. Those fellows had the deck looking like a fish market, with an assortment of tuna, dolphin, mackerel, bonito and horse-eye jacks. One bonito and two tuna were lost to big marlin that rushed up under the stern and knocked them off the hook. We didn't stop to fish for them, as we felt there would be plenty of time for that later on. Instead, we spent the remaining daylight ashore, chasing and capturing iguanas, after which the island is well named.

The following morning we did some trolling around the island, with feathers and the Trix-oreno No. 999. Cut bait was out of the question, for we would have spent all our time tying on bait. We caught fish of one kind or another as fast as we could turn one loose and drop the artificial bait overboard again. Among the species taken were yellowtail, dog-tooth snapper — some weighing as much as eighty pounds — seabass, grouper, tuna and any number of the very sporty papagallo, with their beautiful dorsal fin, resembling a rooster comb. These latter strike with a great shock and make long, speedy runs, often breaking clear of the water.

Our tackle was mostly heavy, 9-0 reels and 24 thread line, which in most cases was ample, though we did find it inadequate on one occasion which I shall come to later. I am not a light-tackle enthusiast when it comes to fishing for big salt water fish, particularly where unfamiliar species are concerned. After all, the fish that count are those that are caught. The ones that get away don't mean a thing to the museum, nor in the trophy room. Other anglers may not agree with me, but I say use heavy tackle for heavy fish, at least when fishing strange waters. If you are lucky enough to get a big fish on your line you needn't worry about having some sport; the fish will take care of that. I don't claim, by any means, that big fish cannot be landed on light tackle, but I do claim that the largest game fish are seldom taken on such equipment, except by anglers who have had a great deal of experience and, even then, much depends on the skill of the man handling the boat.

Rounding Cape Mala, we proceeded up the coast of the Fraile Islands, small but dangerous rock islands jutting up out of the blue, where hosts of sea birds nest and roost.

A bait had only been dropped a few feet behind the boat when a grouper took it and started for the bottom. When that fish was brought back up to the surface, I can truthfully say that a ton of fish followed it up. I couldn't name all the different species, but there were yellowtail, dog-tooth snapper, amberjack, spanish mackerel, shark, tuna and a fish which we called redfish, for want of a better name. They were a brilliant red, with a dark blue eye, and I am sure there must mave been a ton or more of these fish alone. They lent the blue water a fiery red color.

We cut the motor and caught fish until we were tired of pulling them in. After several hours, we put on full speed and headed up the coast in pursuit of the mother ship, which had dropped us off at the Frailes. We passed through school after school of tuna, feeding on still more schools of smaller fish, but we didn't stop. We had had exercise enough for one day and the mother ship, while only capable of ten knots, was four hours ahead of us. A stern chase is always a long one, but our fishing boats made twenty knots, so in a little over two hours we made fast astern and were quite ready for a little rest and food.

Fish and birds were as usual everywhere. We saw any number of sailfish breach, in fact one breached so close that I thought it would hit one of the boats towing astern. As night closed in on us, we rounded Governador Island and dropped anchor in Montijo Bay, a snug harbor and a very pretty one.

After an early breakfast we again cut loose from the ship, which proceeded to Bahia Honda while we cruised along the coast looking for whatever Father Neptune had to offer. As usual the first line wasn't well out when a tuna took it. After that, feeling pretty well caught up on tuna, we kept all lines inboard for a while, hoping to see bigger game.

After about a six mile run we saw a sailfish breach close by and, putting the cut baits over, it was only a few minutes until business picked up. There must have been a school of them, as five sails rushed our bait, along with several tuna, and we hung one of each. Meanwhile the other boat had hung two sails out of the school, but they only managed to land one of them, which evened our scores. We didn't weigh or measure either fish, but I know they were well over nine feet.

Several other sails were sighted that day, though we did not catch any more.

Instead we caught amberjack, papagallo, tuna, snapper and grouper, also several fish which the natives called blue jacks and which on light tackle would give a good account of themselves. We saw a few schools of smaller mullet close in-shore but in deep water these fish would average eight to ten pounds. Some of this species we managed to snag, a few days later, by casting across them with a three-hook jig. They looked exactly like our Atlantic silver mullet, except for the great difference in size. I never saw any of these larger mullet in shoal waters, although the small ones up to eight or ten inches were quite numerous in the shallow bays and rivers.

Late in the afternoon we arrived alongside the mother ship in Bahia Honda, which is a beautiful, deep, landlocked harbor, surrounded by mountains. In the center is a pretty little island on which a few natives live. This spot would make an ideal location for a fishing club if it were a bit more accessible.

There is almost no limit to the varieties of fish that can be caught within a radius of five miles of this harbor. Also it is possible to fish three hundred and sixty-five days in the year, as the Japanese current maintains an even temperature of about 80 degrees Fahrenheit the year around and one can always find a lee in which to fish in comfort. Wind or calm seems to make little or no difference in the fishing.

The fish caught on our run from Montijo Bay were taken ashore by the crew and given to the natives, who sat up all night smoking them, this being their only means of preserving them. They seemed very grateful and reciprocated by bringing us bunches of bananas, green cocoanuts and yams.

After a good night's rest, we made an early start in the two fishing boats, heading for Afuera, an imposing island which towers 650 feet above sea level. No lines were put out until we were within half a mile of shore, when we promptly hooked a pair of horse-eye jacks. These landed, we approached closer to the island and then dropped a teaser off the stern about twenty-five feet.

Before any of us could get a line in the water, the largest wahoo I had ever seen jumped clear of the water, with the teaser in his mouth, snapped the heavy teaser line and was gone — teaser and all! We were all so astounded that no one seemed able to speak for a moment. When we realized that we hadn't just been seeing things, it didn't take us long to get our baits overboard. Not more than ten feet from the boat, and at the same split second, both baits were struck with tremendous force. I almost lost rod, reel and all.

Balanced Rock — Perlas Group.

Part of a few hour's catch of wahoo, etc.

World's record and three to spare.

Captain Herman P. Gray holding a papagallo.

There was no mistaking the species, as both were in plain sight. In less time than it takes to tell it, and before the boat could gather momentum, the wahoo had cleaned off two 9-0 reels of 400 yards of 24 thread line. Snapping when the spools were reached, the double report of the parting lines could be heard above the roar of the motor and left two fishermen looking at each other, wondering what it was all about.

Unfortunately we had neglected to put extra 24 thread lines in our boat. Light tackle being out of the question, we decided to go to the other boat and see if they had some extra lines. They had, meanwhile, disappeared around a nearby point of the island, but we weren't long in overtaking them. They had no spare lines either, but they offered to let us use their outfits and they would stand by and see whether we had been dreaming or had discovered some new and unheard of sea monsters.

Returned to the spot which we had pointed out to them, however, they evidently decided to show us up, for instead of turning their outfits over to us they put out their own lines and proceeded to troll. But, instead of keeping their baits close in and all drags set, they made the mistake of having long lines out. Those fish seemed to be waiting for them and when they presently pounced on the baits the result was the same as in our case — except, of course, that their lines didn't last even as long as ours had.

Determined to at least stop one of these fish, we decided to try a heavy hand line, with extra heavy wire. This line, however, lasted but little longer than that on the reels and when it had sizzled through gloved hands and reached the bitter end, which had been made fast to a cleat, its parting snap was even more impressive. The heaviest lines we possessed were only 24 thread and it was too late in the day to return to the mother ship for them anyway. We were forced to concede defeat for the time being. That we might have resorted to harpoon lines didn't occur to us until later — at which stage many a good idea is born.

Sighting several manta or devilfish, we decided to try our luck with these large rays, often referred to as blanket fish. They are quite plentiful in these waters and anyone looking for excitement shouldn't overlook — nor under-estimate — these monsters. Singling out one that looked larger than the rest, we manoeuvered within striking distance and one of the boys made a clean center shot with the hand harpoon.

The huge ray flashed clear of the water four times, the harpoon line smoking through the chock on the bow. As the fish made a right-angle turn, we managed to get a turn on the snubbing post and when it straightened out again we were going places.

After over three hours of hard fight, sore backs and blistered hands, we were willing to call it a day and let the tiger sharks finish a job they had already started.

We didn't turn in very early that night although all of us were dead tired. The more we discussed the wahoo experience, the more excited we became and I believe that, had we not known that heavier tackle was not available in the Canal Zone, we would have headed straight back there that night. We agreed, however, that on another trip we would bring lines capable of stopping whales if we found them. We did just that, by the way, the following year, but the largest wahoo we landed weighed only ninety-six pounds. Whether the larger fish were still there, and the smaller ones beat them to the bait, or we had just run into a school of extra large fish on our previous trip, I cannot say. I have been back to the same spot a number of times since, but have yet to find those big ones.

After several days in the Bahia Honda section, we moved on to another harbor between the Panamanian prison islands, Quibo and Rancheria. Boats are usually not allowed within three miles of shore, but by special permission of the President of Panama we were privileged to go ashore at any point. From this anchorage we were able to cover Contreras, Jicaron, Jicarita, Montuosa and Secas Islands.

It seemed as though all the fish in the Pacific were on hand wherever we fished. On runs from one island to another we made no attempt to fish, confining our activities to waters around each island. While at this anchorage, we saved all the fish landed, taking them to the prison where they were welcomed, as they had no means of catching fish other than a few speared from shore by prisoners. Every species brought in was eaten, the surplus being salted, as there was no ice.

Tuna seemed to be the most numerous of the surface fish, schools of smaller tuna, estimated as averaging about twenty pounds, being very common; I didn't see any that I would judge to weigh over 150 pounds and the largest we landed scaled 122 pounds. Seventeen sailfish and four small marlin were taken by us in this territory. The latter were all of the silver variety, the largest weighing

171 pounds. We did see one large black marlin but were unable to induce him to take the bait of cut tuna belly, though he followed it for a time.

All of these outlying island waters were teeming with fish. One could cut the motor and drift over the shelf rock and see any number of fish, some of which I would make no attempt to name. I have spent many pleasant days at the Smithsonian as well as the American Museum of Natural History, but I am positive that I saw many fish out there on those ledges that I have not seen among either collection.

Trying to see and do as much as our limited time would permit, we soon moved on up the coast to Parida Island, where by skilful manoeuvering on the part of the captain, the mother ship was anchored in a suitable cove. Here we caught an abundance of amberjack, papagallo and grouper. At Ladrones Island, a rock formation rearing one hundred and fifty feet out of water, about twelve miles west-southwest of Parida, we caught one sailfish, seven wahoo and a number of snapper.

A couple of days later found us at Puerto Armuelles, where the United Fruit Company has large banana plantations and a concrete dock running two thousand feet out into Chaco Azul Bay, on which batteries of banana loading machines operate. Here we were able to replenish our supply of ice, which was about gone. At this point, too, we had scheduled a trip into the interior and had arranged for transportation over the fruit company's railroad as far as their steel went; from there we continued by pack horse.

On arriving at our headquarters camp, we were told of the rainbow trout fishing to be had thereabouts. As we were primarily on something of a hunting trip, and five or six thousand feet above sea level, fishing was the farthest thing from our minds — nor could I associate trout tackle with the tropics.

Our guide was enthusiastic, however, and one could hardly say that he lacked a responsive audience. The result was that three of us set out in the early morning, armed with one dilapidated trout rod that might have seen better days along about 1910. The equally ancient reel held about twenty-five feet of what once probably had been a silk line, backed up by some yards of store string. With this amazing paraphernalia, augmented by two home-made trout flies and an assortment of small hooks, we mounted our horses.

After an hour's ride from camp we halted beside a swift, deep stream. The guide rigged up the antique outfit and handed it to my companion. On his second cast the fly landed about ten feet from the end of the rod. It had hardly hit the water when a beautiful rainbow trout that would go close to three pounds came out in a gracefully curved jump, then started across and down river. Slipping and sliding over the rocks, my companion followed in hot pursuit, finally falling full length into the river. Perhaps this frightened the fish into turning back upstream, which was his undoing. It gave my friend a chance to get most of his line back and with a skilful manoeuver he grounded the trout in the lee of a big boulder.

Taking the eyes and throat for bait, I rigged up my own line on a pole cut from a tree on the bank and went into action. Between the three of us we soon had a beautiful mess of rainbows to take back to camp, not to mention the generous number consumed for lunch, broiled over hot coals. I am well aware that to the dyed-in-the-wool fly fishing purist, our crude methods of taking these fine sporting fish will appear little short of blasphemy. I am not advocating the system described, however. We wanted trout, and — with trout tackle probably some three thousand miles away — we got them as best we might.

Since this is a fishing story, I shall confine my observations to the subject, but I want to say in passing that our fortnight in the interior convinced me that the hunting in the mountains of Panama has not been overrated.

Returning to sea level and finding the ship restocked, the crew rested and everything in readiness, we sailed out of Chaco Azul Bay, rounded Burica Point and headed into the Gulf of Dulce.

Soon after rounding the point, we saw a sailfish cruising around, its huge sail high above the water. Not having seen a sailfish in over two weeks, the impulse prompted by such a sight was irresistible. Laying the mother ship to, we all hopped into one of the fishing boats and were off after our fish.

The big sail didn't wait for the bait to come to him; he made a dash for the tuna belly when it was still fifty feet or more away and it wasn't long before the reel was screaming, water flying and about one hundred and fifty pounds of sailfish was giving an exhibition such as only one of this long-billed family can give. Yells and cheers from the crew, watching from the ship, seemed to encourage the fish and it was a good hour of constant fight before he was brought alongside and released.

Boarding the ship again, we were soon booming in past Banco Point. Devilfish seemed to be holding a convention at this particular place, as we counted eleven in less than twenty minutes. There were acres of jellyfish in the tide streaks and I believe this accounted for the presence of so many of these giant rays, jellyfish being one of their main items of diet.

It was a calm day and the smooth surface of the water was alive with small fish, skipping in all directions, with dolphin, tuna, bonito and porpoise in pursuit. Shark fins might be seen at any point of the compass. With big fish charging the small fry from beneath, of course the pelicans, boobies and gulls were enjoying a Roman holiday. One of the many mysteries of the sea, to me, is how any fish survives the onslaught of almost limitless enemies long enough to attain a weight of one pound. Sea life affords endless fields for investigation and study, and it is my opinion that man's knowledge of it will never be complete.

Perhaps it is the mystery of it all that holds the angler in its spell. One never knows what he will see next. One might fish over the same ground for years, using the same bait and methods, yet no two days' fishing will be exactly the same. The fish will be larger, smaller or of a different kind; they will behave and even bite differently — in fact, may not bite at all.

Cruising on up into the Gulf of Dulce, all hands scanned the surface in hopes of spotting a swordfish. But it wasn't our day, and late in the afternoon we dropped anchor in a mountain-fringed harbor, with a 1726-foot peak due north of us.

We took a fish boat and spent the rest of the day harpooning sharks and sawfish, while the crew went ashore and returned with a good bag of snipe and two crested guans, a large fowl of a fine flavor, similar to that of wild turkey. It was no trouble at all at any time to stock our larder with game.

The following day we fished close to shore, taking the usual snapper, grouper and ground fish. There was one species which we hadn't caught before; in color and stripes it resembled our sheepshead, but it had a true grouper mouth. Running near the surface and with mouth closed, it put up a much better fight than any grouper, a trait of the latter being to sound and then come up open-mouthed, with scarcely a struggle.

Off Copaiba Point we hooked into what I believe was a very large jewfish, or giant sea bass. My companion had hooked a good-sized horse-eye jack which I could see very plainly. In fact, I had put down my rod and was pulling on canvas gloves preparatory to unhooking the fish, when it suddenly made a desperate run, with a huge black object in pursuit. The jack didn't get far when the rod bowed sharply and yards of line began disappearing off the reel. The boat was shot ahead, and it looked for a few minutes as though we were in for a repetition of our experience with the wahoos. The fish changed its course, however, and headed for the 100 fathom curve that makes in close to this point, my companion regaining quite some line during this manoeuver. It was give and take, then, for the best part of two hours. The fish slowed down to a slow, steady swimming speed that convinced us that we were fast to a big jewfish — just how big, we were anxious to see.

It wasn't a question of where we wanted to go but rather where that fish wanted to take us. Evidently he was seeking a shelf rock to get under. Not finding such a place in deep water, he headed toward shore and, on the west side of the point, he must have found what he wanted, perhaps his old home. At any rate, we couldn't budge him and, so far as I know, he is still there. The end of the line appeared to have been cut against the rocks.

When I spoke of this jewfish having a home, I meant just that. I know of many cases of individual jewfish occupying a certain hole over long periods. In clear southern waters, such individuals are often readily identified by scars or other peculiarities and, once located, a daily inspection will nearly always find them at home. As they are far from being a game fish I seldom molest them, but the big fellow we had lost intrigued us and the next day we set out to get him, armed with a lot of bright ideas.

It didn't take us long to catch another horse-eye for bait and we were ready to go into action. On approaching the scene of yesterday's sudden activity we baited a shark hook with our vigorous 15 pound jack and, letting out about twenty fathoms of 9 thread manila rope, hung on, waiting for something to happen. The jack soon began tugging and jerking in a manner that spelled danger and a moment later something grabbed him with a rush that took at least four fathoms of rope without half trying. We let about ten more go and then, when it came taut, lay back with all our weight. Right then and there, there was plenty of action. We finally got a couple of turns around a bit on the foredeck and our fish laid a course for deep water, towing the boat along at good speed.

After about thirty minutes the pace slackened, and we were able to heave in line, a few inches at a time. Every so often the fish, in turn, would take a few feet. Finally the coil of rope began to pile up in the boat, but the fish hadn't

LEAPING RAY.

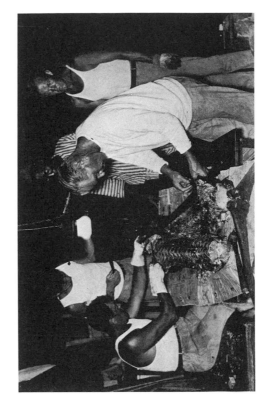

SKINNING SAILFISH FOR MOUNTING.

Photos by Paul Burress.

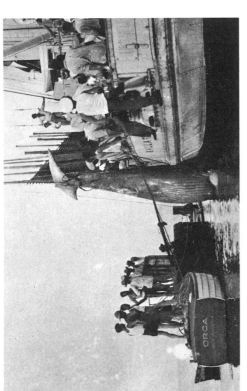

FINBACK WHALE.

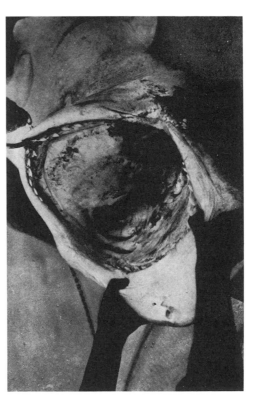

MOUTH OF TIGER SHARK.

given up by any means. Whatever it was, we were agreed that it couldn't be jewfish; we felt sure they didn't grow to such size.

At last a glimpse of the fish, far below, told us the sad story, color alone sufficing to identify him as a tiger shark. The only thing to do was bring him in and get our hook back. The closer he came to the surface, the larger he got and the more distinctly his stripes stood out. At length his back was clear of the water and a well-placed soft-nosed bullet from my companion's .33 Winchester, at the base of the dorsal fin, slowed him up. After two or three more shots for good measure, he was made fast astern and we headed for the ship with our questionable prize.

This tiger measured a good sixteen feet in length, its open jaws being large enough to accommodate a man's head and shoulders, with room to spare.

Proceeding next day we found a new anchorage in a well-protected cove just east of the Dulce River. Several rivers empty into the Gulf of Dulce, but they are mostly small streams, navigable only to boats of very shallow draft. Crocodiles are quite plentiful in these rivers and creeks and the bird life along the banks very interesting. To the north, the shoreline of the gulf is mountainous, affording deep water close in, in contrast with the south and southwest shores which are low and fringed with cocoanut and mangrove. We were here during the rainy season, but didn't let the showers interfere with our fishing. As is sometimes the case in Florida, it might rain in the stern of your boat while the sun shone in the bow.

Several finback whales were sighted, one mother coming so close to our anchorage with her offspring that we thought she was coming aboard for a visit. In fact, that night we thought the whole school was coming aboard. They thrashed and blew around us off and on all night and were still there at sunrise.

I had a hunch that a school of orca had driven them in, which is often the case, particularly when there are baby whales in the school, as they make tidbits for the killer. Hoping for action with orcas, we put extra harpoons, lines, rifles and plenty of ammunition in the small boats and quickly headed out to sea, the two boats spreading out so that we could just see one another.

A white shirt, waved aloft on a harpoon shaft, was to be the signal for battle in the event orcas were sighted, but an all-day search covering considerable territory failed to produce any trace of the marauders. I never consider a day wasted, however, when spent on the trail of these terrors of the sea.

BIG GAME FISHING

Rounding Matapalo Head early one morning, we headed west along the coast toward Salsipuedes Point. The ocean was like a mirror, affording excellent opportunity for observation of the usual survival-of-the-fittest struggle.

Using feather bait, we ran into a school of bait fish resembling our sardines and immediately hooked a pair of tuna. Releasing them, we headed for another school of small fry, with the same results except that the tuna were smaller.

Sharks were beginning to appear on the surface in very noticeable numbers. I believe that on calm days, they, like the swordfish, rise to the surface to rest when full of food. The shark, however, doesn't hesitate to grab another mouthful, no matter how full he may be, whereas the swordfish, unless the bait is a particularly choice morsel, or passes close enough to annoy him, will turn away from it more often than toward it.

Preferring to try for something other than tuna we headed closer inshore. There were many green turtles in practically every piece of water over which we had passed and, our supply of fresh meat being low, my companion harpooned a good fat one of about a hundred pounds to replenish the larder.

Dropping inside the thirty-fathom curve, we dropped a spoon and a feather bait over the stern, but nothing happened until about three hundred yards from shore, when two large amberjacks struck simultaneously. One of these was soon cut in two by a big hammerhead shark that came from under the boat. Not satisfied with a half of the fish, he made a rush for the rest of it, which we were pulling in by hand, and in his excitement ran headlong into the side of the boat with such force that I feared the side had been stove in. Being light and of shallow draft, however, the boat must have been more or less shoved to one side by the terrific impact, for we found no leaks upon removing the floor boards.

Hoping the shark had broken his neck, we resumed our fishing, working closer inshore and toward the mother ship, which had disappeared around the point. Our catch was the usual run of ground fish. Though we saw any number of devilfish we made no attempt to engage them.

The ship had anchored between a shoal and a high rock reef and, going aboard with our turtle, we soon enjoyed a dinner of roasted "conao" such as only our cook could prepare.

After several days at this anchorage, during which we landed seven sails, four silver marlin and a goodly number of small wahoo, we decided to return to Coiba and the Perlas Islands.

Just around Anegado Point, on the southeast end of Coiba, we again found a suitable berth for the ship and, on our first day there, set out in the small boats for Jicaron Island which rears its head 1500 feet into the blue. When about a mile from this island, I saw a great splash a quarter-mile away and jerking the throttle wide open we speeded toward it. Occupants of the other boat had seen it too, however, and their position was closer than ours. Also, though the two boats were identical in size, design and engine, theirs was the faster of the two, by a margin of about a mile per hour. Nevertheless, we gave them a race.

Meanwhile seven more splashes were seen, affording a view of a long keen streak of silver that could mean only silver marlin; even the huge sailfish of these waters, we felt sure, did not grow to such size.

Nearing the spot where the frolicsome marlin had been taking his setting-up exercises, both boats slowed to about six knots and with cut bait and teasers began covering the area, which was still a mass of foam. In perhaps two minutes, excitement on the other boat became intense; the teaser was being pulled in and a great stick-like object was splitting the water about thirty-five feet from the stern. Abreast of their boat, we stopped ours and waited for the climax which wasn't long in coming.

The fin disappeared and we saw the angler lean forward for a long tense moment, then strike for all he was worth. Like a flash the marlin was on his way, headed straight for Cocos Island. He didn't break water until a full two hundred yards away, but made up for it then with a dozen or more jumps, one following another as fast as he could strike the water and get new momentum. The boat swung around quickly and headed full speed in the direction the fish had taken. The marlin was still taking line and showing no signs of sounding or changing his course and it looked as though another good line would soon be trailing loosely behind a fish in the Pacific.

At last the course changed, giving the boat a chance to regain considerable line for the angler. The fish put on another exhibition of fancy jumps, back flips and side skimming, then sounded again and headed for deep water on the west side of Jicaron and Jicaronita Islands. The fight went on for three hours, until one of those major disasters, well known to all anglers, occurred. The line, which from all indications had been tight until that moment, went suddenly and sickeningly slack. Line, leader and hook were reeled in intact, unchanged in appearance except that the leader was coiled like a spring, as is often the case after a fight with any of the billed species. There was nothing left to do but estimate the weight of the lost prize, which we conservatively placed at 450 pounds, and call it a day.

That night we moved our headquarters again, sailing east along the Panama coast, past Cape Mala, then northeast to the beautiful island of San José, southernmost of the Perlas group, arriving just before dark the following evening. All day long we had seen fish of some kind, particularly along the tide rips off Cape Mala. Breaching sailfish were numerous along this stretch and quite a number were also seen while crossing the Gulf of Panama, but we didn't stop, feeling that we had our share of them if we didn't land another one, and being anxious to spend the rest of our limited time in the waters of the Perlas group.

We nosed in past the point just as the sun was sinking and the sky was full of endless strings of sea birds mingled with flocks of parrots winging their way to roost, either on some of the islands or on the mainland.

Out in the fishing boats again, early next morning, we had only cleared the island De Hicaco when not fifty feet from the boat, a beautiful sailfish broke the glass-like surface with four consecutive jumps, almost covering the four points of the compass, then continued to swim slowly on the surface, with its great, black-spotted, deep purple sail high in the air — a memorable picture, accentuated by the glint of the early morning sun.

The engine was promptly stopped and there was a scramble to get cut baits overboard. Fumbling with rods and dropping this or that, we made noise enough to frighten off an orca, to say nothing of a timid sailfish, but we finally managed to get baits in the water and, starting the motor, described a wide circle in order to get the bait close to the fish, yet keep the boat well away. The fish quickly turned and rushed one of the baits, then stopped almost still, apparently changed its mind and swung over to the other bait, taking it with a rush, and we were treated to the spectacle of another fight of indescribable beauty. About an hour later the fish, a good ten-footer, doubtless weighing near the 140-pound mark, was brought alongside and, as usual, released.

Our friends had, meanwhile, taken four sails and one marlin, also reporting the loss of one small marlin. That our luck was no better was due in large measure to the boobies, which were very annoying, diving and grabbing our bait most consistently. We did manage to add another sail, of about nine-foot-six, to our score, but we raised no marlin this day.

Five more thrill-packed days were spent at this ideal spot, including one devoted to the pursuit and capture of a fifty-foot finback whale, at Isla Pacheca, some fifteen miles north-northwest of San Jose.

This was the expedition's final fling at fishing, our schedule calling for a return through the canal and a hunting trip into the interior of the San Blas Indian country — which, however, is another story.

Space has not permitted much more than a superficial account of this trip, my first of several, to these almost untouched waters. During our brief stay at the Perlas Islands, for instance, our total catch of sailfish was twenty-two, including the present world's record, which tipped the scales at 180 pounds and measured 10 feet 8¼ inches; it was, incidentally, caught by my brother, William B. Gray.

Our total of silver marlin during this same short period was seven, the largest weighing about two hundred pounds. Dolphin were plentiful, our largest weighing fifty-six pounds — and for fighting and jumping qualities these fish need offer no apologies. Spanish mackerel, jacks, yellowtail, amberjack, various snappers, bonito, papagallo, wahoo and many other game species were abundant.

I venture to predict that when these waters are more extensively fished, sailfish weighing well over two hundred pounds will be taken. I also believe that these same waters will produce marlin as large as have ever been taken anywhere, for I have seen black marlin there whose weight I would hesitate to estimate for fear of being made an honorary member of Lowell Thomas' tall story club; at any rate I'd rather prove my story by bringing in one of these gladiators of the tide rips.

A recent communication from the Pacific Sailfish Club at Balboa, to the effect that two silver marlin weighing 250 and 356 pounds had been taken in this area, further strengthens my belief that new records may be expected.

Increased transportation facilities, both by air and water, are gradually making this spot more accessible, perhaps largely due to the universal interest being shown by anglers of both sexes. In my experience, incidentally, the supposedly weaker sex can easily hold its own with the stronger where fishing is concerned. Women anglers of today are, if anything, keener and — pound for pound — will fight their fish harder than the average man.

As for the mysterious matter of bait, nearly every one has his own trick, or supposedly secret lure. I regret to say that I have never been fortunate enough to find such a thing, though I have cut them of every kind, shape and size, even resorting to making some of whale blubber on which I painted a red head, dots, dashes and hieroglyphics with mercurochrome; incidentally, this rather unusual bait accounted for a ten-foot-six sailfish. My conclusion, based on personal experience, is that bait cut from any kind of fish, if it "swims" properly, will bring results.

Tackle, of course, is more or less a matter of personal preference; my own preference has already been expressed elsewhere — heavy tackle for heavy fish.

For the waters covered in this chapter I believe the months from May to November to be the most desirable fishing season; this is the so-called rainy season and not at all uncomfortable.

As for boats, I am informed that there are now a few available for charter for fishing with headquarters at Balboa, Canal Zone. Just what they are like, or what the tackle consists of, I do not know but I believe that the Pacific Sailfish Club would gladly furnish any information desired.

This does not purport to be a technical treatise on the fish or fishing in certain waters; life histories (such as are known), food, habits, et cetera are treated in chapters concerning individual species, elsewhere in this volume. Rather, I have attempted to portray accurately the highlights of a single trip to these fascinating waters. If I have succeeded in taking the reader along with me — if he or she has been able to visualize some of the beauties and thrills of the jaunt — my purpose has been accomplished.

Courtesy of Thomas G. F. Aitken.

J. B. Stickney of Honolulu with 124¾ pound, world's record wahoo, caught on regulation heavy tackle, January 1935, off coast of Oahu, Hawaiian Islands.

Courtesy of Ernest Hemingway.

Captain Joe Russell and Karl Pfeiffer
with a Cuban wahoo

CHAPTER XII.

WAHOO

BY

THOMAS G. F. AITKEN

THE saga of the wahoo is shrouded in mystery, conflicting bewilderment and a pitiful absence of authentic scientific data. The species has been neglected by all scientists but not entirely by anglers.

The only really definite phase of the activities of the wahoo on which all anglers agree is its magnificent and sustained fighting proclivities when on moderately light tackle. The fish will be an interesting possibility for future achievements by the younger generation of angling-ichthyologists.

The wahoo likes little known and untraveled waters. He is rather rare and both elusive and exclusive.

The wahoo has many aliases in different sections of the world but universally comes under the general classification of a tropical game fish of the first order. The scientific name is *Acanthocybium solandri,* after Solander, an early explorer, and the name wahoo is said to have been corrupted from *guahu.* In the Bahamas the species is commonly known as *peto;* in the Caribbean as queen fish; and Brazil calls it a springer. In the Pacific, where it is also found, it has the shortest name in Hawaii, being called the *ono* and its longest title is found in the Philippines where they candidly refer to it as a great fighter under the name of *tanguingni.*

The species is an immense, sharp-nosed, swift-swimming, member of the mackerel family to which the majority of our better known big game fishes belong.

There have been many claims for record fish and as late as ten years ago a photograph was used extensively of a "world's record" wahoo taken in the Pacific and said to weigh exactly 50 pounds. This is obviously possible because of lack of previous competent authority over the fast-growing sport of big game fishing. My records, which were recently verified by Miss Francesca R. La Monte, Associate Curator of Ichthyology, of the American Museum of Natural History, show that from 1911 to January, 1935 the world's record rod and reel wahoo belonged to William C. Carlin with a fish weighing 86 pounds which he caught in the Bahamas near Nassau.

The new world's record properly substantiated by competent witnesses goes to J. B. Stickney of Honolulu, who in January of this year (1935) brought to gaff on a 24 thread line and regulation heavy tackle, a fish so much larger than the previous record that it gives you a rough idea of the possibilities, when an influx of Hawaii-bound Amercan big game anglers really gets under way. Mr. Stickney's fish weighed 124¾ pounds and was not taken off the famous Kona Coast of the Island of Hawaii, but near the small Rabbit Island, off the Coast of Oahu, on which Honolulu is situated. It is of course referred to as an *ono*, the Hawaiian name indicating "sweet," which incidentally is very descriptive of the fish when properly cooked and served. The meat is firm, white and of exceptionally good flavor. When alive, the wahoo lacks a sweet disposition, however, being ill-tempered and the possessor of exceptionally bombastic fighting characteristics.

If you have never hooked a wahoo, this new record fish may not sound like a giant, but after thirty years spent at the sport of hunting big fish I know of nothing that would thrill me as much as the good fortune to bring to gaff a wahoo of over one hundred pounds. This is not the only wahoo ever taken in Hawaiian waters as they are there in sufficient numbers to satisfy the most ruthless sportsman. The average weight of a wahoo in these mid-Pacific waters is around forty pounds and almost every angler who has been lucky enough to encounter one in the past would travel many miles and undergo excessive hardships for a chance at a twenty pounder.

The species is widely scattered but each season quite a few are taken along the lower east coast of Florida, but never when after this particular fish. Florida anglers never expect to catch a wahoo and are naturally delighted if the Goddess of Luck comes their way. I know many thoroughly competent anglers who have fished Florida waters consistently, year after year, and have never even seen a wahoo. To these gentlemen I extend my condolences. There is nothing about the fish that may be catalogued as common for it is indeed a stout-hearted fellow.

Perhaps my usual luck is accountable for my wahoo, taken at intervals, much too infrequent, but each one still fresh in my memory. The speed of this fish is phenomenal and the application of propulsion appears effortless. It is the most graceful fish that swims, with a possible exception of the dolphin.

The strike of a wahoo is a detail that beggars description. Their excellent eyesight may have something to do with this. From a distance of between one and two hundred feet I have seen a wahoo approach a bait like a projectile — straight and true — with dorsal and part of back cutting the waves. At the impact the fish usually veers off at a sharp right angle giving the angler a terrific shock, even if prepared.

Its characteristics when hooked are uncertain and I have heard of a single run at lightning speed of around a thousand feet. They are naturally surface feeders but will use every artifice to free themselves from a hook, frequently jumping to great heights, but more often sounding to a considerable depth. One of my greatest thrills was many years ago while fishing outside one of the reefs near Key Largo, when without warning a forty pounder went straight in the air with my bait in his mouth. When I struck, the hook was outside of the fish's mouth and the end of the cut bait was all the fish secured. My hook, with half of the bait still on, hit the water at about the same time as the fish and, before I could speak, he again went in the air with the remainder of the bait and this time I successfully set the hook. I was using 6/9 tackle and despite every effort on my part to get my fish, it required nearly an hour to bring it to gaff.

I have frequently expressed the opinion that the wahoo is the fastest game fish that swims as well as the hardest bait hitter. I retract nothing.

I have heard of many reports of large wahoo in the Tongue of the Ocean amidst the Bahama group. I have seen very large fish taken near Nassau. One of the best spots so far uncovered in that locality is from Clifton Point to Goulding Cay at the west end of New Providence Island and about fourteen miles from Nassau. In these waters market fishermen have recorded hand-lined fish of ninety-seven pounds and report that they frequently see them exceeding one hundred pounds.

The construction of the body of this species is somewhat similar to the large Florida kingfish, but in appearance more like that of a sailfish, except the form, which is almost round, instead of compressed at the sides, and with a radically altered set of fins and, of course no bill. The first dorsal is long and low, having about twenty-five spines, instead of ten to sixteen as in the other mackerels. A second high, pointed dorsal is slightly to the rear of the center of the back. Between the second dorsal and the caudal will be found about nine dorsal finlets which are matched with eight anal finlets. The anal matches the second dorsal in size and shape, while the ventrals are small and negligible. The caudal is typical of most salt water game fish but it is smaller than either a sailfish or marlin, although widely forked and gives every indication of an ability for maintained high speed work. The pectoral fins are short and similar in construction to the Florida kingfish. The teeth are irregular, the posterior much the largest. The eyes which are of good size are set well back due to a long tapering and very pointed head.

Some anglers believe the wahoo, before evolution set in, once carried a bill similar to a sailfish, but this theory is discredited by scientists. There is something akin, however, and an opinion has been expressed by others that the wahoo is possibly the "missing link" between the sailfish or marlin and the more conventional species of the mackerel group. This is something for future anglers and ichthyologists to solve and until more definite data is compiled we must be content with its status as a great fighter and continue to look for more productive waters. The wahoo is a perfect example of streamlining and is really something of great beauty, usually a rarity in the world of ichthyology. The color is variable but will usually be found with a very deep blue back, which, however, in the green water inside of the Florida Gulf Stream, changes to a peculiar pale golden green. Although varying in number according to the size and age of the fish there are more than twenty, purple-tinted, lead-color stripes across the back continuing below the lateral line and fading into the silver sides. The under side is white but the entire fish carries a beautiful opalescent silver sheathing which blends into the white.

The Atlantic species is presumed to spawn in Cuban waters but I believe this is a matter of mere conjecture, each authority apparently requoting the previous one without giving a statement of fact. Little or nothing is known of the Pacific spawning waters. The migratory habits are also based on theory only, but the northern Atlantic limit is the mid-Florida east coast and in the Pacific along both coasts of Lower California. Most of the Pacific Coast species so far recorded were in the vicinity of Cape San Lucas, although the range is south to Panama. It inhabits most of Polynesia and probably occurs in the Indian Ocean as well as both coasts of Africa. The large variety of local names makes it difficult to trace without either specimen or photograph to assist in identification purposes.

It is surprising how little has been written about this fish but the reason is obvious. It is one of the really marvelous big game fishes that for many anglers may always remain somewhat of a myth. Charles M. Breder, Jr., Research Associate at both the New York Aquarium and the American Museum of Natural History, in his *Field Book of Marine Fishes of the Atlantic Coast* has only this to say regarding the wahoo:

"Tropical Atlantic, north to southern Florida where it is not uncommon. Known to spawn in Cuba. A large species valued as food. Reaches a length of over six feet and a weight up to one hundred pounds."

This is one species that would make an expedition for the study of our big game fishes a very much worth-while enterprise. Our lack of knowledge and our inability to find ways and means of getting at the fundamentals is appalling. We know all about almost every other living thing, permitting only the lives and habits of our big game fishes to remain unsolved mysteries.

The inexperienced angler suffers the loss of many of these fish through the inadvertent belief that in order to sink the hook the drag must be set up hard when striking. With a light drag the wahoo will practically hook himself, and it is only natural that many anglers are usually unaware that they may have had a wahoo strike. Of all the hard-hitting fish I consider the wahoo most likely to pull or rip the hook loose right at the time of striking. Its momentum will simply snap the hook out of its mouth on encountering a stiff drag. Another fault of the novice which accounts for the loss of many fish is the consistent failure to soften the drag after several hundred feet of line has been stripped from the reel. The weight of one or two hundred yards of line is a good substantial halter on any fish.

The best bait for wahoo is an open question. Like most mackerels they will hit almost anything that is moving, if of a light color. The feeding policy of most hard-hitting fish appears to be to stop the feed promptly, before another fish gets it, and investigate the digestibility at leisure. The most frequently used bait in Florida waters is naturally the cut variety, as the wahoo is almost invariably taken while trolling for sailfish and the same tackle is considered adequate. In other waters it has been found that a feather lure or any type of trolling squid, wooden plug or large spoon is effective. The feathers are used almost exclusively in Hawaii, but some fish have been taken on live bait while still fishing. A large specially-cut strip of pork rind will prove most effective when trolling with a conventional sailfish rig and it has the practical feature of being almost indestructible.

The discovery or development of a new and more palatable bait may reflect the necessary improvement in wahoo angling. Anything that can be done to produce more fish and better sport will be most welcome. An excellent opportunity for bait research work is offered in Hawaii as the *ono* is present in these waters every month of the year which, incidentally, would also indicate the probability of spawning in the same locality.

The comparatively recent discovery of large wahoo around the Hawaiian group is really not a new discovery at all. Because of its relative distance from the great centers of population and also due to the absence of modern advertising, its angling secrets have been carefully guarded by local sportsmen. The Kona coast on the western side of the Island of Hawaii has become the best known spot and a hotel at Kilula started the news of their giant fish on its way around the world. It is inevitable that all of the islands in this group can produce good angling if they possess the proper reef construction.

The failure of most tourists — who might also be anglers — to take their tackle along when visiting the islands has of course interfered with the progress and further development of the fishing. It may be expected that rod cases will be very much in evidence on future trips to Hawaii. It is a fact, however, that for centuries past the giant game fishes have afforded sustenance to a large native Hawaiian population. Prior to the recent world's record fish taken by Mr. Stickney, another rod and reel wahoo was reported weighing 92¼ pounds but this was never properly substantiated.

The many luxurious steamships from California to Hawaii, coupled with their excellent hotels and satisfactory charter boats, now adds big game angling to the previous Hawaiian appeal of climate, blue sky, volcanic marvels, soft music, gentle breezes, a profusion of flowers, the beach at Waikiki and the inevitable proffered leis. Unquestionably Hawaii has "reel" appeal.

Our Atlantic Seaboard has the necessary facilities and equipment at Miami and along the Florida Keys, but the wahoo are too scarce to make this a fish to be sought to the exclusion of other species. The Bahamas in the past have offered a rather poor type of charter boat, but many Miami anglers make the forty-five mile trip in chartered boats or private yachts across the Gulf Stream to Bimini and Cat Cay for the sport. Here, also, a predominance of other species has made exclusive wahoo angling almost unknown. Big wahoo are frequently taken nevertheless.

The new progressive interests controlling the large hotels at Nassau are now formulating plans for much better angling equipment, and in the future it is absolutely assured that the famous Tongue of the Ocean waters may be fished in comfort and security. It will be an interesting contest between Hawaii and the Bahamas for future record honors.

Another excellent possibility is in the offing, as Bermuda — only two days by steamer from New York — has finally been made to appreciate the commercial value of big game fishing. With no charter boat on the island, two New Yorkers during the past winter were forced to borrow a cabin cruiser and in doing so were able to show the Bermuda officials that big fish and great fishing were just outside of the harbor. Bermuda, which is on the warm water side of the Gulf Stream, must have wahoo in both size and quantity, and my guess is that as soon as they secure satisfactory boats they will be in the contest for recognition and subsequent honors.

No matter how many names the wahoo may now possess in various parts of the world it has only one meaning to me — a brilliant performer and a great game fish.

Photo by Beers, Miami.

CAPTAIN GIFFORD'S "LADY GRACE" EQUIPPED WITH OUTRIGGERS.

CHAPTER XIII.

FISHING BOATS AND SAFETY AT SEA

BY

FRANCIS H. GEER

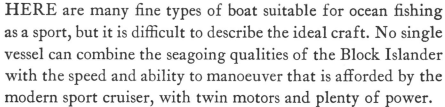

HERE are many fine types of boat suitable for ocean fishing as a sport, but it is difficult to describe the ideal craft. No single vessel can combine the seagoing qualities of the Block Islander with the speed and ability to manoeuver that is afforded by the modern sport cruiser, with twin motors and plenty of power.

We may have a boat that is built to "take it" day in and day out, nine months of the year, or the year around in anything like a moderate climate, like those used by the commercial fishermen of the Block Island-Montauk district and further east; a boat that will knock off 8 or 9 knots in anything except half a gale and a storm sea — and even then will get you home without making you wish you hadn't come. But such a staunch old friend will make it a long day for you if you want to go off twenty miles or so and fish four or five hours and then either quit early to get in for dinner, or devote the evening to the run home, and snug up just as the lights ashore are blinking out for the night.

But you will have been safe, relatively that is, and comfortable, and you will be glad you went.

Or we may have a boat that is fast enough to reach the fish within an hour's run from our harbor, where we can keep an eye on the changing weather and the state of wind and sea. If we don't care for the prospect, just hook her up and take it on the nose for an hour or so. Then we slip in around the point or behind the jetty and drop off the oilskins and say "Well, that was a dusting. How about a little scoop?" This type of boat may make us miss or shorten many a good day or stay out when it's risky and we ought not to — considering what is under us — or else miss out when it looks messy, but really is good enough.

One summer we were offshore in the "Iris," a beautiful little auxiliary sloop, built to race in Great South Bay. No further description of her need be given. We were bound for Chincoteague Inlet on the Eastern Shore of Virginia. We had enjoyed head winds and engine trouble the whole day's run down from Cape May, and our gasoline was all but gone. The clouds were lifting out in the west, the tide was just beginning to ebb and night was falling. It wasn't bad, but it wasn't good either, and one of us turned to the man and said, "Well, Thompson, it looks as if we might have to stand on and off all night." His answer was "Yes, sir, it does, and I wouldn't mind if I had something to stand on and off in."

There are countless good types between these two extremes and only men of wide fishing experience can know more than a few of them.

The sea-skiff is a great favorite, ranging from an open boat 22 feet or so, to the fast cabin skiffs of 38 or 40 feet. Such boats can be driven at about 8 knots for the smaller ones and 10 knots for the larger ones, with moderate power and slight gasoline consumption. When higher speeds are wanted, more power is necessary, of course, and these models are modified, given a slightly longer, flatter run, with a view to their planing at high speeds. This power is extremely useful to reach fish seen at distance in the shortest possible time. There is real danger, however, in going far offshore, where rough weather may be encountered unexpectedly, in a craft of light construction.

The dead-rise boats so much used in the Chesapeake and off the Maine Coast are fine sea boats — heavily built and very serviceable. The principal objections to them are low freeboard and slow turning.

The operation of a fishing boat with twin motors is steadily gaining favor and there are many advantages to such an installation. If one motor lets go, the other furnishes adequate power to get home at reasonable speed. The ability to manoeuver is tremendously increased and this is of great value, both in working on fish before they are hooked and in the successful consummation of the ensuing battle. The disadvantages in the main are two: the center of gravity is raised because off-center installation of two motors has to be higher, and the center line installation of one motor on the keel is much stronger from a structural point of view.

A number of successful boats have been built with one powerful high-speed motor and an auxiliary — say in the 15 to 20 hp. range — installed off-center and operating with a shaft and propeller separate from that of the main motor. The chain or gear drive from a small auxiliary motor to the main propeller shaft has not been successful and few boats are now put out with this arrangement.

In operating a boat with main power plant and a small auxiliary, the auxiliary should always be regarded as a unit by itself — separate gas tank and, as pointed out above, separate propeller and shaft. The small motor should be turned over by its own starter and run for a quarter to half an hour every day and should be regarded always as a vital part of the ship's power plant. No one can tell when his main motor is going to fold up on him, and to have something that will run you home at four knots or so, or that will keep the sea for forty-eight hours or more, may mean the difference between a fishing incident and a tragedy.

Let us suppose that your main motor will burn twelve gallons of gas per hour and that you carry 150 gallons. You run off for a day's fishing and burn a third of it, say 50 gallons, and then your propeller drops off or you strike some obstruction and bend your shaft hopelessly. You have in the little motor something which burns one-third or less of the gasoline consumed by the main motor and which can run for twenty-four hours on the gas you have left in your tanks.

Whatever we have, efficiency of equipment should be a vital consideration. First — the motor, or motors. Manufacturers have made great progress in stepping up the reliability of the power plants they offer for small boats. Marine motors are approaching the consistent performance of automobile motors, although they can not reach it yet. Generally speaking, they are all good and getting better, and can be counted on to do the necessary, if they are given the care to which they are entitled.

It is bad enough to knock around the Chesapeake or Long Island Sound or farther east in waters that are more or less in touch with the land, relying on a motor that may get you home and may not. Offshore conditions are very different. The time and care and money you devote to keeping the motor in A-1 condition is the premium you pay for "return insurance." If you don't pay the premium, you don't get the insurance and it is too late to sign up when something lets go about four o'clock on a September afternoon and you find yourself alone and in supreme command of 150 square miles of open ocean, and looking not too hopefully for someone from the old home port — or any other port as far as that is concerned.

Know the motor. Watch it as a doctor watches a patient. Note every flicker of its pulse, every change in its breathing, every lift in its temperature, every stutter, every blush — if a motor can blush — and surely they all must at times. Remember we haven't a nice suit of sails that will get us home — a day or two later than we intended, perhaps, but home nevertheless.

Spare parts. One of my friends carries all he can — almost enough to build a new motor. Fuses, gaskets, condensers — all the obvious things, and then some. He took the combined advice of the service man of the company that built his motor and of a yacht captain who had run motor boats all his life. Result? He gets home, even if it is an hour or so late once or twice a year. Expensive? Yes, but not in relation to the other expense factors.

When we go fishing in the ocean, we usually have three things in mind: to find the fish, to have the fun of catching them and to get home again without incident or accident. This last is merely routine most of the time, but occasion does arise when it calls for a considerable amount of experience, skill and preparation.

Fire is the worst hazard, of course. Statistics are not available, but it must be close to the truth that there are more fatal accidents on small motor yachts from fire or explosion than from any other single cause.

When a boat is built, suitable ventilation ought to be planned. This should give positive circulation of air when the vessel is at anchor as well as when she is under weigh. Many accidents occur when the motor is started immediately after gassing up and before the normal circulation of air caused by the forward motion of the craft has had a chance to carry off the fumes.

Gasoline vapor is the most unaccountable explosive. Sometimes you can not set it afire, and again it will go off on any excuse. Without getting too scientific, sixteen to one seems to be the deadly combination — sixteen parts of air to one part of gasoline vapor. This will explode if you look at it. One of the big gasoline distributors had a whole tank wagon of gas standing still, on four rubber tires, with no one near it, blow up from static electricity touching off the vapor.

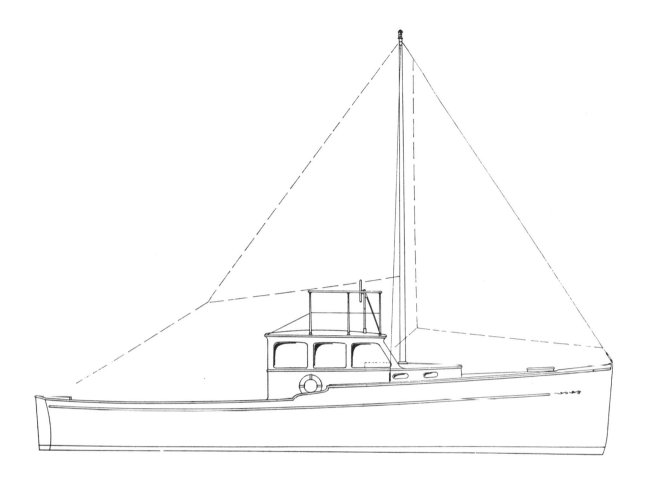

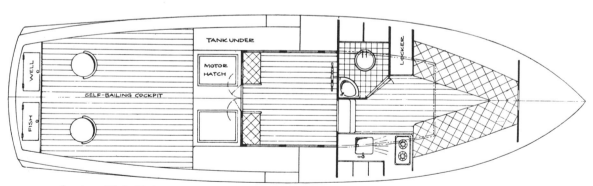

AN IDEAL OCEAN FISHERMAN.

These sketches of a fine 36-foot vessel designed by Cox & Stevens, Inc., P. L. Rhodes, Associate, show most of the features necessary for an efficient Ocean Fisherman.

Note the topside controls, steadying sails, twin motor installation, good deck room forward. The chairs are sensibly placed where the angler can brace his feet against the after bulkhead or the gunwale, depending on whether his fish is astern or abeam. Generous cockpit with no top over it, so that the sky's the limit when it comes to waving around rods and gaffs and outriggers. Good fishbox and good bait box 'way aft where they ought to be, with scuppers overboard to carry off the blood and water.

Courtesy of Lynn Bogue Hunt.

THE FLEET OF GUIDE BOATS AT THE LONG KEY FISHING CAMP.

Courtesy of The Matthews Company.   *Rosenfeld Photo.*

MATTHEWS "38" SPORT CRUISER. THIS IS A FINE, FAST AND ABLE CRAFT, EQUIPPED FOR
OCEAN FISHING.

Clean bilges. Sawdust is a fine cleaner of the bilges. Tight tanks, gas lines and connections; drip pans, non-leaking carburetors — non-back-firing devices — convenient and efficient extinguishers — plenty of them, and a great big hatch over or into the engine compartment, which can be opened, and ought to be opened, to free the boat of gasoline fumes before touching the starter; suitable vents from each tank to the outside air. These are the ordinary precautions and need not be dwelt upon.

The combination of a competent designer and a careful owner is the best safeguard against the fire hazard. The odor of leaking gasoline is easily perceptible. One sniff, and stop to learn the why of it!

Another consideration, and of great importance on any craft that has the engine compartment or tanks closed in, is the fire extinguishing system — automatically or manually operated. All the recognized ones are good and any one of them may be worth the lives of everybody on board if and when it is needed.

It goes without saying that our vessel should have the equipment required by the Government. A little emphasis on this at present, however, will not be out of order. Some of us have been obliged to try to explain to the Coast Guard or to U. S. Navigation Service officers the absence of required equipment, and many boat owners have had heavy penalties assessed against them for minor infractions. Someone protested at the right time to the right person and most of these fines were remitted and the imposition of them—except in flagrant cases—was abandoned. Boat owners generally must see to it that they adhere to these regulations and avoid an accident due to neglect that might again focus the attention of the authorities on this matter and restore the severe supervision and penalties of a few years ago.

Stout pumps, intelligently located and of substantial capacity, have saved many vessels which might have been lost without them. The ordinary boat pump has its place aboard; but a permanently installed three-inch galvanized pump or one of the box type or both ought to be aboard as well. With this equipment a pooped or stove boat may be saved where otherwise she might be lost.

The small balsa life rafts are well worth taking to sea. One can be stowed inconspicuously on top of the pilot house where it can be reached readily if needed. It will increase your ease of mind very materially and it is a swell place to curl up in for a little outdoor bunk fatigue.

Their usefulness can be materially increased by splicing on five or six lengths of six-thread rope. It is a grim thought, but if the life raft is to be used at all, it will be in a pretty hard chance and if you can make yourself fast by the belt or under the arms, you will be a little better fixed. This is good to remember, in any event. If you find yourself overboard, try to make yourself fast with a line or with your belt to something that floats — even if it is your fat friend from the city.

GROUND TACKLE. On the subject of ground tackle there is little to be said except that it must be sound and adequate. A big anchor and a small anchor — according to the size of the boat — and at least two good lines 40 to 75 fathoms each, depending on the depth of water in the locality where you propose to work.

Getting up the anchor of a small cruiser by man power, even in a moderate sea, is a tough go at best and will break the backs of two men and a boy if it is really rough. When you anchor frequently at sea, as for example when you chum, and perhaps change your position two or three times a day, a tremendous amount of unnecessary work can be saved by carrying and using a light grapnel — say 25 pounds — or a light sand anchor of similar weight bent to a long line, about one-half inch. Getting this rig aboard is a very different matter from heaving up a 75 pound anchor on the end of 30 fathoms of 1½-inch manila rope. This is well worth remembering. It won't hold you in a strong breeze and a heavy sea, but it will hold you many times when you think it won't.

Always carry a sea anchor or its equivalent and know how to make it effective. Claude Worth says in *Yacht Cruising*: "If one carries a sea anchor for thirty years and only really needs it once during that time, it will have been well worth its stowage room." There is nothing to be added to the three or four pages devoted to the subject in that fine book. His rule is to have the warp five times the length of the vessel, and it must be remembered that it should be cared for when you don't need it, so that it will be ready when you do.

NIGHT SIGNALS are of four types:

1. The ordinary red or white flares — Coston Lights — which have a tip covered with a sulphur combination which can be struck like a match and which burns brightly for about a minute. The tips are protected from moisture by tin foil and they come eight or so in a water-tight copper container.

2. Rockets — not carried often on small boats — difficult to protect from moisture and rather unmanageable under most conditions which might call for their use.

3. "International Flares" — a valuable method of signalling your position

to any one within a distance of a few miles. This equipment has been out of the range of the purses of most of us until the last year or two. The company has now put on the market a "dory set." It consists of three cartridges and pistol packed in a water-tight container. When shot into the air from the pistol, the cartridge explodes and releases a lighted magnesium flare on a small parachute. The thing gives a brilliant light and stays up for a minute or more. Cost $25, if my memory serves me.

4. The old shotgun has told the story of boats in distress for many years and should not be left behind. Remember the shells, too.

Under the present regulations it is useless to give much consideration to two-way radio communication as safety equipment in the type and size of boat we have under consideration. The Federal Radio Communications Commission requires that all transmitters be operated by men whom they have examined and licensed. The larger type installations which operate on the commercial traffic channels require an operator holding a commercial grade license. These men are too expensive for most of us, and all messages ashore are charged for at regular radio rates. Mobile transmitters are forbidden on the useful amateur frequencies. The range on the ultra-high frequencies, on which there are no restrictions except the operator, is limited from sea level and can not as yet be relied upon to call for help.

The radio receiver which includes the radio compass and direction-finder features is another matter. This apparatus will come into general use and be very helpful in thick weather for taking bearings, checking watch or chronometer with time signals and for ordinary radio reception purposes. A direction finder which will give the bearing of every light vessel and most of the shore stations, can be had for $150. Range 50 miles. If it is kept in operation the chance of being lost in a fog is reduced to a minimum.

Now for some of the things that help to fill the fish box:

First — outriggers. Whether they were invented by Tom Gifford, I do not know, but certainly he brought them to this coast and developed them to what they are today. While they look horribly expensive and very difficult to handle, the cost *can* be kept down and, properly designed, they should give little trouble.

A drawing is shown of a medium sized power cruiser with the port-side outrigger set and ready to use, and the starboard rigged in, as is usual when not working.

The view is from aft looking forward and shows two light spruce uprights at the sides of the pilot house, with halyards through two masthead sheaves to bridles on the outboard end of each of two 30-foot light spruce spars. A stiffleg or "holder outer" keeps the outrigger from coming aboard with every roll of the vessel.

The whole thing is surprisingly simple and the rig can be — and ought to be — as light as possible to reduce windage and to make for ease of handling.

Each outrigger can be set by one man standing on top of the house and can be brought in by one man as well. This should be done in smooth water inside, before leaving the inlet and after returning from the ocean, although it can be done at sea in moderate weather and even in rough water if necessary.

The balance of such a rig as is sketched is most satisfactory and even tends to reduce the motion of a small boat in a seaway. Forward guys from the outboard end of the spruce spar to the bow are a necessity, and after guys may be desirable.

Outriggers should be installed with a small pulley at the upper or outboard end, through which an endless light linen or cotton line should be rove. This line carries a snap clothespin and is so rigged that the clothespin can be hoisted on the pulley to the outboard end of the outrigger or brought down to the deck with ease and dispatch.

When it is desired to troll the bait from the outrigger, the baited hook is run out from the tip of the rod, say 40 or 50 feet. The bight of the line is then engaged in the clothespin and the clothespin hoisted up to the outboard end of the outrigger, the reel paying out line meanwhile.

For some reason or other, the tuna are not anything like so ready to take an outrigger bait as dolphin, marlin and sailfish — that is, in our experience. Perhaps that is just bad luck — like the man described recently in one of the newspapers, who had fished for thirty years without catching a single fish — because others report having been successful with the tuna using the outrigger. The tuna, even with a hard mouth, seems to be able to feel the hook and throw it between the time he disengages the line from the clothespin on the end of the outrigger and the time he fetches up and you can "give him the butt."

The cockpit of a fishing boat should be equipped with *one* proper fishing chair, a swivel chair, and fitted with gimbal rod holder. One is enough, provided you have one or two other seats in which a man can sit with comfort and

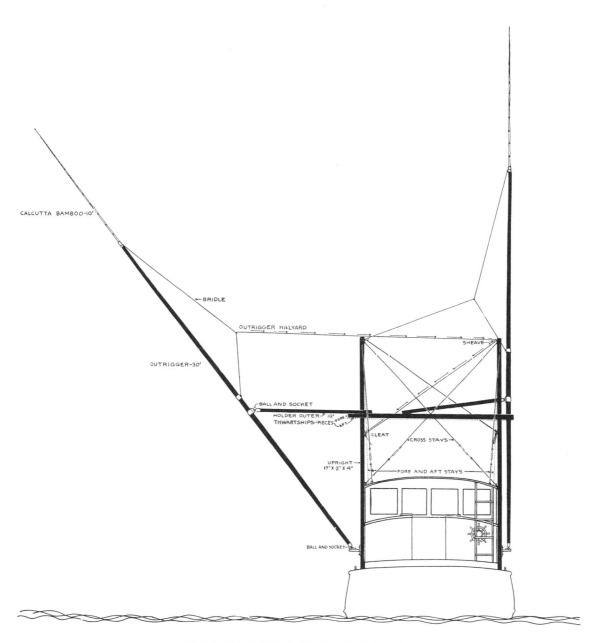

CALCUTTA BAMBOO-10'

←BRIDLE

OUTRIGGER HALYARD

SHEAVE

OUTRIGGER~30'

BALL AND SOCKET

HOLDER OUTER - 10'
THWARTSHIPS-PIECES
FORE
AFT

CLEAT

CROSS STAYS

UPRIGHT
17'X 2" X 4"

FORE AND AFT STAYS

BALL AND SOCKET

OUTRIGGER DESIGNED BY FRANCIS H. GEER.

Wood parts black. Metal parts white.

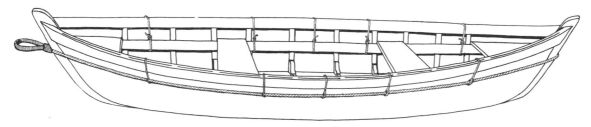

Drawn by Lynn Bogue Hunt from information supplied by Francis H. Geer.

DORY RIGGED WITH SLING FOR TOWING AT SEA.

hold a rod. You seldom hook two fish at one time, both of which call for the chair. If you do the impossible and hook two giants at once, simply tie the Samson of the party to one of them, put a knife in his teeth and lower him gently over the side!

The seats of the chairs should be almost level with the gunwale — or within two inches. Many a good fish has been lost and many a good rod broken by the sudden decision on the part of a large fish to sound — and a rod "fetched up" on the rail.

Behind the fishing chair, toward the bow, the cockpit should be clear overhead of awnings, stanchions, davits, railings, etc., for about eight feet. A big fish must be followed and any such obstructions may put an end to the show.

The freeboard abreast the cockpit should be low in order that a fish may be grasped by reaching *into* the water at exactly the right moment, or gaffed before he knows what goes on. One of my friends *hooked twenty-one marlin* in three trips to the Gulf Stream, ninety to one hundred miles or more about E S E from Barnegat Inlet — and landed but one. Name on request — it was not the writer. He had a fishing cockpit aft, but his boat was a large one and the freeboard was so high that he was licked when it came to getting his fish aboard. Also, his boat was equipped with a Diesel engine and auxiliary ketch rig and was not easy to manoeuver.

A good fishing boat must be provided with a suitable fish box draining overboard for cleaning and to allow the blood to run out through the scuppers. This will sometimes keep schools of bluefish, dolphin or tuna under the stern for a considerable time. If it fetches the sharks, a cork or a glove in the scuppers will stop it at once.

A well or a tank for live bait is good. I haven't one on my boat and it is really impossible to keep bait alive without one. Fish of the mackerel family will die anyway — well or no well. Ling, porgies and sea bass will live for a while and so will bunkers; but to get live bait ashore or on the way out and keep it alive for five to ten hours, takes infinite patience and interest and care.

We have just ordered a tank for the "Seven Stars," galvanized, four feet long, nine inches wide and one foot deep with a hose connection and check valve as intake at one end at the bottom, and an outlet at the other end about two-thirds of the way up. The idea is to run the intake hose out through one of the scuppers with a bent fitting on the outboard end, so that it will scoop up a little water when the boat is under weigh. Whether or not it will work remains to be seen.

The Lehmann Bait Box is the last word in keeping bait fresh and firm. It is fully described in the chapter on swordfish.

KITES. Very few of our Atlantic Coast fishermen seem to warm up to the kite. This is probably because it is "just one more thing" and partly, no doubt, because a kite is not easy to handle for one who has not practised with it. It can be most helpful, however, in catching fish and there are times when they cannot be taken without it. One day in early September, running across from Manasquan to East Rockaway, we passed through acres of tuna and albacore, tearing around on the surface as if the devil were after them. They apparently weren't feeding and wouldn't take any ordinary bait, but a feather skipped on the surface by a kite did something to them that made it a day.

There are two main methods of kite fishing: 1. The one where the strike of the fish drops the kite in the water. This makes it necessary to retrieve the kite before you begin to work on the fish and may cause the loss of much valuable time when time is of the greatest importance. 2. The method where the strike of the fish disengages the fish line from the kite line, the kite is hauled in and the fish . . . , well?

In rough weather the bait from a kite should be trolled pretty well astern, as otherwise it is out of water practically all the time. In smooth water, the bait can be trolled wide of the wake to be sure, but nearly abreast of the stern of the boat. The lift of the kite skips the bait on the surface and gives it a glamorous allure that only the most unemotional of fish can resist.

It is a fascinating way of hooking a fish. There are those who don't approve of it because they say you lose some of the thrill of the strike, and that the kite method calls for less angling experience and skill, but there really is no doubt that the kite and the long outrigger take more fish than the system of trolling directly astern, and they certainly furnish more cases of heart failure.

Kites come for the most part in three sizes for breezes of varying strength, and the bought ones are the best. They can be made up, however, with a little care, but should be thoroughly experimented with before they can be expected to function as a real aid to the fisherman and not as an efficient "builder-upper" of profanity in its more advanced forms.

The kite can be used when chumming — when the wind is with the tide —

to carry a bait well down the chum streak and still keep it on the surface, with a view to luring some unwary denizen of Tunaville to an untimely experience with an uncompromising gaff.

THE PULPIT. If a boat is so constructed as to permit carrying a pulpit, the owner must make the decision for himself. Some do and wish they hadn't, and some don't and wish they had. Unless the bow is fairly high, there is a definite danger of burying the pulpit in a sea and carrying the whole business away. And what a job to clear up! A pulpit which combines usefulness and comparative safety, can be made of two stout oak pieces bolted through the deck at the inboard end, running out one on each side of the stem and joined at the outboard ends with an oak block between them, by long, stout bronze bolts. Platform, guardrails and lifeline to suit individual preference.

THE TENDER. Every man must decide for himself what he wants in the way of a tender and where he wants it. There is one thing sure, however — that something of the sort ought to accompany a fishing boat, of adequate size, when she goes to sea. In case of accident, it will prove invaluable, and a man fast to a big fish may be put over in a dinghy with someone on the oars and left to work out his own salvation without putting a stop to everybody else's fishing from the big boat. Last summer, Buss Hall took a 96-pound tuna from our 9-foot sharpie and Pete Goodwin took a 231-pound tuna from the same boat. This latter fish towed the sharpie with two men in it for three hours, then broke the rod and was hand-lined to gaff after another half hour on 24-thread line.

The ideal is a sixteen foot lap-strake dory, but it calls for a big boat to bring it aboard. If it is to be towed, it should be fitted with a sling completely around it and hitched to the rail with short lines. Otherwise there is a severe strain on the small boat and an excellent chance of taking out the stem.

"And now let's call it a day."
"Suits me. What's the course for the Inlet?"
"Hasn't this wind hauled down?"
"Gee, it's thicker'n I thought."
"When is high water?"
"I don't feel very good, do I?"
"How fast do we go at ten-hundred revolutions?"
"Who invented this pump and who on earth put it in this death trap?"

"Can you see anything, you four-eyed Dutchman?"

"How long did we run sou'west after lunch?"

"This compass is cock-eyed."

These questions and observations mean something to all of us. How often we've heard them depends pretty much on how old we are. They are frequently accompanied by considerable profanity, most of which can be saved for a more suitable occasion if we review them before we go out, rather than when we start home.

In the first place, trust your compass. Get it right and check it frequently and then when necessary to bet on it, shoot the pot! Have two of them — compasses, I mean.

In the second place, watch the weather. Read the reports, note the force and direction of the wind; watch the sky and watch the other boats, who may know more about it than you do. Study the barometer and write it down or remember it, and try to know what it means.

Fog is the double-crossin'est, stab-you-in-the-back enemy of those who love the wind and the wave and who get a thrill out of a few white splashes — "just ahead of us — watch yourself — we're right over them now." Fog is mean and prayerfully to be avoided, but it catches us now and then, and there are even times when we must lose a day altogether or else walk right out into it.

"Stop, look and listen" and don't allow yourself to be confused, and remember why you carry a fog horn and a bell and that a good pair of eyes up aloft or on top of the pilot house is a good complement to a pair on the bow and at the wheel. Sharp eyes see fish, too, and they see driftwood, and they see landmarks and they see other ships. And they may see buoys or breakers or fish-pound stakes.

In the third place, try to know where you are — all the time. Know the speed of your boat when the motor is turning up 600 revolutions, 800, 1000, 1200 and know your course and keep track of them, both in your mind and on paper.

An excellent method of keeping continuously informed of your position is to run off, say 15 miles, on a course to a point X and then to work in a square, or back and forth, figuring on returning to point X and then retracing the course home.

Have a good pair of 6 power binoculars — some men can use 7½ or 8 power at sea — and a lead and line *properly marked, and use it*; and a patent log unless you have an accurate idea of your speed at varying rpm's.

A good idea is to leave word at home or at the dock or yacht club where you *think* you are going and when you hope to return.

Watch the color of the water when approaching the shore and uncertain of your position, and have the tide tables and current tables and know how to use them.

A LAST WORD. Safety at sea calls for that priceless combination of experience, constant vigilance and presence of mind which some men seem to have by nature and which others will never come by. If you have it, Lady Luck perches on your shoulder. If you haven't, she'll not be at your elbow when you're in a tough spot.

WORLD'S RECORDS

Heaviest Big Game Fish Of Various Species (Over 100 Pounds) Caught With Rod and Reel.

Corrected to April 1, 1935 — Copyright 1935, *Outdoor Life*.

Species	Weight and Year		Angler	Where Caught	Locality
SWORDFISH (Broadbill)	837½ lbs.	1934	W. E. S. Tuker	Chili	Off Tocopilla
MARLIN (Black)	976 lbs.	1926	Laurie D. Mitchell	New Zealand	Bay of Islands
MARLIN (Striped)	692 lbs.	1931	Alfonse Hamann	California	Off Balboa
MARLIN (Blue)	*				
MARLIN (White)	161 lbs.	1938	L. F. Hooper	Miami	Off Miami Beach
SAILFISH (Pacific)	180 lbs.	1931	William B. Gray	Panama	Gulf of Panama
SAILFISH (Atlantic)	106 lbs.	1929	W. A. Bonnell	Florida	Off Miami Beach
TUNA (Blue Fin)	851 lbs.	1933	L. Mitchell-Henry	England	Off Whitby
TUNA (Allison)	*				
TARPON	232 lbs.	1911	W. A. McLaren	Mexico	Panuco River
WAHOO	124¾ lbs.	1935	J. B. Stickney	Hawaii	Off Oahu
MAKO	798 lbs.	1931	H. White-Wickham	New Zealand	Bay of Islands
YELLOWTAIL	111 lbs.	1926	Zane Grey	New Zealand	Bay of Islands

The earlier records on this chart are taken from the list of records compiled by Van·Campen Heilner of *Field & Stream* and Francesca R. La Monte of the American Museum of Natural History.

* Confusion of species and failure to file complete data leave records open.

No fish are considered eligible for records unless unmutilated, witnessed and taken by angler unaided on rod and reel and according to tackle specifications and accepted angling club rules and practices of the locality where caught.

UNITED STATES BIG GAME FISH RECORDS
(Including U. S. Island Possessions.)

Heaviest fish of all recognized game species caught on rod and reel.

Corrected to April 1, 1935 — Copyright 1935, *Outdoor Life.*

Species	Weight and Year		Angler	Where Caught
ALBACORE	64 lbs. 4 ozs.	1912	Frank Kelly	Catalina, Cal.
AMBERJACK	~~95~~ 166 lbs.	~~1916~~ 37	S. W. Eccles	~~Long Key,~~ Passagrille, " Fla.
BASS (Channel)	74 lbs.	1929	Chas. D. Beckmann	Chincoteague, Va.
BASS (Striped)	73 lbs.	1913	Chas. B. Church	Vineyard Sound, Mass.
BASS (White Sea)	60 lbs.	1904	C. H. Harding	Catalina, Cal.
BLUEFISH	25 lbs.	1874	L. Hathaway	Cohasset, Mass.
BONEFISH	*			
BONITO	*			
DOLPHIN	*			
KINGFISH (Florida)	58 lbs.	1927	May Haines	Long Key, Fla.
MARLIN (Black)	*			
MARLIN (Blue)	*			
MARLIN (Striped)	692 lbs.	1931	Alfonse Hamann	Balboa, Cal.
MARLIN (White)	161 lbs.	1938	L. F. Hooper	Miami, Fla.
POLLOCK	*			
SAILFISH (Pacific)				
SAILFISH (Atlantic)	106 lbs.		W. A. Bonnell	Miami, Fla.
SWORDFISH (Atlantic)	505 lbs.		A. Rex Flinn	Montauk Point, N. Y.
SWORDFISH (Pacific)	573 lbs.		Geo. C. Thomas, III	Catalina, Cal.
TARPON	*			
TUNA (Allison)	*			
TUNA (Blue Fin)	705 lbs.		Francis H. Low	New York, N. Y.
WAHOO	124 lbs. 12 ozs.	1935	J. B. Stickney	Honolulu, Hawaii
WEAKFISH	17 lbs. 3 ozs.	1933	F. J. Conzen	Peconic Bay, N. Y.

The earlier records on this chart are taken from the list of records compiled by Van Campen Heilner of *Field & Stream* and Francesca R. La Monte of the American Museum of Natural History.

* Proof of records lacking and/or angler's failure to substantiate claims.

No mutilated fish accepted and proof of ethics required before acceptance.

INDEX

INDEX

INDEX

INDEX

[243]

INDEX

INDEX

INDEX

INDEX

INDEX

INDEX

INDEX

INDEX

White seabass (*Cynoscüon noblis*), 193; record, 237
White-Wickham, H., 236
Whitman, Edmund S., 10
Wicht, Captain Fred, 145, 146, 147, 149, 150
"William A. Morse" (cruiser), 148
Wirtheim, Jacob, 145
Women anglers, 213
Woodward, H. L., 72
Worth, Claude, 228
Wright, Mrs. Edith, 42
Wright, Hamilton M., 5, 6
Wright's sailfish. See Sailfish

X

Xiphias gladius. See Swordfish, broadbill

Y

"Yacht Cruising" (book), 228
Yellowfin tuna. See Tuna
Yellowtail (*Serioia dorsalis*), 188, 194, 197, 236

Z

"Zebra fish." See Marlin
Zeiss Contax camera, 124
Zeiss field glasses, 124